TACOMA

Puget Sound Ferries

For my parents, Earl and Bernice Ferguson. They taught me to love
Puget Sound. And for my dear husband, Tony Neal.

Carolyn Neal

This book is for Elizabeth Kilday, my wife and inspiration, and
Natasha Rossle, my dear daughter.

Tom Janus

American Historical Press
Sun Valley, California

Puget Sound Ferries

From Canoe to Catamaran

An Illustrated History

Carolyn Neal & Thomas Kilday Janus

Right: Map of Puget Sound and the surrounding areas. Courtesy, Washington Department of Energy

Previous page: The mills at Teekalet, Washington Territory, approximately 1863. Teekalet was later renamed Port Gamble. Reproduced from a lithograph in the George A. Pope III collection. The barkentine Jenny Ford is in the left foreground. Courtesy, Port Gamble Historic Museum

Endpapers: From 1913 to 1930 the Tacoma carried passengers between Seattle, the "Queen City," and Tacoma, the "City of Destiny." Courtesy, Kitsap County Historical Museum Archives

Image of ferry throughout text: The 93-foot steamer Dauntless was built in Tacoma in 1899 and eventually ended up on the Whidbey, Irondale, Hadlock run as part of Hastings Steamboat Company in Port Townsend. Courtesy, Puget Sound Maritime Historical Society, 709-4 Seattle

© 2001 American Historical Press
All Rights Reserved
Published 2001
First Edition
Printed in the United States of America

Library of Congress Catalogue Card
Number: 2001095443

ISBN: 1-892724-19-7

Bibliography: p. 208
Includes Index

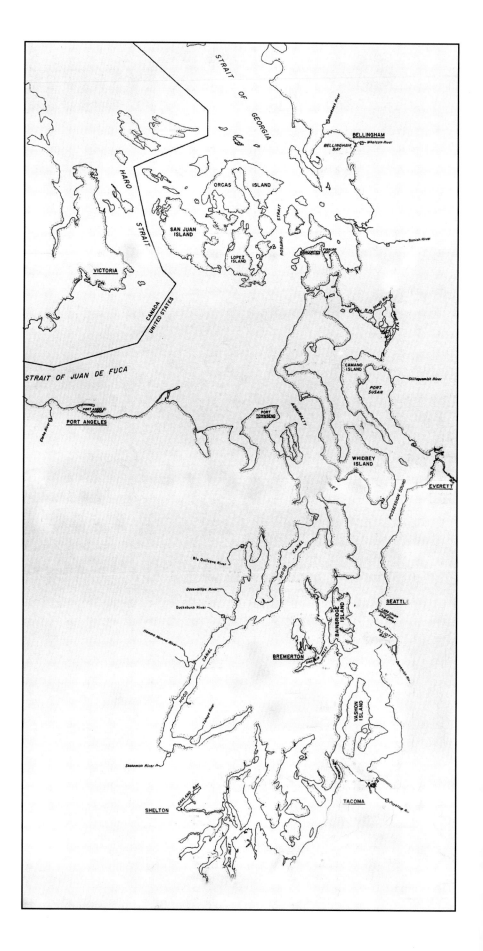

CONTENTS

Details from Cory Ench's Innis Creek. This portion of a larger mural found on a building in Port Angeles, WA displays the sleek elegance and distinctive prows of native canoes. More than one European explorer expressed admiration for these vessels. Photo by Tom Janus

FOREWORD

If you were raised near a ferry landing like I was, you know a million stories about the boats; the antics that occurred on the ferries themselves or while waiting for an arrival or departure.

The fellow that heard the whistle of the departing boat and was frantic to make his appointment in town. He jumped four feet across the open water to catch the ferry, only to find out it was arriving instead of departing.

A neighbor who arrived at the dock with a snoot full of moonshine and didn't realize the boat was not at dock when he proceeded down the ramp in a brand new Chevrolet; the swim ashore certainly woke him up.

The lady who thought the whistle on the *Willapa* sounded just a bit too close and went out on her front porch on a foggy morning to take a look. The *Willapa* was in her front yard, the captain looking her square in the eye across the beach as the ferry was grounded firmly next to her rowboat. And, of course, we all have friends who were born on the boats whose mothers did not quite make it to Swedish Hospital or Tacoma General.

As the years go by, the tales get taller and the stories get richer. But, in fact, Puget Sound's water transportation has provided an abundant layer of life, legend and lore to Washington State.

From the early mosquito fleet boats that filled Puget Sound to the most modern, up-to-date car ferries, this book tells it all. It is a wonderful description of our marine transportation system. It is history!

Enjoy *Puget Sound Ferries* and then go take a ride on the ferries.

Ralph Munro
Secretary of State, Retired

PREFACE

The Indians called it "Whulge," (whuh-ul-ch) the word for sea, ocean, or in general, a big area of saltwater. British explorer Captain George Vancouver, sailing the waters of the vast inland sea in 1792, chose instead to call it Puget's Sound in honor of his expedition's second lieutenant, Peter Puget. Over the years the possessive "s" disappeared and today Puget Sound is the defining geographical feature in the northwest corner of the continental United States.

As the heart of Washington State's "Evergreen Playground" and a major part of the state's economic backbone, Puget Sound is extraordinary. Its waters are deep and cold but they hold unimaginable beauty in the variety of life that the ecosystem supports. From the bald eagles soaring above to the mainstay of Native American culture, the salmon, to the smallest creatures like mussels, and the oddest creature, the geoduck, there is an enduring sense of wilderness that connects present to past.

Geologically Puget Sound is still a work in progress. Its waters hide an array of seismic faults capable of causing catastrophic earthquakes and its shores are ringed with volcanic peaks—Mt. Baker, Glacier Peak, and Mt. Rainier—all capable of hurling hot gasses or mudflows, the kind of activity that led to the present landscape. Some 20 to 40 million years ago the crunching, mashing, and folding of the earth, resulting from volcanic action and the movements of the region's tectonic plates, created an indentation called the Puget Lowland. Stretching from Canada to Oregon's Willamette River and surrounded on each side by mountain ranges—the Olympics on the west and the Cascades on the east—these Lowlands are an alluvial plain drained by rivers running out of the mountains. In perhaps as many as four eras popularly called the Ice Age, these Lowlands became a frozen ice-covered wasteland. In the fourth period, about 15,000 years ago, a great ice sheet, or glacier, moved southward from Canada. When it reached the Olympic Mountains the ice split into two sections. One part, the Juan de Fuca Lobe moved off to the west while the other section, the Puget Lobe, flowed into the Puget Lowland, gouging and scraping in bulldozer fashion as it inched its way southward. The glacier extended as far as what is now Olympia, Washington, burying what is present-day Bellingham, the San Juan Islands, and the Seattle-Tacoma-Olympia metropolitan area. At the current site of Seattle, the ice was more than a half-mile thick and covered an area 60 miles wide. Some 2,000 years later the receding glacier left a giant U-shaped trench to be flooded by the melting ice sheets and the rising waters of the Pacific Ocean. The northern portion of the Puget Lowland became the sheltered saltwater sea called Puget Sound. Other troughs cut by the glacier became channels that include Hood Canal, and Lakes Washington and Sammamish along with a network of smaller canals and inlets sometimes called the arms of Puget Sound.

While Puget Sound is a defining feature for Washington State, its boundaries are not so easily defined. Nautical charts place it within the area from Point No Point on the Kitsap Peninsula in the north to Tacoma in the south. The definition on file with the U.S. Board of Geographic Names expands the area to roughly 90 miles south from the Juan de Fuca Strait to Olympia. If a man-on-the-street survey were taken in the cities bordering the Sound, most residents would probably agree with those perimeters. The third definition, identified by Arthur Kruckeberg in *The Natural History of Puget Sound*, is the most generous of all and comes from the Puget Sound Water Quality Act. It defines Puget Sound as "all salt waters of the state of Washington inside the international boundary line between the state of Washington and the province of British Columbia, lying east of Ediz Hook at Port Angeles." Agencies operating under the Act recognized that oil spills and other types of water pollution follow the currents and know no boundaries.

Regardless of which perimeter is used, Puget Sound is one of the world's largest inland seas as well as one of the deepest water basins in the contiguous United States. Water depths range from 300 feet at its southern end to 600-800 feet in the north. The deepest hole, just northwest of Seattle, is 930 feet. Its waters average a chilly 50 degrees Fahrenheit year round and provide a vital biological habitat for more than 220 species of fish, along with a variety of marine mammals, waterfowl, birds, shellfish, and other organisms.

Two of Puget Sound's most interesting life forms are on opposite ends of the scale when measured according to size. The single-celled dinoflagellate produces flashes of pale blue fluorescent light that sparkle magically in the water on dark summer evenings. The wake of a passing boat or even the splash of a hand can cause the effect. By contrast, the depths of the water shelter the largest species of octopus found anywhere in the world. The Giant Pacific Octopus may weigh 100 pounds and can have a tentacle-spread of over 20 feet.

With its 10 major deep-water access ports, Puget Sound is a marine highway for world-wide commerce and a major element in the Pacific Northwest economy. Writer Murray Morgan calls it a "liquid highway." The waters are also home to a transportation system of ferryboats. From the time that the first inhabitants settled on its shores Puget Sound has hosted ferries—whether they be Indian canoes or large modern vessels filled with electronic marvels. These ferries transport commerce, daily commuters, local residents, and tourists. They are an intrinsic part of the area's history and culture, used on logos, tourist brochures, and as illustrations depicting the area. As a part of the Northwest lifestyle, ferries inspire art, music, and merchandise and occasionally serve as backdrops for motion pictures and television. There is even an Internet site featuring a virtual ferry where viewers can tour a ferry interior as well as witness the live action at the ferry terminal. Northwest  ferries are an icon of Puget Sound.

Washington State boasts the largest public ferry system in the United States and one of the world's most unique mass transit systems. Owned and operated by the state since 1951, the Washington State Ferry System carries over 27 million passengers and over 11 million vehicles each year. Its 29 vessels operate on 10 routes and travel over 900,000 miles annually. Ferry connections such as Bremerton–Seattle, Kingston–Edmonds, Vashon–Seattle, Bainbridge–Seattle, and the route through the San Juan Islands link the various communities on the Sound. For residents on some of the islands in the Sound, the ferries are the only public transportation system carrying passengers and autos to the larger metropolitan areas.

It may be that we Puget Sound residents get a little too complacent about our ferryboats. Those of us who commute every day are momentarily amused by tourists who thrill over the boat ride on the "lake." We habitually complain about ferry service, ferry costs, ferry crews, and ferry breakdowns that disrupt our daily schedules. Perhaps we should take some time to marvel over the simple pleasure of drinking that morning cup of coffee or that occasional evening glass of wine while we sit safely in our seats, away from the gridlock of traffic lights and merging traffic. We are privileged to enjoy the stunning scenic beauty of snow-capped mountains and blue waters complete with seagulls, cormorants, the occasional jumping fish, harbor seals, and sometimes orcas and gray whales. Even on the numerous gray days marked by drizzle or pounding rain, there is an awesome quality to the scenery. Take a fresh look at our amazing marine highway and the ferryboats that travel on it.

Carolyn Neal and Tom Janus

1921:—"THE NEW FLAGSHIP OF PUGET SOUND, M.V. CHINOOK."

Left: Seasonal ferry schedules have long been a part of life on Puget Sound. Courtesy, Raplh White Collection, Kitsap Regional Library, Bremerton, WA

Above: The luxurious 1947 ferry Chinook sailed on the overnight Seattle–Victoria run. She was anticipated as the new flagship of the Black Ball fleet. Courtesy, Author's collection

Below: In her later years the Indianapolis was a regular on the Seattle-Tacoma route. Courtesy, Author's collection

12726. S. S. Indianapolis, Seattle-Tacoma Passenger Boat, Seattle, Wash.

Above: Set against the backdrop of the Olympic Mountains, the ferry H.B. Kennedy approaches the Port Orchard dock in the early part of the last century. Ward Collection, Kitsap County Historical Society.

Right: Alex Young's paintings have been made into the annual Washington State Ferry commemorative posters for more than a decade. Courtesy, Alex Young

Above: Life sized figures on a Kalakala mural, painted by Cory Ench on the side of a bank building in downtown Port Angeles, WA are joined by Beth Kilday from Port Orchard. Photo by Tom Janus

Left: Colorful life rings provide a spot of brightness on ferries that are painted white and green. Photo by Tom Janus

Opposite page, top: Commuters lined up on the Bremerton boardwalk, waiting to board the catamaran Chinook to Seattle. Photo by Tom Janus

Opposite page, bottom: A Bainbridge Island ferry is framed by signage at Seattle's Pike Place Public Market. Photo by Tom Janus

The first mode of transportation in Pacific Northwest waters were the canoes belonging to the various Indian groups which inhabited the shores of present day Washington and British Columbia. An essential part of life, the vessels carried religious significance as well as cargo, families, fishermen, and warriors. This painting, entitled Return of the War Party by Paul Kane, was photographed at the Maritime Museum of British Columbia, Victoria, B.C., where it was on loan. Courtesy, Royal Ontario Museum

Chapter I

From Canoe to Steamboat

For more than 150 years, ferries have been a continually-evolving transportation mode on Puget Sound. Each of the eras—from the earliest canoes to the paddle-wheelers, steamboats, passenger ferries, auto ferries, and still faster passenger ferries—offer a history rich in personalities and lore. The Washington State Ferry System (WSF) was not created out of whole cloth—it has a colorful heritage—fascinating to anyone who has ever been on a Puget Sound ferryboat and wondered how it all began.

The recorded history of ferryboats on Puget Sound begins with the arrival of European and American explorers, traders, and, ultimately, with the settlers on the shores of a vast inland sea bordered by forests, rivers, prairies and towering mountains. These varied peoples who came to Puget Sound may have been seeking wealth, trade routes, the fulfillment of a national agenda, or simply a new home. What they found was a "marine highway" teeming with fish and wildlife, its shorelines occupied by indigenous peoples who plied the waters in canoes unlike anything Europeans had ever seen. As the two cultures met on the great salt waters called Whulge. Puget Sound sailing vessels co-existed with canoes. By the 1830s the canoes and schooners were joined by steamboats. To connect the growing numbers of settlements, the transportation system that began with a paddle evolved to a paddle-wheeler and later mushroomed into a swarm of steamers following the old canoe routes.

Explorers and fur traders were the first non-Indians to note the potential value and natural beauty of the Pacific Northwest. Two expeditions most closely related to Puget

British explorer George Vancouver first visited the Northwest as an able seaman on Captain James Cooke's ship Resolution. *The young Vancouver is pictured in part of a larger painting honoring explorers.*

The entire work, The Explorers, *is on display at the British Columbia Maritime Museum, Victoria B.C. Photo by Tom Janus, courtesy, The Maritime Museum of British Columbia, Victoria, B.C., and The Royal British Columbia Museum.*

on the land by these two explorers. Elliott Bay, Bainbridge Island, Port Orchard, Eagle Harbor, Port Townsend, Blake Island, Mt. Baker, Mt. Rainier, Mt. St. Helens, and even Puget Sound, are among the hundreds named by Vancouver or Wilkes. Wilkes holds the record, having named 261 places. Ironically, while he honored his subordinates such as Midshipman Samuel Elliott with the naming of Elliott Bay and Passed Midshipman George W. Colvocoresses with Colvos Passage, no geographical site has been named after Wilkes. There is, however, a Captain Wilkes Elementary School on Bainbridge Island named in his honor. In giving Wilkes the title of captain, school officials actually elevated Wilkes to the rank he felt that he had deserved as commander of the Expedition. The United States Navy had disagreed, refusing Wilkes' request for promotion. Not one to bow to authority, Wilkes reportedly wore a captain's uniform during the voyage.

Captain George Vancouver sailed to the northwest coast on behalf of the British Government in 1792. His purpose was twofold: explore in the hope of finding the long-sought Northwest Passage—an all-water route through the North American continent—and transact diplomatic business with the Spanish representative at Nootka Sound, a maritime fur-trading port on the western side of the island that the Europeans named Quadra's and Vancouver's Island (now shortened to Vancouver Island). The diplomacy foreshadowed Spain's abandonment of claims to the Pacific Northwest. In his role as explorer, Vancouver successfully entered, charted, and named much of the Puget Sound area.

In the last significant northwest exploration by a European power, the 34-year-old Vancouver commanded an expedition of 145 men and two vessels, the sloop *HMS Discovery* and the armed tender *Chatham.* Only two of the men were over 40 years of age; most were under 20. Some, like Lieutenant Joseph Baker and Lieutenant Peter Puget, were immortalized as names on the landscape of the Pacific Northwest, but the majority, like Vancouver himself, were to remain relatively unknown in their own country.

While Vancouver's published journals extol the wonderful nature of the still waters and deep anchorage of Puget Sound, his records also provide more spontaneous comments illustrating the confusions of discovery and exploration. Lacking the advantage of a map or an aerial

Sound are the explorations of the British under George Vancouver in 1792 and the United States Exploring Expedition of 1838–1842, more commonly known as the Wilkes Expedition, after its commodore, Navy Lieutenant Charles Wilkes. Both expeditions are significant because of their charts and notations on local geographical conditions and indigenous cultures of Puget Sound. Even more relevant to the lives of contemporary northwesterners, although they may not realize it, are the names bestowed

shot and forced to view the area from a small ship or even the equivalent of a rowboat, Vancouver had trouble distinguishing inlets from channels and islands from peninsulas. He was lucky enough to spot the San Juan Islands from the height of the bluff on Protection Island, where he could see the archipelago. Yet, elsewhere, forested headlands hid the bays and the marshlands hid the rivers. He completely missed a 12 mile stretch of Hood Canal, or, as he more accurately named it, Hood's Channel. Vancouver, complaining about the labor-intensive chore of gathering "correct or satisfactory information," called it a "broken country." But he also declared it "the most lovely country that can be imagined."

During his tenure in Puget Sound, Vancouver engaged in activities that have since become traditional in the Northwest—brewing, harvesting timber, and heading for warmer climates. While spruce twigs are no longer used, brewing is still a flourishing industry in the Northwest. In the process of making new topsail yardarms for the *Discovery,* his carpenters became the first white men to choose from among the "thousands of the finest spars the world produces." Some 60 years later these carpenters would be followed by the buzzing of steam-powered sawmills. Vancouver no doubt realized that Puget Sound weather can be wet and miserable. He named Foulweather Bluff and then declared the site not "ill named." Not surprisingly, in the best of Northwest tradition he spent the winter weeks of his voyage in Hawaii (Sandwich Islands).

In honoring his young lieutenant, Peter Puget, Vancouver did not name the entire inland sea after him. At the formal ceremony for taking possession, the explorer called the major body of water the Gulf of Georgia, after King George. Originally only the southern portion with its narrow fingers and shallow bays was named Puget's Sound. However, because the earliest settlements were in the southern portion and spread northward, the Sound's inhabitants adopted the designation Puget Sound and applied it to the entire area. Georgia was retained as the name for the straits separating Vancouver Island from mainland British Columbia. In a strange twist of fate, Lieutenant Puget, of whom little is known and no likeness has ever been found, usurped the British monarch in the naming of the waters of Whulge.

A half-century after Vancouver's voyage, it was an American's turn to chart the waters and give place names to the nooks and crannies of Puget Sound. The complete story of the United States Exploring Expedition has all the elements of a good "potboiler." A concise account of the voyage can be found in *The Wilkes Expedition: Puget Sound and the Oregon Country,* edited by Frances B. Barkan. The official five-volume *Narrative* compiled by Wilkes himself was also published. "The United States Ex Ex" as it was known, was an expression of American desire to practice Manifest Destiny and to show European powers that the United States was poised and ready for expansion.

An abundance of adventure marked the years 1838-1842 of charting the Pacific, including Fiji and the Sandwich Islands. There were murders, retributions, a volcano Mauna Loa, and an international controversy over whether Wilkes was the first to sight the shores of Antarctica, which apparently he was. Ships were lost, enemies made, and a mountain of grudges were yet to be settled by the time the expedition returned to New York. Much of the difficulty was owing to Wilkes' own abrasive, combative personality. After the expedition he was publicly reprimanded for his treatment of sailors under his command. His controversial behavior continued through to the Civil War years when Wilkes, acting on his own, used a naval squadron to seize British ships carrying mail and supplies to the Confederacy. Court martialed in 1863, he was found guilty of charges which included insubordinate conduct, disrespect, disobedience, and conduct unbecoming an officer. The punishment, three years suspension from all naval duties, was reversed after President Lincoln, a personal friend of Wilkes, reviewed the case and canceled both the charges and the verdict. However, the court martial proceedings were made public and Wilkes retired in disgrace.

Wilkes' shortcomings do not diminish the achievements of the United States Exploring Expedition—a major scientific accomplishment resulting in, among other things, charts so accurate they were in use well into the next century. The northwest part of the voyage occurred in the spring and summer of 1841 when Wilkes sailed his two ships, the *Vincennes* and the *Porpoise,* into Puget Sound. From those ships a number of smaller vessels were dispatched to survey and chart the waters. Wilkes benefited from Vancouver's charts, though he made corrections in some areas, such as Hood Canal. Using geographic names already bestowed by Vancouver, he added names of his own and also honored names given by local residents.

As well as recognizing its exceptional suitability as a deep water harbor, Wilkes observed and duly noted the natural attributes of Puget Sound. "Nothing can be more striking," he wrote, "than the beauty of these waters without a shoal or rock or any danger whatever for the whole length of this Internal Navigation the finest in the world accustomed as we are to prize that of our own country." Along with charting the waters he took time to calculate the height of Mt. Rainier, setting it at 14,850 feet, modern sources placing it at 14,410 feet. He even complimented the smells of the trees lining the shorelines, saying, "It was found by all of us . . . delicious . . . it savoured of civilization..."

Significantly, members of the Wilkes Expedition staged the first formal celebration of July 4th held on Puget Sound.

The celebration, featuring American flags, a dress parade, a 26 gun salute by the ship's howitzers, and a picnic of roast ox along with games and libations, highlighted an underlying purpose of the Wilkes Expedition—to expand American presence in the Northwest.

From 1818 to 1846 ownership of the Pacific Northwest was under terms of a joint occupancy treaty with Great Britain. Citizens and ships of any nation were allowed to occupy the territory up to the 49th parallel. The success of the Wilkes Expedition and the increased number of American settlers in the region made occupation of the Oregon territory a political issue. Presidential candidate James Polk's slogan in 1844 of "54°-40' or Fight" resulted in a new treaty placing the Northwest in American hands. Under the 1846 Oregon Treaty the boundary was set at the 49th parallel, with Vancouver Island going to the British and the San Juan Islands going to the United States. The actual San Juan boundary was not fully settled until 1872, when arbitration by Germany's Kaiser Wilhelm established the present border.

The Hudson's Bay Company vessel Beaver *steamed around the various ports of Puget Sound for more than 50 years. Her pace was sedate and her boiler consumed enormous amounts of cordwood, but the* Beaver's *success paved the way for other steam vessels. Courtesy, Special Collections Division University of Washington Libraries, Negative No. 7612*

Oregon officially became an organized United States territory in 1848. The present day state of Washington remained a part of the Oregon Territory until 1853 when it gained territorial status of its own and narrowly missed being named Columbia—congressmen paradoxically were concerned about potential confusion with the named District of Columbia.

Sandwiched between the first explorers and the United States Exploring Expedition were the fur traders, specifically Hudson's Bay Company. In 1833, this British-owned giant business established a post at Fort Nisqually. Located in the southern Puget Sound region, it served as a station on the route between company holdings in Fort Vancouver on the Columbia River and Fort Langley on Canada's Fraser River.

When company officials became impatient with the problems encountered by their sailing vessels trying to cross the dangerous river bar at the mouth of the Columbia, they voted to provide Fort Vancouver with a British-made steamboat. Instead of being delighted by the move from sail to steam, John McLoughlin, Fort Vancouver's legendary manager, or chief factor, balked at having to pay the operating expenses for a steamship. He was pleased only after the 100-foot vessel, the *Beaver*, turned out to be too underpowered for use on the Columbia River; thus he was able to exile her to service on Puget Sound.

The *Beaver* was unique. Her engines and boilers built by one of the inventors of the steam engine, James Watt, she was the first steam-powered side-wheeler on the Pacific Coast and for more than half a century—from 1836 to 1888—a familiar presence on Puget Sound. She worked mostly as a trading vessel but also did duty as a passenger carrier, a warship, and a towboat. Like other early steamers, the *Beaver* was slow and inefficient. Her limited twin 35-horsepower engines propelling her dual 13-foot paddlewheels meant that for every day of travel she needed to stop for two days so that Indian laborers could cut the 40 or 50 cords of wood necessary to keep the *Beaver* going.

The *Beaver's* tenure concluded in 1888 when a careless crew grounded her on the rocks at Prospect Point near Vancouver, Canada. To add to the indignity, the ship sat on the rocks for four years until the wake of another steamer washed her off and down to the bottom in 20 fathoms of water. Ironically, the passing steamer was the *Yosemite*, who would herself end up grounded and broken on the rocks of Puget Sound near Bremerton.

The fur company's other vessel, the *Otter*, was an equally well-known presence on the Sound. Longer than the *Beaver*,

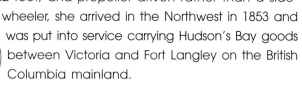

at 122 feet, and propeller driven rather than a sidewheeler, she arrived in the Northwest in 1853 and was put into service carrying Hudson's Bay goods between Victoria and Fort Langley on the British Columbia mainland.

Both of these Hudson's Bay vessels were years ahead of the heyday of steam on Puget Sound. As the harbinger of steam navigation in the Northwest they encouraged demands from the Sound's American population for whatever modern means of transport the mid-nineteenth century could offer.

Even as a derelict shipwreck lodged on the rocks near Vancouver, BC, the Beaver attracted notice. This commemorative plaque exhibits a Northwest maritime tradition—recycling vessel materials. It also notes that the Beaver, built in England, crossed the Atlantic, a crossing made under sail, with the paddle wheels carried as cargo and attached after the ship's arrival at Fort Vancouver on the Columbia River. Courtesy, Special Collections Division University of Washington Libraries. Photo by Info-Services, Negative No. 5326-B

In a landscape where dense forests, thick undergrowth, and steep slopes rendered the land nearly impassable, the sheltered waters of the Sound and its estuaries were natural highways. The first traditional craft on those highways were Indian canoes. The Indians of Puget Sound and southern British Columbia share a common linguistic background defining them as Coast Salish. Prior to contact with whites their economy centered on the bounties of the salt waterways, the tidelands, and the rivers. Canoes enabled them to maintain a marine lifestyle that involved seasonal migrations to follow fish runs. Tons of smoked and dried salmon, cod, and halibut could be transported along with shellfish and smelt to their winter lodgings. Canoes were also used for social interaction, carrying the populations of entire villages to dances and potlatches.

The cedar dugouts carved by hand from a single log combined speed and seaworthiness with grace and sleek elegance. The largest canoes belonging to the Haida of Vancouver Island could carry 100 warriors. Generally, however, they used smaller canoes that carried 20–30 people. European explorers who obviously knew something about boats admired the frail-looking craft, often noting in their journals the numbers of canoes they had

seen. In one 1791 account, the captain of a trading ship in the Queen Charlotte Islands mentions that 600 Haida canoes surrounded his vessel. American explorer Lieutenant Charles Wilkes, who mostly wrote in uncomplimentary terms about the Indian population, described their canoes as different from anything he had seen on his voyage. "They are made from a single trunk and have a shape that may be considered elegant..."

The canoes, along with most of the implements of everyday life, came from cedar. Lightweight, easily worked, and durable; the wood and the bark were perfectly suited to meet the Indians' needs. The organic toxin thujaplicin, which gives cedar its uniquely pleasant aroma, also acts as a preservative to stave off insect pests and rot. The sacred tree, or "Great Life Giver," provided clothing, waterproof hats (a necessity in the Northwest climate), baskets, boxes, mats, ropes, houses, and canoes.

Canoe-making was a special skill possessed by a select few. Even today, knowledge of the specific tricks is not widely shared. A master carver could create a canoe ranging from 8 feet to 72 feet long from a single cedar log, or he could craft as many as three smaller canoes from the same log. Although red cedar was most frequently used, carvers could also use yellow cedar, spruce, and sometimes cottonwood. A master carver usually worked a few hours a day with one or two assistants as well as a spirit helper. The most common dream spirit for the canoe builder was, appropriately, the redheaded woodpecker. It was also important for the craftsman to observe traditional rules such as abstinence and not combing his hair. These rituals helped prevent the cedar from splitting. It took about two months to complete a 25 foot dugout. Amazingly, a canoe of that length would typically be three-quarters of an inch thick along the sides and gradually thicken to one and a half inches on the bottom. Sources disagree over the average lifespan of a canoe, placing it from 10 to 70 years. Perhaps the most reliable

opinion comes from an 84-year old canoemaker who claimed that a well-maintained canoe could last 30 years.

Canoes were designed for special functions. Large sea-going canoes manned by warriors were used by the Indians of Vancouver Island in raiding expeditions to Puget Sound, where they captured slaves and booty. The Makah Indians of Cape Flattery, located on the most northwestern tip of Washington State, used, and are once again using, ocean-going canoes to hunt migrating gray whales. The Indians of Puget Sound relied on two basic types of saltwater canoes. One version averaged about 40 feet in length and was used for carrying cargo or freight; the other was a smaller, more graceful hunting canoe intended for pursuing porpoise, seal, and ducks.

Tribes such as the Snohomish, Snoqualmie, Nisqually, and Skykomish, that resided near the rivers flowing into Puget Sound, used shovel-nosed dugout canoes in the fresh water. Ranging in length from 10 to 40 feet, they were suited for shallow water and stable enough to survive the rapid currents of swift rivers. It has been suggested that the shovel-nosed canoe was actually the first type used in the Northwest and that later versions evolved from that style.

Canoes were among an Indian's most important possessions and a symbol of his wealth. It was not unusual for Indians living on the Puget Sound to bury their dead in canoes tied onto a tree or mounted on cross pieces laid on posts. Sometimes the canoe was set under the trees and a shed was built to cover the body. Both men and women were buried in this fashion.

Commonly painted black with red interiors, other decoration on canoes could include small shells embedded in the vessel's gunwhales. However, the major expression of the carver's artistic vision was to be found in the carved prow. Those unique images reflected birds, whales, fish and other figures common to the Indians' environment or mythology.

While Indians were out on Whulge, they talked to their boats, calling them by name and verbally giving them directions. Canoe names were inspired by either the owner's family or by some idiosyncrasy of the canoe itself, such as Crooked Canoe, Lazy Canoe, or Dancing Canoe. Women,

just as adept at paddling as the men, used a lighter and smaller paddle. In smaller boats such as the shovel-nosed river craft, women often took the helm, shouting orders to their male companions. In family travel, children paddled so that they could "learn by doing." If conditions were favorable, they might abandon their paddles in favor of sails made of woven cedar that could catch the wind.

Indians used songs and chants to learn proper breathing, set the pace, and maintain rhythm while paddling the canoe. When they wanted a favorable wind they might splash their paddles in the water or drum on the sides of the canoe as if urging it along. Early white settlers noted that they often heard Indians approaching by canoe long before they could see them. Imagine the rhythmic pounding of paddle on wood and the sing-song voices of the canoe's occupants carrying across the waters of the Sound on a still and foggy morning.

Recently those songs have again been heard on Puget Sound and in the waters around British Columbia's Vancouver Island and the Queen Charlotte Islands. Northwest Indians are using canoes as a tool for cultural renaissance. Beginning with the Washington State Centennial celebration in 1989, they scheduled a series of gatherings that ceremonialized the old custom of using canoes as a means of travel between tribes. Tribes in Canada and Washington are resurrecting the art of canoe carving with the help of modern technology such as chainsaws. One thing that has not changed is the

deep respect for the spiritual characteristics of the cedar tree and the canoe. The process of shaping a 400–800 year old cedar tree into a canoe has brought Native American communities together and acquainted their younger generations with the traditions and culture of their ancestors.

The influx of permanent settlers into the lands and waters of the canoe Indians was largely the result of the Donation Land Claims Act. Somewhat a precursor to the 1862 Homestead Act, the September 1850 legislation included the provision that every male settler over 18 years of age who became a resident of the Territory before December 1, 1850, and who lived on the land for four years, could be granted 320 acres. If he was married, his wife was likewise entitled to 320 acres in her name. The Act also provided that for the period between December 1, 1850 and December 1, 1853, any male settler over 21 years of age was entitled to 160 acres of land plus an additional 160 acres for his wife. In both cases the male settler had to be a United States citizen or have declared an intention to become a citizen. Subsequent legislation extended the Act until December 1, 1855 and provided

Opposite page: Canoes have the advantage of not requiring docks. The larger cedar models did, however, require some manpower to move from the beach into the water, especially at low tide. Courtesy, Jefferson County Historical Society, Port Townsend, Washington

for the settler to purchase the land for $1.25 an acre after two years (later reduced to one year) residency.

Attracted to the free land granted by the Donation Land Act, settlers lodged claims ranging from 60 to 640 acres on the lands bordering Puget Sound, Hood Canal, the Straits of Juan de Fuca and the Straits of Georgia. It was believed that ultimately white society would replace the indigenous residents. If the goal was to make Indians irrelevant, that goal was unattainable in the 1850s, simply because the 2,000 whites living on the Sound and its adjacent waters were neighbors to 12,000 or more Indians. Writing in 1893, pioneer steamboat captain J.G. Parker noted that in 1855 "Indians were more numerous on the beach and waters of Puget Sound than gulls are now." Indians were unavoidably relevant. They provided food and labor in the early sawmills and on farms and also worked as domestics. White Americans, or "Bostons" as they were called, paid to travel or ship goods by Indian canoe.

For white settlers on Puget Sound, canoe travel was considered the first type of ferry travel. For a price, Indians would transport settlers from one place to another. The accommodations may not have been comfortable, the schedules non-existent, and the pace a little slow, but the Indians did generally deliver the customer safely to his destination.

Descriptions of these trips are recorded in the letters, journals, and reminiscences of Puget Sound's early white inhabitants and visitors. Some accounts, like the letters of Methodist Episcopal missionary David Blaine and his wife Catherine, are highly critical of Indians and of everything about their lifestyles. Others, represented by Whatcom County pioneer Phoebe Judson, Port Townsend icon James Swan and the lyrical prose of Caroline Leighton, show a greater curiosity, understanding, and appreciation of Indian culture.

Phoebe Judson observed an interesting tidbit of Indian canoe etiquette. When two canoes encountered each other on the water, no one spoke until the canoes had passed each other. Then they would shout greeting as long as the canoes' occupants were within hearing range. Judson also noted "It was a common saying among the old settlers, when our journeying was mostly by canoe, that one was perfectly safe anywhere on the water in the hands of an Indian." Problems occurred when white men insisted on telling the Indians what to do. A case in point was the deaths in 1854 of Captain Barstow, owner of the barque *Mary Melville*, and George N. McConaha, a member of the territorial legislature. The men insisted that Indians transport them from Olympia to Seattle even though the Indians argued that the water was too rough for the trip. A few miles short of Seattle, the canoe hit a violent squall and overturned. Barstow, McConaha, and two of the six Indians drowned.

Even Catherine Blaine, who experienced the Indian War and generally had nothing favorable to say about local Indians, had enough common sense to note in her

THE TRAVELS OF THEODORE WINTHROP

One of the best written, although quite acerbic, accounts appears in Theodore Winthrop's classic book *Canoe and Saddle*. The 25 year-old Yale graduate traveled through the Northwest from April to September, 1853, visiting many sites in Oregon and Washington. The manuscript, originally entitled *Klalam and Klickitat,* finally appeared as *The Canoe and Saddle* in 1862, more than a year after Winthrop was killed in the Civil War. The book's exotic locale provided popular escapist literature for readers on the war-torn East Coast and quickly became a best seller.

For two days Winthrop traveled on Whulge, as he preferred to call it, from Port Townsend to Nisqually. Although he expressed disdain for the indigenous residents of Whulge, he had nothing but praise for the geography—calling Whulge a "vast fiord, parting rocks, and forests primeval with a mighty tide." He went so far as to declare Whulge more interesting, and its salmon better, than those in the waters of the eastern United States. He even suggested that its "cockney misnomer," Puget, be dropped in favor of the more melodic Whulge.

Winthrop's description of the trip begins with the sentence. "The Duke of York was ducally drunk." The reference is not, of course, to British royalty but rather to Chetzemoka, brother of the Klalam Chief King George. It was a British and American convention to christen Indians with the names of more famous figures simply because they could not pronounce the Indians' real names. Consequently Klalam Chief S'Hai-ak became King George, his wife Queen Victoria, and their sons, General Jackson and Thomas Jefferson. Other Indians were known by names such as the Duke of Clarence, John Adams, and Patrick Henry.

The Duke of York succeeded his brother as Chief of the Klalams and by all other accounts he was a popular and generally sober leader. He quickly realized that the white population had come to stay and that the Indian's best hope was to seize the commercial opportunity for trade with the Europeans and Americans. He fostered friendly relations with whites, signing the 1855 Point-No-Point Treaty and refusing to join with the hostile tribes during the Indian War. Today Chetzemoka Park in Port Townsend is one of the loveliest spots on the Olympic Peninsula. Another honor which is not surprising given the Northwest's caffeine oriented culture is a blend of coffee bearing the name Chetzemoka. One of Washing-

Theodore Winthrop's colorful, if exaggerated account of his 1853 journey to the wilds of the Northwest, including his trip with the "Duke of York", was a popular tale with readers in America's more urbane East Coast cities. Courtesy, Special Collections Division University of Washington Libraries, Negative No. 18578.

ton State's ferries also bears his name. Given Winthrop's account of being ferried by a canoe commanded by the Indian, it is an appropriate name.

In Winthrop's episode the Duke is an insolent player in a comedic farce. Although displaying Winthrop's contempt for Indians, the story does reveal something about the process of traveling by chartered canoe. Price negotiations for canoe-hire were conducted in the Chinook jargon, a combination of English, French, Spanish, Chinook, Haida and other dialects widely used in commerce between Europeans, Americans and the Indians. It was so widely used that the territorial newspaper in Olympia printed a glossary in one issue and then repeated it so settlers could more easily communicate with their Indian laborers. For canoe travel one of the most valuable words was "hyak," meaning hurry. Lacking knowledge of that admonition, a traveler could find himself at the mercy of Indians who tended to move at their own pace. Like Indian time, the pace was apt to be slower than most "Bostons" were happy with.

For the cost of one blanket for the canoe and one for each paddler, Winthrop hired a 40 foot dugout manned by Olyman Siwash, the Duke of York, one of his wives, Jenny Lind, and three other paddlers. After they started on the trip, Winthrop, unhappy that the Indians were passing a cupful of alcohol for general consumption, seized the cup and emptied its contents into Whulge. The angry paddlers displayed guns and knives to which Winthrop responded by producing his own Colt six-shooter. In a sullen form of work stoppage, the Indians decided to take a nap. Sitting in the drifting canoe, Winthrop was able to calm himself by enjoying the surrounding scenery. Likewise, the nap seemed to calm the Indians. When they awoke, relations were once again amicable. At Winthrop's suggestion they stopped for a picnic and then continued the voyage with renewed paddling and songs Winthrop seemed to enjoy, even though he labeled them as "grotesque combination of guttural howls."

Two things of interest noted by Winthrop were, first, his observation that his canoe transport was not alone on Whulge. He commented on the number of lumber ships visible on the opposite shore. The export of trees to San Francisco formed the basis of a growing economy that would ultimately draw more settlers to the shores of what they would call Puget Sound. Secondly, Winthrop noted that canoes often faced lengthy delays on windless summer days because the smoke from burning forest fires obscured all vision. In the absence of a compass there was nothing to do but wait until friendly breezes pushed the smoke along and created clear conditions for navigating by sight.

After spending the night by a campfire on the beach, Winthrop and the Indians set off for the second and last day of their trip. As they entered the southern waters near present-day Puyallup, Winthrop looked up to see the giant mountain dome of snow. "Only its splendid snows

were visible, high in the unearthly regions of clear blue noonday sky. The shore line drew a cincture of pines across the broad base where it faded unreal into the mist." He was experiencing Mt. Rainier with the same awe that anyone who sees it today cannot help but feel.

Along with his description of the beauty of Mts. Rainier, Baker, and St. Helens, Winthrop launched into a written tirade on the naming of the mountains. He called Rainier "stupid nomenclature perpetuating the name of somebody or nobody." He preferred the Indian designation of Tacoma. Years later his comments apparently swayed one group of settlers residing at the foot of Mt. Rainier. In 1868 they changed the proposed name of their city from Commencement City to Tacoma.

The mountain that George Vancouver had christened Mt. Baker the Indians called Kulshan, and Winthrop agreed. "Mountains should not be insulted by being named after undistinguished bipeds nor by the prefix of Mt...." Theodore Winthrop would be pleased that Kulshan is a familiar name on Puget Sound. It graces a ferryboat. Now, if there were only a ferryboat named Whulge.

Although Indian adoption of the clothes worn by "Bostons" was ridiculed by Theodore Winthrop in Canoe and Saddle, Chetzemoka *aka Duke of York apparently took great pride in this outfit and in his visit to San Francisco in 1852. Courtesy, Jefferson County Historical Society Museum, Port Townsend, WA*

description of the same incident that "the Indians...were always to be trusted as to the propriety of going out in a storm...." Aside from that comment, Catherine Blaine was quite forthcoming about her unwillingness to travel by canoe. Calling them those "dreaded canoes," she wrote that they were a terror to her. Her husband, the Reverend David Blaine, was more annoyed at the cost of canoe travel and complained that Indians expected to be paid for the use of their vessels!

Caroline Leighton was a marked contrast to the Blaines. The Indians called her "Closh tum-tum," meaning good heart. As the wife of a Treasury Department agent and customs collector, Caroline arrived in the Northwest in 1865, living first in Port Angeles and later in Port Townsend. She also had the opportunity to travel with her husband throughout the territory. Her *Life at Puget Sound*, published in 1884, is a charming pioneer memoir distinguished by its literary quality and Leighton's emphasis on delighting in all of her experiences. She did not judge,

but observed. Reporting on her first encounter with Indians at Port Angeles, her first thought was to get dictionaries of the Haidah, Chinook, and other Indian languages so that she and her husband could communicate in a more satisfactory manner with their guests. "At present we can only smile very much at them."

Like other early settlers ferried by Indian canoe, the Leightons preferred sobriety in the paddler. In one instance they politely declined the services of the intoxicated Duke of Wellington, choosing instead an Indian reputed to be a teetotaler.

One person who may have best understood the effects of alcohol and most opposed the liquor trade was James G. Swan, himself, ironically, a practicing alcoholic. Based on Swan's journals and diaries, Ivan Doig's 1980

A Washington pioneer who settled in the Bellingham area at Lynden, Phoebe Judson recorded several journeys made by canoe. In a trip up the Nooksack River with an Indian couple hired to transport the Judsons, Phoebe noted with interest the skills used in tricky navigation around fallen logs and other obstructions. Indian women were often in charge of the difficult navigating, shouting out orders to the men as they paddled. Courtesy, Special Collections Division University of Washington Libraries, Negative No. 18584.

book *Winter Brothers: A Season at the Edge of America* is the beautifully told story of a thoroughly likeable man. In the 1850s Swan abandoned his middle-class Boston life in favor of the wet wilderness of the Northwest Coast. There he became, among other things, an Indian Agent, teacher to the Makah, collector of Indian artifacts for the Smithsonian Institution, booster for the city of Port Townsend, and friend to Chetzemoka (Duke of York). Of all the "Bostons," Swan was probably the best known among the Indians.

Swan's canoe trips between Washington's northwestern tip of Cape Flattery and the town of Port Townsend on the Strait of Juan de Fuca typically took three days. Like other observers, Swan praised the skillful and elegant workmanship that went into carved canoes. He compared them to the finest clipper ships. And, like the unfortunate drowned "Boston" men in Blaines's account, Swan, on one occasion, insisted that his paddlers continue a trip after they had beached the canoe about six miles short of Port Townsend. The Indians argued that the weather was ominous; they were right. A ferocious tide caught the vessel, nearly swamping it, as the paddlers' usual songs gave way to the death song. In this instance the Indians were able to get the canoe safely back to shore and a wiser James Swan learned firsthand the respect that Washington pioneers generally held for those who transported them via canoe.

Prior to the arrival of steamships on Puget Sound, sailing vessels supplemented Indian canoes in providing water transportation. Schooners, barks and brigs, distinguished by their masts and riggings, carried log piles, square timber, and sawed lumber away from the heavily forested shores of the Sound bound for San Francisco, the Sandwich Islands (Hawaii), and even Australia and China. They returned such goods as sugar, salt, syrup, rice, dry goods, paints, liquor, tobacco, nails, and window glass.

The seemingly endless supply of trees and the profits attached to logging attracted the earliest industry to the shores of Puget Sound. Starting with Henry Yesler's Seattle steam mill, other mills were established at Bainbridge Island, Kingston, and Seabeck on Hood Canal. Any place with suitable anchorage offered a prospective mill site. One of the premier mill towns was Port Gamble on the Kitsap Peninsula. Founded in 1853 by William Talbot, A.J. Pope, Charles Foster, and J.P. Keller, the Puget Mill Company, later Pope & Talbot, became the longest continuing operating sawmill in the United States before it closed in 1995 after 142 years. Thanks to its status as a National Historic Site, the town of Port Gamble has maintained its 1853 era appearance to such a degree that visiting the site is like stepping back into Washington's territorial days.

With 33 sawmills operating in Washington Territory by 1854, the trade in lumber fostered a growing economy that attracted new settlers. The ships carried passengers from San Francisco to Puget Sound and within the Sound from port to port. While sailing vessels may have been considered more civilized than Indian canoes for passenger travel, they were also slow, not always available, and not really suited for the tides, currents and eddies that existed on portions of the inland sea.

The idea of introducing American steamships onto the waters of Puget Sound generated excitement for local boosters who wanted to develop the commercial interests of the region, attract settlers, and gain bragging rights over Portland, Oregon—the main settlement on the Columbia River. In 1852 Olympia's weekly newspaper, *The Columbian*, declared that "the businessman on the Sound, as well as the traveling public, have heretofore experienced the most serious inconvenience, arising from the want of a comfortable and speedy means of transportation up and down the Sound." So long as white residents continued to depend on the canoes and the Indians for their transit, they could expect to "suffer from their implacable extortiens (sic), annoyance, disappointment, and the chagrin consequent upon the repining of strangers." This was a call for improvements in the transportation system. Dressed in modern verbiage, it could have just as easily been written in any of the decades of the twentieth century. The desire of the "traveling public" for a comfortable and speedy transportation system has long been cause for discussion in the Puget Sound region.

One of Seattle's founding fathers, Arthur Denny, reported that the trip from Seattle to Olympia by canoe took at least two and sometimes three days in the winter. Travelers had to camp on the beach. Puget Sound beaches tend to be rocky or covered in gravel, a reminder of their Ice Age origins. In the winter they are also likely to be cold and perpetually wet. The "traveling public" may have indeed had something to complain about. Steamers were faster, more comfortable and, once the fare dropped from $10.00 to $6.00, were considered reasonable by Denny's count. The entrepreneurs who put steam into motion on Puget Sound were generally regarded as "public benefactors."

The pioneer steamship intended to be a "regular accommodation packet," or ferry, was a side-wheeler steamer named the *Fairy*. In late 1853, she arrived from San Francisco, not under her own power but aboard the bark *Sarah Warren*. Her name reflected her diminutive size—less than 100 feet long. She left Olympia every Monday and Wednesday bound for Steilacoom 25 miles away, and made the return voyage to Olympia on Tuesdays and Thursdays. On Fridays she followed an Olympia-Alki-Seattle route until she was forced to give up the run. The *Fairy* was too small and unseaworthy to work on the northern part of the Sound during winter weather conditions. In pioneer parlance, traveling north on Puget Sound, i.e., from Olympia to Seattle, was referred to as going down the Sound. The trip down the Sound was a problem for the wee *Fairy*. Rounding Alki Point on her approach to Seattle, she always lay so far over on her side that one paddle-wheel came completely out of the water. Despite popular support for the venture, people were reluctant to travel on her. Her career ended abruptly when her boiler exploded, sinking the ship at the Steilacoom wharf in 1857. Despite the fact that she sunk at the wharf, nothing was found when a search was conducted for the *Fairy* a few days after the sinking. A week later she was found floating 15 miles away from Steilacoom, her machinery mysteriously absent.

Maintenance on early steamships presented a problem since new parts and supplies were difficult to obtain. Even lubricating oil was in short supply until the Indians discovered how to extract oil from dogfish. Consequently, mechanical problems and even boiler explosions were fairly common occurrences in Sound transportation. One ship's captain, the victim of a boiler explosion, was scalded in the blast and ended up in Olympia for medical treatment. He had been engaged in towing logs at the time of the explosion and informed his employers by stating simply, "*Resolute* blown up; boom gone to hell, and I'm at the Pacific Hotel."

The next phase in the evolution of steam navigation on the Sound began with the arrival of the Sound's first ocean-going steamer, *Major Tompkins*, owned by John M. Scranton. The initial appearance of the 97-foot wooden steamship in Port Townsend in September 1854, inspired local residents to issue a noisy salute. Normally this would have been done with artillery, but, lacking the proper guns, Colt revolvers were called into action as a satisfactory form of greeting. The citizens of Steilacoom, faced with the same absence of artillery, showed their excitement and their creativity by blowing up stumps as a welcoming gesture for the vessel.

The *Major Tompkins* was the object of intense scrutiny by the local press. In hyperbole typical of the time, ship's Captain James Hunt and his crew were found to be gentlemen who not only performed their duties with ability but were also kind and courteous toward passengers. Crew demeanor has always been an important and controversial part of ferry travel in Puget Sound. It was also worth noting whether or not the *Major Tompkins* was really a seaworthy vessel. Emphasizing that she was built of live oak by master carpenters, and had safely made the trip from San Francisco, seemed proof enough of the ship's suitability. The fact that the normal 12 day trip was accomplished by the *Major Tompkins* in three weeks indicated her general tendency toward slowness. However, it may have been the viewpoint of early settlers that a slow steamer was better than no steamer and that the propeller driven *Tompkins* was a technological step up from the earlier side-wheelers. It was reported that a steamer on the waters of Puget Sound would add more toward the growth and prosperity of the territory than any other project.

A general declaration of praise for the *Major Tompkins* was accompanied by other regular news of the "Pumpkins," as she was known. The nickname reflected the ship's "broad in the beam" and "round in the stern" appearance. The time and place of every stop on the ship's weekly Olympia to Victoria route were duly noted in the Olympia newspaper. It took three hours to make the 25 mile run to Steilacoom, five hours from Steilacoom to Seattle, and another five hours on the 50 mile journey from Seattle to Port Townsend. Even the list of passengers was published, reading like a who's who of early pioneer society. Clearly the *Major Tompkins* was destined to be

a valuable commodity on Puget Sound because she provided not only passage for people, stock and freight; she was also fitted out to provide towing service for other vessels.

For the adventurous few who had left families and friends behind, pioneer letters and early newspaper rantings reveal what might be considered an obsession with the mail. How, when, and even if letters were received was a major topic in correspondence sent back East. The lack of regular mail service outranked the weather as the most irritating feature of life on Puget Sound. Located at Olympia, the first post office received mail once a week from Rainier, Oregon. Carried by canoe up the Cowlitz River to Cowlitz Landing, the mail was then transferred to horseback for the overland trip to Olympia. From Olympia it was distributed to Puget Sound settlements via canoe in an enterprise referred to as the "Canoe Express," although "express" may not have been the right word to describe the speed of the service. By carrying the mail in addition to her other cargoes, the *Major Tompkins* was heralded as the source of a "healthy postal communication."

As it turned out, the "Pumpkins" relationship with Puget Sound was not of long duration. The *Major Tompkins* left Olympia on February 8th for what would be her last trip. Two days later, on February 10th she left Port Townsend bound for Victoria on Vancouver Island. Midway across the Straits of Juan de Fuca, gale force winds hit the ship. Captain Hunt turned back toward

Port Townsend, the wind abated, and he once again turned toward Victoria. Darkness and the revitalized storm kept the captain from finding the entrance to Victoria harbor so he headed the ship toward nearby Esquimalt. Two hundred yards short of safety, the storm combined with the tide to smash the ship into the rocks at the harbor entrance. Passengers and crew saved themselves by scrambling across the rocks just before the breakers swept the upper deck away.

While the *Major Tompkins*'s arrival and activities were big press items, her sinking after six months service on the Sound received only perfunctory notice and a comment that the Sound community would be without a steamer for awhile. And it was not long before other steamers took up the position left by the *Major Tompkins*. The *Water Lily*, *Traveler*, *Resolute*, and *Constitution* were all operating on Sound waters in the 1850s.

Like the *Major Tompkins*, the *Traveler* also met a tragic end. She had left Port Townsend with one passenger bound for Port Gamble early in March 1858. Her crew, trying to wait out a storm and a strong tide, anchored her in a sheltered spot 400–600 yards off the tip of the Kitsap Peninsula. During the night, the *Traveler* started to take on water and gave every indication of sinking despite the frantic efforts of the eight men aboard who tried to bail her out and pole her towards shore. The engineer, Thomas Warren, and two Indians were able to swim safely ashore. The other men remained behind, clinging to the cordwood that had been on the *Traveler's* deck. By the time that Warren made his way along the beach the eight miles to Port Gamble and returned with help, five men, including the captain, Thomas Slater, and the purser, Truman H. Fuller, had drowned. Slater, a popular maritime figure in the Northwest since 1853, was buried in Port Townsend. Fuller, ironically, had also been the purser aboard the *Major Tompkins* and had survived that wreck. The *Traveler* disaster was a low point in early Puget Sound steamship lore.

In more positive developments, by 1858, the same year as the *Traveler* sinking, steamboats were being locally crafted. The first was the *Julia Barclay*, constructed by the Port Gamble mill workers. The 145-foot vessel, built entirely of Douglas fir, ushered in the change from side-wheeler to sternwheeler although side-wheelers continued to be built.

Two of the most famous of the later side-wheelers, the *Eliza Anderson,* and the *George E. Starr* had careers that spanned the second half of the nineteenth century. The *Eliza Anderson* enjoyed the distinction of having been the first ocean-going steamship built in Portland, Oregon shipyards. She arrived in Seattle in 1858 and was undoubtedly a welcome sight simply for her size. At 140-feet-long, the *Eliza Anderson* was among the first substantial vessels to operate in Puget Sound waters. For 12 years she steamed along at a leisurely pace of nine knots on her routine trips between Olympia and Victoria, B.C, with stops at Yesler's Wharf in Seattle as well as stops in Steilacoom, Port Madison, Port Gamble, Port Ludlow, and Port Townsend. Travelers going the whole distance paid $20.00 while those who boarded in Seattle got a lower fare of $15.00, along with cattle which also traveled for $15.00 a head. Sheep could be shipped the distance for a mere $2.50 a head.

Like other steamships operating on Puget Sound, the *Eliza Anderson* offered more than just transportation. Her captain, D.B. Fitch, served the smaller communities such as Port Gamble and Port Ludlow as a banker, handling money needs in the absence of more formal financial institutions.

As a pioneering vessel and the only one on the route for the first two years, her profits supplemented by a lucrative mail contract, the *Eliza Anderson* was enough

of a money-maker that she could easily face down competition when other steamships challenged her dominance. Her owners, John T. Wright and sons along with the Bradford Brothers, were able to inaugurate rate wars so vicious that at one point the cost of travel between Olympia and Victoria dropped to less than a dollar.

In 1870, the *Olympia*, a newer and more elegant steamer, replaced the sturdy old *Eliza Anderson*, which continued to run as a spare boat until 1877. In 1882 her career seemed permanently over when she sank at the Seattle wharf. For a year she sat in the mud until raised, rehabilitated, and restored to the Victoria run in 1884. Her owner, one of the Wrights, Captain Thomas Wright, was well-known for his sense of humor. The *Eliza Anderson* was equally well-known for her steam calliope. The two became even more famous when Wright chose to enter Victoria's harbor on the Queen's birthday with the calliope playing "Yankee Doodle."

A year later, in 1885, the *Eliza Anderson* was seized by Port Townsend-based customs officials on a charge of carrying contraband Chinese laborers. By the time that owner Captain Wright was exonerated of any knowledge of the Chinese passengers, it was too late. He had suffered financial ruin and the loss of his boat.

The *Eliza Anderson* moved on and from 1886 to 1890 she was part of the Washington Steamboat Company fleet owned by Port Gamble pioneer Daniel B. Jackson. Sold to the Puget Sound & Alaska Steamship Company, she remained moored in the Snohomish River until the Klondike Gold Rush promised premium prices for anything that could float and make it as far as Nome. The veteran steamship made it to Dutch Harbor, Alaska in March 1898 where she was stranded on the beach, broken and in pieces. A sad end, far from home for one of Puget Sound's favorite pioneer vessels.

One of the steamships that challenged the *Eliza Anderson* on the Sound was the *George E. Starr*. Built with great care and attention to detail in Seattle by J.F.T. Mitchell and launched in 1879, the *George E. Starr* was owned by the Starr brothers, Louis and George. The boat had been intended to run as partners with the Starr's other vessel, the *North Pacific*, on the all-important Olympia–Victoria mail route. The 148-foot side-wheeler can best be described as elegant. She was also a smug-

last years on the Sound, 1908-1912, were occupied with excursion cruises of happy summertime picnickers who could count among their memories a day spent on the *George E. Starr.*

As the decade of the 1850s ended, the era of the steamboat continued in earnest, fostering the development of numerous shoreline communities. For the next 60 years Puget Sound residents depended on the services of little steamers known collectively and affectionately as the Mosquito Fleet.

Above: Sources vary on the size of this elegant steamship. She was either 148-feet long or 154-feet. In any case she was well built and traversed the Sound's waters for many years. Courtesy, Puget Sound Maritime Historical Society, Seattle, 1018-11

Right: Photo of Charles Wilkes. Photo by Asahel Curtis, courtesy, Washington State Historical Society, Tacoma, Neg. No. 11507

gler, although that was certainly not part of her intended function. Extra space in her oversized paddle boxes made it possible for Chinese immigrants to enter the United States illegally.

Sold in 1881 to the Oregon Railway & Navigation Company, the *George E. Starr* kept on her usual run with the added task of taking out the competition—the reactivated sentimental favorite *Eliza Anderson.* The ensuing rate war dropped the cost of travel to a laughable 25 cents, a fare that might have gone lower if the *Eliza Anderson* had not been seized on the smuggling charge.

Besides being a popular excursion boat, the *George E. Starr* was also one of the boats that transported the circus across the Straits of Juan de Fuca for performances in Victoria, B.C. Somehow the image of elephants pushing circus vans up the loading ramp onto the gaily festooned white boat seems appropriate for 1890s America.

During her long tenure, the side-wheeler operated between Port Townsend and Port Angeles, ran on the Columbia River, transported prospectors and their horses to Skagway for the Klondike Gold Rush, and worked the Bellingham-Seattle route as one of Joshua Green's LaConner Trading & Transportation Company vessels. Her

Opposite, right: Nathanial Crosby III (1836-1886) performed purser's duties on early Puget Sound steamers. Traditionally, pursers also fulfilled the role of communicator by delivering newspapers and breaking news to their ports of call. Courtesy, Jefferson County Historical Museum, Port Townsend, WA

Opposite, left: Famous crooner Bing Crosby displayed the same relaxed style that made his grandfather Nathaniel one of the most popular steamboat men on Puget Sound. Courtesy, Gonzaga University Library

THE CROSBY CONNECTION

Steamboating on Puget Sound tended to be a family affair; the Wright Brothers, the Hunt Brothers, the Barlows, Hansens, Moes, Morans, Skansies, and Starrs represent a few but certainly not all of the Sound's maritime families. Another family, most famous for its non-maritime progeny, was the Crosby clan.

The Crosby's maritime traditions stretched all the way to Maine and Massachusetts where five of the Crosby men were sea captains. Captain Nathaniel Crosby Jr. first reached the Northwest in the mid-1840s and was so impressed with the area's possibilities that he convinced his brothers to move the entire family westward. Some immigrants made the trek overland as part of the annual wagon trains. Others were booking passage on the sailing ships for the long voyage around South America or the shorter route by ship and then overland across Central America to another ship. The Crosbys accomplished the trip in a slightly different style. Elder brother Clanrick Crosby purchased a brig named the *Grecian* and transported the whole family, about 20 members, including the family patriarch Captain Nathaniel Crosby Sr. as well as wives, children, in-laws, a housekeeper, and one passenger. Clanrick was captain and another brother, Alfred, second officer. The first officer slot was filled by brother-in-law Washington Hurd. The group left the East in 1849 and arrived in Portland, Oregon in March 1850.

From Portland, Clanrick moved north to Tumwater on Puget Sound. Alfred became a well-known ship's pilot in Astoria, Oregon where piloting across the Columbia River bar was an enviable skill. A presumably homesick Nathaniel Sr. returned to Cape Cod. Nathaniel Jr. first helped to found the town of Milton, Oregon and then began an international trade carrying northwest timber spars to the Orient, pausing long enough to join brother Clanrick in a general store and flour mill venture in Tumwater. Nathaniel Jr.'s wanderlust and foreign business interests took him and his family to Hong Kong where he died in 1856. Son Nathaniel Crosby III returned to the Northwest, working for his Uncle Clanrick in Tumwater as part of a company known as Hale, Crosby and Winsor. Nat, as he was called, served as purser on the company steamboats

where he was popular as "one of the few men who know how to tender the ordinary civilities of life in a gracious manner," as quoted in the *Washington Standard* newspaper in 1866.

Clanrick Crosby and his partners, H.C. Hale and Henry Winsor, united in 1866 for the purpose of competing with the *Eliza Anderson*. Like the other enterprises taking on Puget Sound's reigning cash-cow, the Hale, Crosby, and Winsor steamers *Josie McNear* and then *New World* engaged in price-cutting that made it impossible for either side to operate without losing money. The conflict ended late in 1867 when controlling interest in the *New World* shifted to another entrepreneur, Joseph Kamm, who reached a gentleman's agreement with the owners of the *Eliza Anderson*.

Hale, Winsor, and the two Crosbys turned to other pursuits. Nat Crosby went to work for the prestigious Wells Fargo company, and while he continued to live in Tumwater, one of his sons, Harry L., took up residence in Tacoma. Harry's son, Harry Lillis Crosby, was born there in 1903. In 1906 that branch of the Crosby family left Puget Sound for a new life in Spokane. Oh, and the famous progeny? While he was sometimes pictured in a yachting cap, Nathaniel Crosby III's grandson, Harry Lillis Crosby, became far better known for his singing than his sailing. He was also better known by his nickname—Bing.

Holiday crowds at the Poulsbo dock in May 1902 probably indicate the celebration of the Norwegian Independence Day. Courtesy, Kitsap County Historical Society Museum Archives

Chapter 2

The Mosquito Fleet

Along the various shorelines of Puget Sound, one can still see remnants of what were once docks. Solitary pilings, abandoned and decaying, mark the places where a fleet of small vessels, fondly remembered as the Mosquito Fleet, stopped to pick up passengers—transporting people and their goods between the bustling and growing metropolises of Seattle and Tacoma and the smaller, more rural, communities that dotted Puget Sound.

Communities with picturesque names of Suquamish, Indianola, and Olalla were less isolated—they had direct links to Seattle. By stopping at every waterfront community where there was a dock or a float, the fleet supplemented the larger steam-powered sternwheelers and side-wheelers. Some of the boats were even able to beach themselves in order to load passengers and freight. Eventually the smaller, agile, vessels became the mainstay of Sound transportation and remained so until the demand for auto carriers led to the next stage in ferryboats in the 1920s.

Defining the Mosquito Fleet is tricky. The Puget Sound maritime era, spanning the decades from the 1860s through the 1920s, has numerous fans and devotees. These local experts are drawn to their definition of the Mosquito Fleet for different reasons. Some are steamboat hobbyists prepared to cite the litany of vessel names and specifications with detailed descriptions of the various engines, accompanying each recitation with a number of anecdotes about the vessel. Needless to say, the depth of knowledge possessed by this group is a valuable addition to the region's maritime heritage. Others, pursuing the study of local history, appreciate the Mosquito Fleet for its role in the shaping and development of many of the Sound's waterfront communities. Ferryboat and

transportation enthusiasts maintain the lore of an industry comprised of numerous small companies engaged in building a marine highway system for people and freight on Puget Sound.

Each of these groups include purists who may not agree with others about the exact parameters of the Mosquito Fleet. Some would limit the fleet to only those passenger vessels with wooden hulls and steam-powered engines easily identified by their narrow hull and sharp bow—the "pointy-enders." A broader interpretation would include the later steel-hulled, diesel-driven passenger ferries. A 1908 feature article in the *Seattle Post-Intelligencer* defined the fleet as everything from the modern steel vessels down to the old flat-bottomed boats which ran on the Skagit River, as well as similar vessels on the rivers and marshes bordering Puget Sound. The *Post-Intelligencer* also clearly defined the Mosquito Fleet as a "vast ferry system centering in Seattle and spreading out all over the Sound."

True steamboat men and some ferryboat scholars have been known to distinguish the Mosquito Fleet from ferries. Ferryboats carried automobiles and in *Steamer's Wake*, author Jim Faber quotes legendary Captain Everett Coffin's assessment of ferries as "steam-powered garages." By those criteria, the first ferryboat on Puget Sound may have been the side-wheeler *City of Seattle*.

For our purposes, any vessel used to carry people and

goods back and forth across a stretch of water qualifies as a ferryboat. So, while the vessels of the Mosquito Fleet were certainly unique and special in their design, they were still ferryboats.

Mosquito Fleet vessels are often recalled as "jaunty," "trim," or "smart." They were, in reality, practical. By transporting passengers, mail, livestock, and freight from just about any shoreside community that could build a dock or place a float where the vessels could stop, the boats played a direct role in the development of Puget Sound towns. Places that could not have existed in the isolation of the heavy forests and absence of roads prospered because they were linked to bigger metropolitan areas. Their link, the Mosquito Fleet, used the water highway provided by nature.

The original if unofficial "fleet" was made up mostly of side-wheelers and stern-wheelers, while the boats of the later period were propeller-driven, steam-screw ships. Size was not a classifying factor since boats varied from 30-feet to more than 200-feet in length. Most measured an average of 100-feet and carried about 300 passengers. Using the broad definition, the number of Mosquito Fleet vessels has been estimated at 2,500 boats. At the turn of the century, the steamers were serving approximately 25 routes on the Puget Sound.

For most of the era the first generation of Sound steamboats, those with visible paddle-wheels mounted at the

Below: During 1907 and 1908, an average of 60,000 people a day traveled to and from Seattle on Mosquito Fleet vessels. Courtesy, Puget Sound Maritime Historical Society, 5011-17 Seattle

Right: Launched in 1889 and named State of Washington *to commemorate the achievement of statehood, this stern-wheeler was a popular vessel on the Bellingham route until 1907. Courtesy, Special Collections Division University of Washington Libraries, Neg. 18579*

sides or in the stern, shared the waters with the propeller-driven craft. Together these vessels contributed to the nostalgic memories that permeate the region's transportation history. The intent here is to give a general overview of some of the many vessels in the Mosquito Fleet. Those seeking detailed information on the technical aspects of the various engines in the boats are referred to the standard reference for Puget Sound vessels, *H. W. McCurdy Marine History of the Pacific Northwest,* which offers a wealth of technical and background information on the individual ships of the Mosquito Fleet. *McCurdy's* also aids in sorting out the transient nature of Mosquito Fleet vessels. Boats that appear on one route under the ownership of an individual or company show up again and again with different routes, different owners, and often even different names. Mobility, as applied to these boats, meant more than just steaming from one place to another.

Some of the vessels, such as the *Bailey Gatzert*, survived beyond the heyday of the Mosquito Fleet and went on to join boats of the later era as auto ferries. Named after Seattle's pioneer booster, businessman, and former mayor, the sternwheeler was built by John J. Holland in Ballard shipyards in 1890. Her owner, Seattle Steam Navigation and Transportation Company, was headed by John Leary, a friend and business associate of the man he honored with the vessel.

Unlike the *Eliza Anderson*, the *Bailey Gatzert*, at 177-feet long, was a floating palace and a suitable representative of the over-indulgences of the Gilded Age. Her décor included artwork hand-painted onto her interior paneling. The elegant touches made the steamer a beauty; her 1,300 horsepower engines, a far cry from the 70-horse capacity of the *Beaver,* made her a contender in the speed category.

Not only did the *Bailey Gatzert* provide first-class transportation, she initiated a new sport that would have been unthinkable in the days of the early plodding steamers. Steamboat racing found its way into the popular culture of Puget Sound. Running between Seattle and Tacoma, the *Bailey Gatzert* engaged in spirited competition with the appropriately sleek and fast *Greyhound*—a competition that the *Bailey Gatzert* started by sporting on her pilothouse an ornament depicting a gilded greyhound on a broom. The dog with the broom sticking up out of its back became a sought-after trophy. After the *Bailey Gatzert* defeated the *Greyhound*, the competition widened to include the *T.J.*

Potter. It was easy to tell when the steamboats were racing since the challenges were issued via boat whistles. One Tacoma wharf agent attributed the whistling impulse to some "savage blood" in the captain's veins. "They have got to using combinations to deepen the soul-rendering shrieks. The *Bailey Gatzert* has a triple affair that is enough to turn a man's hair grey. Her captain holds onto her rope as if it were the ladder to salvation. It is fiendish…hair-raising." (quoted in Alcorn, Rowenea and Gordon, "Puget Sound's Great Sternwheeler Days," *Sea Chest,* March 1982). Passengers apparently enjoyed the "fiendish" sport since they filled the ships to capacity when they knew a race would occur. In the middle of the big showdown between the *Bailey Gatzert* and the *T.J. Potter,* the *Bailey Gatzert* suffered a mechanical problem that caused her to stop. The *T.J. Potter* reigned as ultimate champion and kept the dog on the broomstick.

In 1891 the *Gatzert* was sold to the Columbia River & Puget Sound Navigation Company (PSN). She spent some time on the Seattle-Olympia route before being moved to the Columbia River where she served as an excursion ship and for several years was the Royal Barge for the Portland Rose Festival. After an extensive overhaul in 1895 she started a new career on the upper Columbia River.

Another renovation in 1910 converted the *Bailey Gatzert* from a wood-burner to an oil burning steamer and she returned to Puget Sound in 1918 to become the regular boat on the Navy Yard Route's Seattle–Bremerton run. A final stay on the Seattle-Tacoma route for two years, she could travel at speeds of 16 knots.

Although both the *Bailey Gatzert* and the *Greyhound* carried passengers on the Seattle-Tacoma route, they did not share the longevity of the *Flyer*. The *Flyer* started service between the two cities in 1891 and remained on the route for 21 years. Using the slogan "Fly on the Flyer" the steamer, noted for its speed, made four round trips daily. Single fare was 35 cents while a round trip cost 50 cents. The slogan, along with a graphic of a large detailed drawing of a house-fly, was catchy by early century advertising standards.

While the larger turn-of-the-century boats are perhaps more famous and carried more passengers on their routes, they were not the backbone of the Mosquito Fleet. In addi-

conversion in 1920 made her the first automobile ferry to run between Seattle and Bremerton; she was capable of carrying 27 cars. Retired in 1926, her dismantled hull remained moored in Lake Union until it was converted to a floating warehouse at the Lake Union Drydock and Machine Works. Her whistle, considered the best of all the Puget Sound steamboat whistles, was transferred to the *City of Bremerton* ferry. The *Bailey Gatzert* had spanned three eras of Puget Sound maritime history. As part of the Mosquito fleet she participated in the period most fondly remembered by contemporary steamboat aficionados as the high point of ferryboat history.

One of the *Gatzert*'s racing opponents, the *Greyhound*, deserves a mention here simply because of her somewhat unusual proportions. Like the dog whose name she shared, the *Greyhound* was noticeably streamlined—139-feet long and only 18-feet wide. In contrast to the low-slung boat, her more than 20-foot stern-wheel seemed to loom above the ship's structure. Her too-tall stack was also out of proportion and earned the *Greyhound* the label of a "homely" boat. Likewise, her interior was plain. Despite her odd appearance, the *Greyhound* was fast and reliable. A main-

tion to the ships that regularly connected the larger cities of Seattle, Bremerton, Tacoma, Bellingham, and Olympia, there were hundreds of smaller vessels that linked places like Chico, Lemolo, and Seabold with Seattle. They were the boats that could stop at any local dock or float, the boats more likely to be compared to the insect mosquito because of their numbers and the fact that they always seemed to be buzzing around.

In some beachfront neighborhoods, one of the residents would donate part of his land for a dock and a

Below: Smaller vessels like the Florence K *connected communities such as Eagledale on Bainbridge Island with the outside world. The vessel's captain and crew, pictured here, are in a standard steamboat man pose for the era. Courtesy, Puget Sound Maritime Historical Society, 970-9 Seattle*

Right: "Fly on the Flyer" captured imaginations to the extent that people took the trip between Seattle and Tacoma just in order to say they had been on the famous steamer, the Flyer. *Author's collection*

Opposite page: Scandia, *situated across Liberty Bay from Poulsbo, was a regular stop on the Poulsbo-Seattle route. Courtesy, Kitsap County Historical Society Museum Archives*

community landing place would appear. Today's waterfront land owners might well be mystified by such a generous sharing of shoreline, but at the end of the nineteenth century farmers placed high value on their crop-growing areas and not much value on their beaches. The beach was only valuable if a vessel could stop there to pick up whatever the farmer was trying to market or to deliver whatever goods a settler needed.

Other settlers would form a group, join together cedar logs with three inch wooden pins, use split cedar planks for a floor, attach the whole structure to a chain or thick rope, then move it out to deep water and anchor it with a rock. This "float" became the stopping place for Mosquito Fleet steamers. Passengers would have someone row them out to the float so they could hail a passing ferry. In some places it was generally necessary to be on the float by 6 A.M. and since that hour falls in darkness during much of the year, the prospective passenger waved a lighted lantern to hail the passing steamer. Pity the poor traveler who failed to make arrangements to be picked up in case the ferry suffered mechanical problems and did not make the run. Sitting on a float can be a lonely and cold experience. And, for those passengers who did get picked up, navigating the space between the float and the steamer could be a little tricky. It is easy to speculate and harder to document, but the phrase "missed the boat" can have a literal meaning. Missing the leap from raft to boat could result in a very uncomfortable dip in the always cold waters of Puget Sound. Incoming passengers landing at the float also had to be picked up and some floats had an "official" oarsman, sometimes a neighborhood boy, who met the boat and rowed the passengers ashore.

Mosquito Fleet vessels were a major agent for settlement. Free mail delivery was a courtesy offered by the first steamers and it was common for the ships' captains to accept lists of needed items for isolated Puget Sound residents and deliver the goods on the next trip. Livestock, crucial to the success of small farmers, arrived via steamer. When they could not be off-loaded at a dock, the cows and horses were pushed overboard to swim ashore. Bulls were also delivered on steamers provided they came aboard with references attesting to their gentleness.

In his book *One For the Weather, One For The Crow*, Dwight Droz, a poet and resident of the tiny waterside community Scandia, in Kitsap County, noted that the "small ferries were a godsend to people engulfed by trees with few roads to connect them to commerce of any sort... Farm wives were commonplace passengers on these boats. The farmer rose early to pick the zucchini and gather the eggs. All the luggage you could carry on board unaided was scott free. It paid to be a husky so you could tote more stuff aboard...."

One such farm wife was Alice Paulson, the author's grandmother. In the 1920s she and he daughters took slaughtered pullets to sell at Seattle's Farmers' Market. The daughters, now in their eighties, remember the early morning boardings on the ferry, carrying their poultry from Poulsbo to Seattle. The trip took two hours with the boat stopping at Scandia, Lemolo, Pearson, Keyport, Virginia, Suquamish, Indianola, and Seabold as it made its way to Seattle. The trip on what they describe as the sleek and spotlessly clean ferry was a memorable event for little girls who could sit on a bench on the boat's deck and watch the water, the shoreline, the seagulls, and the routines on the various docks where the boat stopped. At the end of the route was a taxi ride to the market and a long day spent sitting in a stall interacting with all the customers and the farmers in other stalls. Evening was time for the return trip—a lighter load and an opportunity to share all the latest gossip with the other farm wives.

Aside from the goods that market-bound farm wives carried aboard the boats, the Mosquito Fleet vessels did depend on freight for half their income. In one year alone, between August 1907 and July 1908. The boats carried outbound cargo from Seattle valued at a total of nearly $16 million and inbound freight valued at nearly $10 million. This was especially true of agriculture-based communities like Poulsbo. Feed for chickens, cows, and sheep was shipped in and stored in wharfside warehouses for sale to farmers. The Mosquito Fleet also aided Kitsap County's flourishing chicken and egg industry by opening Seattle's market connections.

Poulsbo is about 20 miles from Seattle by water although at least one pioneer account claims the distance

was 28 miles. It makes a difference if the means of transportation was a row boat. Early settlers made the trip in two days. The first steamer to make regular trips from the small community was the *Augusta* in 1885. She made the voyage to Seattle three times a week at a cost of $1.00 each way. In a pattern that would become all too familiar on Puget Sound, the arrival of the *Augusta* prompted the owners of Port Blakely Mill Company on Bainbridge Island to place their own boat, the *Detroit*, on the same run but at a lower fare. When the *Detroit* broke down, Poulsbo residents Captain John Hansen and his sons Henry and O.L. began operating the small steamer *Quickstep* in 1890. When the *Detroit* returned to service, the fare was again cut.

The Hansens remained in the ferry business, replacing the *Quickstep* with a larger boat, the *Hattie Hansen*, named after Henry Hansen's daughter. As one pioneer recollection, written by E. Pitzenberger and published in *Kitsap County: A History* recounts, much good timber from the shores of Dogfish Bay (later renamed Liberty Bay) was cut into cordwood to fuel the *Hattie Hansen*. Early steamers burned green slab wood because it was a cheap and plentiful fuel, but it also produced plenty of smoke. Stern-wheelers could burn

up to five cords of wood an hour. Wood choppers earned $2.50 to $3.00 per cord—measured as a pile four feet wide by four feet high and eight feet long.

Seeking to maintain fares at less than one dollar, Poulsbo farmers formed a cooperative around the locally built steamer *Advance*. The Poulsbo-Colby Transportation Company was headed by Thomas Hegdahl and Nils Olson. They succeeded in lowering the fare to fifty cents and then to a quarter.

When Captain John Hansen died in 1896, his sons combined with another Poulsbo steamboat man and Hattie Hansen's husband, Alf Hostmark, to continue the business. In keeping with the small entrepreneurship which characterized the business end of the Mosquito Fleet, another pair of Poulsbo brothers, Andrew and Chris Moe, also started a competing business, running the boat *Dauntless* from Seattle to Tacoma via Vashon Island. Later she ran from Poulsbo to Seattle. When the Moes bought the *Advance* from the failing farmers' cooperative, they sold the *Dauntless* to Captain L.B. Hastings and Captain Mann of Port Townsend. The Moes added to their fleet by purchasing the larger *Reliance* in 1900.

During the period when the Moes ran the *Dauntless* on the route from Seattle to Tacoma they typically collected fares after the boat got underway. This was standard procedure in the early Mosquito Fleet days. But, as the Moes discovered, the procedure encouraged transients to get on the boat with the assumption that once the boat was underway the crew would take no action against individuals who could not pay. To dispel that notion, the boat operators took to lowering a life boat and rowing any non-paying passengers ashore. After a few attempts, the transients gave up on trying to get a free ride to Tacoma.

In 1905 the Hansens and Alf Hostmark, along with Warren Gazzam, bought out the Moe Brothers interest in the *Reliance* and reorganized as the Kitsap County Transportation Company. One of their new boats, the *Hyak*, launched in 1909, was most often associated with Hostmark because he captained her throughout her career.

Hostmark, whose own career spanned over half a century of Puget Sound ferry history, died in 1953 at the age of 78. After his time with the Kitsap County Transportation Company he went on to work for the Puget Sound Navigation Company and then for the Washington State Ferries when the state assumed control of the ferries in 1951. He was captain on the Suquamish-Indianola-Seattle run and then skipper of the Vashon-Fauntleroy route.

The Moes continued to operate the *Advance* on the Port Gamble–Port Townsend–Seattle run. They also expanded their fleet, contracting for a new steamer in 1906. The *Monticello* was a typical Mosquito boat. She was built at Crawford and Reed Company in Tacoma where workers managed to complete her hull in only 21 days. The trees that provided the raw material were winter logged and the wood was air dried for some two years before it was used. Trees felled in winter contain little

sap, and air drying lessens destruction to the cells in the timber.

Once she was operational and on the Poulsbo route, the *Monticello* became part of the competition between the Moes and Captain Hostmark. Kitsap County Transportation Company, Hostmark's enterprise responded to the *Monticello* with a new boat of its own, the 128-foot *Kitsap*. Beyond spirited, the competition could sometimes be reckless. The steamers *Kitsap* and the *Monticello* literally ran into each other in 1906. Captains Hostmark and Moe were both censored by steamboat inspectors who ruled that had the men been on more friendly terms, they would have given each other more room to pass. The Moes continued to operate the *Monticello* for a year until she was sold along with the *Advance* to the owners of the Port Blakely Mill Company.

Poulsbo residents, meanwhile, were still not happy. One of the problems with local steamer service was that passengers competed with freight. A trip that could have taken two hours for a passenger could be extended to four or five hours because of the time spent loading and unload-

Because early crews often lived aboard the vessels, it was not unusual to see a cook as part of the crew. Courtesy, Puget Sound Maritime Historical Society, 1188-18 Seattle

ing freight. Passengers would be stuck within sight of the Poulsbo dock while they waited for freight to be offloaded at Scandia or at one of the other nearby piers. Poulsbo's farmers tried again in 1914 to gain control of water transportation by selling $10 shares and organizing the Liberty Bay Transportation Company under the management of Andrew Moe. Their premier vessel, the *Athlon,* was thought of as "the People's boat" and the emotion surrounding her was packaged in patriotic hyperbole that called on locals to retain their "liberties" in the steamboat service. In 1916, Poulsbo's weekly newspaper, the *Kitsap County Herald,* announced the return of the *Athlon.* She had been temporarily out of service, forcing Poulsbo residents to travel to Seattle on "the other boat,", the *Hyak.* The paper called on locals to free themselves from private domination. "The transportation between this bay and Seattle is something the people must, and will, control for themselves. This freedom is something that will not come without a struggle, but we also believe that the people are prepared for it."

The community continued to be divided between supporters of the *Athlon* and those of the *Hyak,* so much so that personal animosities grow up around who traveled on which boat. The rivalry between the Liberty Bay Transportation Company and the Kitsap County Transportation Company was so bitter that the boats habitually raced each other—straining their boilers beyond optimum steam pressure. The ailing *Athlon* had to be spelled by the *Liberty,* a boat formerly named the *City of Everett,* and purchased by the Liberty Bay Transportation Company in 1917. The *Liberty,* far less popular than the *Athlon,* was regarded as a bad purchase—too much money and not much of a boat. It was indicative of a business enterprise suffering from poor management, sloppy maintenance, and internal bickering. Andrew Moe was replaced by Christian Servold, who was followed by Ed Person. Person was a good manager but his tenure came too late. After a six year existence, the Liberty Bay group went into bankruptcy and the steamer *Liberty* went over to the Kitsap County Transportation Company. In

an effort to salvage something, the company's main asset, the *Athlon* was chartered to a private business. Shortly thereafter, in 1921, the steamer hit a rock near Port Ludlow and sank. Her insurance had lapsed just days prior to the accident.

The company was followed briefly by the Poulsbo Transportation Company and its boat the *Verona*. The *Verona* later served as the stage for one of Washington State's most famous and bloody anti-union incidents. In 1916 a group of IWW (Industrial Workers of the World) activists, more commonly known as Wobblies, chartered the *Verona* to transport 250 demonstrators from Seattle to Everett where they were going to demonstrate in support of striking shingle weavers. Even though it was November, there was a picnic-like atmosphere aboard the boat. But as the *Verona* approached the Everett dock, Sheriff Donald McRae and armed citizens on the shore opened fire on the vessel. At the end of the 10 minute hail of bullets, seven men were dead and 50 were wounded in what came to be known as the "Everett massacre."

In most respects the steamers of Puget Sound were a safe mode of transportation. As maritime historian and author Gordon Newell has pointed out, the most remarkable thing about the Mosquito Fleet was its safety record. Given wooden-hulled vessels with potentially unstable boilers prone to explode if not properly maintained, and operating without the benefit of radar in waters famous for periodic blankets of fog that obscure all visibility, serious accidents were notable because they were such a rare occurrence. Experienced captains relied on their

knowledge of the neighborhoods. Lights from shore, familiar barking dogs, and the distinctive echo of the steamer's own whistle as it reverberated from a high bluff, a gravel beach, or a low coastline were the artful ways in which captains guided their vessels.

While wood and sail complemented each other, steam engines were better suited to steel hulls. Wooden steamers performed stellar service but they were never the equal of a steam engine in a steel vessel. By the first decade of the twentieth century wood was rapidly being replaced with steel in the shipbuilding industry. The transition was hastened by the 1904 maritime disaster considered the worst in regional waters. Puget Sound Navigation's wooden steamer *Clallam* sank in a storm while making the crossing to Victoria, British Columbia. Critics, later proven wrong when human error was determined to be the cause of the tragedy, claimed structural weakness in the wooden hull resulted in the foundering and loss of 54 lives. The casualties were mostly women and children who had been dispatched to life boats when the boat began to founder. The lifeboats overturned with no survivors while those who stayed aboard the *Clallam* were rescued before the vessel rolled and sank.

Both the *Clallam* and a sister ship, the *Jefferson*, had been built by one of the Northwest's preeminent shipbuilders, Edward Heath. A master craftsman, Heath made an art of building wooden ships. Although he was vindicated in the *Clallam* disaster, and continued to build

Opposite page: Ferry Kirkland *on Lake Washington. From* Seattle *(Chas. H. Kittinger, Publisher, 1889). Courtesy, Arundel Books, Seattle*

Above: The Athlon *capsized after hitting a rock, but her machinery was salvaged and used in another vessel. Courtesy, Puget Sound Maritime Historical Society, 251-13 Seattle*

below deck to collect fares, the mate somehow ran the ferry right under the bow of the steam schooner *Jeanie*. How, or why, he turned the ship in the wrong direction was never discovered since the mate was one of the victims of the sinking. The larger *Jeanie* rammed the side of the *Dix*, tearing a huge gash in the ferry's hull. Within a minute of the collision, the *Dix* keeled over and sank, trapping passengers and crew in the cabin. In all the confusion it was never clearly established how many people died, although 45 seems to be the accepted figure. Captain Percy Lermond survived and suffered the penalty of having his license revoked for a year. He returned to work on tugboats and chose never again to captain passenger vessels.

The *Dix* fatalities had a profound effect on the small Port Blakely community. Everyone knew someone who had perished in the accident. In the aftermath of the tragedy, an obelisk was placed in the Port Blakely cemetery and dedicated as a memorial to the five members of the local Knights of Pythias Lodge who went down on the *Dix*. In 1966 a memorial plaque recalling the disaster was placed in a park

near the site of the disaster at Alki Point.

wooden ships, Heath never built another passenger steamer. The *Clallam*'s replacement, the *Indianapolis*, was a steel vessel.

One of the other well-known Puget Sound disasters was the sinking of the steamship *Dix*. The 102-foot long, 130-ton *Dix* had always been a little top-heavy and suffered from stability problems even though she was a fairly new boat, built in 1904. On the clear, calm, and cold night of November 18, 1906, the *Dix* was off Alki Point on her way to Port Blakely with 77 passengers when the captain turned the wheel over to an inexperienced mate. While the captain was performing his other duty as purser and had gone

Most of the early vessel losses were less dramatic. In July, 1903, in what came to be considered annual waterfront fires in Port Orchard, the steamer *Walsh* burned to the water's edge at the city's Bishop Wharf. The sternwheeler, which was being used as an excursion boat, had dropped members from a social group called the Montana Club in Bremerton for a tour of the Navy's shipyard. Because there was no room at the dock, the *Walsh* proceeded to Port Orchard. Shortly after tying up at the wharf, a fire started near the ship's boilers and quickly spread throughout the vessel. Witnesses recounted that it took less than two minutes for the boat to be entirely engulfed in flame. Cut loose from the dock, the burning *Walsh* drifted a short distance from shore and deposited her charred hull in about 15-feet of water. The 238 excursionists, many of whom were bemoaning the loss of their coats left behind on the ill-fated vessel, were returned safely to Seattle aboard the *Inland Flyer* and the *Port Orchard*.

In 1905, in what the local press described as Port Orchard's third annual waterfront fire, the sternwheeler *Garden City* was destroyed in her berth at the city's Kemp & Baker wharf. An early morning blaze of unknown origin resulted in total loss of the two-year-old vessel. Owner Captain C.E. Bergman vowed to continue on the Port Orchard–Bremerton–Seattle run if he could find a replacement boat.

While the north end of Kitsap County typifies the most rural services of the Mosquito Fleet, the urbanized section around Bremerton and Port Orchard represent a more standard model of ferry service. The two towns, along with a third town, Charleston (which consolidated with Bremerton in 1927), are all situated on the shores of Port Orchard Bay, the body of water that divides Bainbridge Island from Kitsap County. It runs from Agate Passage in the north to the Sinclair Inlet in the south. The towns are actually at the southern end and today are commonly thought of as being on Sinclair Inlet. Earlier in the century they were referred to as being on Port Orchard Bay. Also on Port Orchard Bay, but separated from Bremerton by another body of water called Port Washington Narrows, lies what once was a separate community and now is the neighborhood of Manette. These were all areas where water transportation was the most obvious means for residents to get around.

Before Bremerton was platted and the Navy Yard located there, early settlers on the site were served by Nibbeville founder and Bainbridge Island resident Captain John Nibbe who, starting in 1876, provided transportation to Seattle via an 18-foot rowboat. After three years, Nibbe upgraded to a sloop named the *Sea Bird*, and finally to the steamships *Leif Erickson* and *San Juan*. Other individual boat owners provided service via the *Helen*, the *Grace*, the *Mountaineer*, the *A.R. Robinson* and a variety of sternwheelers such as the *Mary J. Perley*, the *Skagit*

Chief, the *Pilgrim*, and others that operated in the area up to about 1900.

The *Leif Erickson* was destroyed in a tragic fire off Seattle's Alki Point on Christmas Eve 1888. Louis Fagerholm's first-hand account of the event, published in *Kitsap County: A History* noted that not only was the boat overloaded with passengers, it was also carrying dynamite! When the fire started, some passengers immediately jumped overboard, others waited, and some, like Fagerholm, went in search of life preservers. Once located, no one seemed to know how to put them on. Crew members, including the captain, had left the ship before many of the passengers. The disastrous scenario was not likely to be repeated. The materials which could be carried aboard ferries became strictly regulated, and contemporary ferry crews are well-trained should there be any need to abandon a ferry.

While several ships shared the duties of providing cross-Sound service, formal transportation service between the adjoining Kitsap communities was provided by Vern C. Gorst, starting in 1904. The son of a pioneer Port Orchard family, Gorst prospered in the Klondike Gold Rush. Upon returning to Port Orchard he started a launch service. His fleet, which included the *Shamrock*, *Crawford*, and *Lady Marie*, connected Port Orchard, Bremerton and Manette.

Gorst's business was doing well when he consolidated with another operator, E. T. Harris and his son Walter. The Harrises took over the business and Gorst moved to south-

Tacoma also had its share of Mosquito Fleet activity. Southern Sound areas like Quartermaster Harbor, Gig Harbor and Anderson Island were connected to *Tacoma by ferries. Photo by Asahel Curtis, Courtesy, Special Collections Division, University of Washington Libraries Neg.25095*

ern Oregon in 1910. There he continued in the transportation business, eventually focusing his talents on air travel. He founded Pacific Air Transport Company in 1920 which evolved into United Air Transport in 1931, the corporate parent of today's major carrier, United Airlines.

The first regularly scheduled service on the Seattle-Bremerton run came via the *Inland Flyer* in 1901. At a cruising speed of 16 knots and room to comfortably seat 200 people, she was easily the best boat on the run at that point. Her owner, the LaConner Trading and Transportation Company under the leadership of Joshua Green, eliminated one rival—the *A.R. Robinson* with hardly a struggle.

Following in the wake of the *Inland Flyer* came the competition commonly called the "opposition" boat. In this case the opposition boat, *Athlon*, of later Poulsbo fame, but here in her first appearance on Puget Sound, was owned and operated by Seattle businessman H.B. Kennedy. After two months of nearly ruinous competition, Green and Kennedy merged their interests into the Port Orchard Route with Kennedy as company president. The move stabilized competition on the route and established the *Athlon* and *Inland Flyer* as the equivalent of the "home team." Thereafter any other boat on

the route became the automatically unpopular opposition.

In 1907 the Port Orchard Route charged 50 cents round trip with stops at Bremerton, Port Orchard, Charleston, and Pleasant Beach on Bainbridge Island. Early in 1908 the routine of the run was "rudely interrupted" by the appearance of the North Kitsap boat, *Monticello*. Owned by the Port Blakely Mill Company, the steamer had a reputation for interloping. It did not help that she was charging 20 cents for one-way fare in comparison to the Port Orchard Route's 25 cents. In response, the "pioneer line," i.e. the Port Orchard Route, lowered the cost of its "commutation ticket" to $6.00. The ticket permitted one round-trip each day of the month during April 1908. It effectively reduced a one-way fare to nine cents, and, as the *Seattle Star* proclaimed, "The knife has been opened, the hatchet thrown into the air and one of the fiercest of rate wars is now on between the steamers plying from Seattle to Bremerton."

The competition was triggered by the arrival of the United States Navy's Great White Fleet, which met with tremendous hoopla when it stopped in Puget Sound in the summer of 1908. The increased tourist traffic between Seattle and Bremerton had steamboat owners scrambling for profits. The most elegant addition to the route was the aging side-wheeler *Yosemite*, which began making three daily trips between the two cities in March 1908. The last trip of the evening offered the extra pleasure of onboard music and dancing plus refreshments and private dining rooms. And, if dancing was not enough entertainment, the *Yosemite* also offered at least one prize-fight. Since the bout between two lightweights had been banned from any shore, the *Yosemite*'s captain, Thomas Grant, circled the steamer south of Whidbey Island in the intersection and therefore legally muddied waters of King, Snohomish and Island Counties. The bout ended in a draw.

In July 1909, with a full complement of tourists on board, the *Yosemite* grounded on Orchard rocks near Bremerton. While the passengers were saved, the ship broke in half, a total loss. It may have been an unfortunate accident; the Orchard rocks had certainly claimed their share of vessels. Or, as widely speculated, the aging *Yosemite* may have been deliberately sacrificed for insurance money.

Opposition boats were generally excoriated in the press because it seemed unfair that the local Port Orchard Route, which provided service all winter, should be forced into ruinous rate wars prompted by summertime interlopers. Although urged to show loyalty to their home-town boat, the public in Port Orchard, Charleston, and Bremerton, who had their own ideas about what kind of service the Port Orchard Route provided, often did not hesitate to take advantage of the lower fares offered by opposition steamers.

Apparently the *Monticello* was an exception, since passengers continued to bypass her in favor of the Port Orchard Route ships. The disgruntled owners of the *Monticello* chided Port Orchard Bay residents for not supporting their vessel and reminded them that the local company had been providing shoddy service until the *Monticello* had given them some competition. The argument may have been valid

but the consumers were not swayed and the *Monticello* owners made good on their threat to withdraw the boat from the route.

One of the most unpopular opposition boats had to be the *Vashon*. Even renaming her the *Wireless* in 1909 failed to staunch criticism and, as one news article pointed out, she was too slow to be called the *Wireless* and would just have to remain the *Vashon*. In other words, no one was fooled, and readers were reminded that the Vashon had been lying underwater for months as a sunken hulk before being raised and refurbished. In one rate war, fares on the Seattle–Bremerton route dropped to a nickel; passengers who chose the lucky boat were treated to free beer and Seattle theater tickets. Competition may have been brutal for the boat owners but it generally provided a brief bit of excitement for the traveling public.

The natural pattern of development of the steamboat business on Puget Sound was toward larger, faster, and more luxurious vessels that could carry more passengers and thus drive competing steamboat operators out of business. Throughout the first few decades of the twentieth century the Mosquito Fleet vessel owners fought for dominance on the Sound.

The steamer *H.B. Kennedy* represents the trend toward amenities in passenger travel on Puget Sound at the beginning of the century. Designed to be a first-class vessel, built for speed, running only during daylight hours and carrying no freight, the *H.B. Kennedy* was intended to be the showpiece for the Port Orchard Route. The connection of the vessel to the company was clearly established by the fact that the president of the Port Orchard Route was, indeed, H.B. Kennedy. Due to the agreement between Kennedy and Joshua Green, the company was actually a subsidiary of Joshua Green's Inland Navigation Company. The steamship was designed by naval architect Fred A. Ballin and built in 1908–1909 at the Willamette Iron & Steel in Portland. Original plans called for a steel vessel of 180 feet, but the *H.B. Kennedy* picked up an extra 10 feet during construction. At 190 feet long with a 28 foot beam and a 13 foot depth, she represented a new class of passenger vessel— one that could carry 1,000 people and use a 2,000 horsepower engine to move them along at a rate of 17 knots. Current passenger-only vessels operating on the same route by the Washington State Ferry System measure 143

feet in length, carry 350 passengers, and are equipped with 7,200 horsepower systems that can produce speeds near 35 knots or 40 miles per hour.

Placing the *H.B. Kennedy* on the Seattle–Bremerton route was timed to coincide with the summer of the A-Y-P (Alaska–Yukon–Pacific) Exposition in Seattle. An early equivalent of a World's Fair, the A-Y-P promoters expected to highlight Seattle as a summer tourist destination. Part of the celebration included a return visit from the U.S. Navy's Great White Fleet. Some of the fleet's battleships were to be docked across the Sound from Seattle at the rapidly developing Puget Sound Navy Yard. Bremerton was touted as a tourist destination representing healthy profits for any company that could provide an attractive mode of transportation between the two cities.

Another aspect of the decision to build the *H.B. Kennedy* for the Port Orchard Route was the company's desire to solidify its position as the one enterprise serving Bremerton and its adjoining communities of Port Orchard and Charleston. The opposition boats that appeared each summer in an effort to take advantage of the recreational travelers were an annoyance that the Port Orchard Route hoped to eliminate with the *H.B. Kennedy*.

To further cement the identity of the company and

The H.B. Kennedy *represented a new standard for luxury on the Seattle-Bremerton route. Her upper cabin sported leather seats and a piano, along with oak and mahogany woodwork. Spitoons were a practical necessity. Courtesy, Kitsap County Historical Society Museum Archives*

the *H.B. Kennedy* with the Bremerton/Port Orchard area, the Port Orchard Route joined with two local newspapers, the *Bremerton News* and the *Port Orchard Independent*, to sponsor a contest to choose a young lady to christen the *H.B. Kennedy*. In the fall of 1908, when an American Presidential election was the most important news for much of the country, Bremerton, Charleston, and Port Orchard, were embroiled in a spirited and heavily publicized competition to determine the most popular girl in Port Orchard Bay.

The voting process itself was a clever marketing tool. Votes were tied to tickets on the Port Orchard Route vessels. Each one-way ticket enabled the purchaser to one vote, a round-trip represented five votes and a 26-ticket commuter book was worth 26 votes. The newspapers benefited by giving votes in exchange for new subscriptions. They also took advantage of would-be voters by offering votes to "hustlers" willing to go out and collect past-due subscriptions. The *Bremerton News* admitted that many of its subscribers were from one to five years in arrears and offered 10 votes in exchange for every dollar collected.

In the final tally, Minna Benbennick, daughter of a prominent Bremerton businessman, won with a total of 35,176 votes. The more than 90,000 votes cast in the contest testify to the success of the marketing strategy. Bremerton, the most populous city of the Port Orchard Bay area had a total population of 5,000 residents at the time.

Miss Benbennick, a 19-year-old graduate of the Wilson Modern Business College in Seattle, was prominent in Bremerton society. In addition to the honor of christening the *H.B. Kennedy*, her prizes included a lifetime pass on the steamer, a souvenir of her own choosing, and a trip to Portland for the ceremony and a celebratory banquet. The pass, engraved on a silver plate with the steamer in gold relief, was designed to last but may not have been too practical for the small handbags of the time. The launching, which was described as one of the most elaborate affairs seen in Portland for many years, took place on a clear Saturday in November 1908 with a full compliment of Bremerton area social elite, as well as Seattlites Joshua Green and H.B. Kennedy.

The completed vessel arrived in Puget Sound at the end of March 1909 and immediately commenced speed trials. An official course of the east side of Vashon Island,

As symbols of an era, the H.B. Kennedy *and the elegant lines of Seattle's Colman Dock are an appropriate pair. Courtesy, Puget Sound Maritime Historical Society, 1108-15 Seattle*

known as the "government mile," was used to benchmark the steamer's abilities. She succeeded in grand fashion with an unofficial clocking at 18 ¾ knots or 21½ miles-per-hour. In the process she passed both the *Indianapolis* and the *Flyer*—ships once noted for their speed. One of the *H.B. Kennedy's* most anticipated features was her running time of 45 minutes on the Bremerton-Seattle run. Other steamers took more than an hour for the trip. While the *H.B. Kennedy* was being prepared for her introduction to travelers on Puget Sound, the Port Orchard Route changed its company designation to the Navy Yard Route. The name reflected the growing influence of Bremerton's Navy Yard as a destination for both tourists and commuting laborers.

When Port Orchard and Bremerton residents finally boarded the *H.B. Kennedy* in April, they saw three passenger decks with outside seating along the sides of the main cabin area and the ladies' cabin. Inside the cabin the ladies enjoyed red plush upholstered seats, carpeting on the floors, and curtains on the windows. The upper cabin housed a piano and featured leather seats. The smoking room, situated on either side of the engines, was elegantly attired in seats made of split cane. Part of the aft space in the main cabin was occupied by a full dining room and a bar. Mahogany and oak made up the interior woodwork. The engine room crew numbered 11 men—three engineers, three firemen, three oilers, and two water tenders. Above deck, the captain was assisted by two mates. The vessel, described as the "most completely and most handsomely finished boat on the Sound," represented a total investment of about $150,000.

Despite the rosy forecasts at her christening, the ferry, according to one creative journalist, was followed by a "hoodoo." The H.B. Kennedy completed her five daily trips between Seattle and Bremerton for about two weeks before a lost rudder sidelined her. In November she broke a crankshaft, ran onto the rocks, and did major damage to her steel plates and machinery. After extensive and expensive ($10,000) repairs at Seattle's Moran Company drydock, she was back on the Bremerton run in January 1910.

The Kennedy's history also included at least one fatality—a popular Bremerton youth, Charles "Jerry" Boyle, drowned while assisting a Kennedy passenger with two suitcases. Trying to jump aboard the vessel, suitcases in hand, Boyle lost his balance, missed the Kennedy and fell into the water, apparently striking his head as he fell. Dozens of witnesses, not realizing that he was unconscious, watched, thinking that he was swimming.

With the initial difficulties behind her, the H.B. Kennedy enjoyed a long and productive career on Puget Sound where she was known simply as the "H.B."

Around 1918 the H.B. was renamed Seattle. Her duties unchanged, she continued to carry passengers from Bremerton to Seattle until 1923 when she fell victim to the demands of the motoring public. The ship's elegantly slim lines were "sponsoned out," a term meaning that she was widened in order to accommodate vehicles as well as passengers. Having been adapted to

the times, the Seattle remained in operation until 1937. Her last service was on the Seattle–Suquamish run where she was replaced by the Klahanie.

On Puget Sound, one of the nation's great recreational waterways, the tradition of getting out on the water and getting away to some other shore began early, fostered by the availability of steamships to move people around the Sound. Numerous West Sound communities, among them, Fragaria, Colby, Indianola, Manchester, Brownsville, and Lemolo, began as summer holiday sites for city dwellers. Those who would never visit the urban waterfront with its unsavory characters and businesses were quick to realize that rural beaches were entirely different and the perfect destination for an outing or a vacation. In Olalla, Saturday nights were lively as steamers dropped citizens of Seattle or Tacoma at the community dock. From there they could walk up the hill to the barn-like building of the Lodge of the Modern Woodsmen of America where entertainment included dances, dinners, and parties.

This unidentified photo shows one aspect of Puget Sound life that has been popular for nearly 150 years—going to the beach. Courtesy, Kitsap County Historical Society Museum Archives

The excursion trade also worked the other direction— west to east. The Mosquito Fleet played a role in any community event that involved travel. There was no practical alternative way for West Sound residents to reach Seattle. Partly from necessity and partly from tradition, the boats became part of any celebration, gaily decorated with flags and blaring whatever music, brass band or steam calliope that might be available. When 4,000 residents of the four towns adjoining the federal shipyard gathered to attend Navy Yard Day at Seattle's Alaska–Yukon–Pacific Exposition in June 1909, the local boats accommodated them with reduced fares and extra trips.

The *H.B. Kennedy, Athlon, Tourist,* and *Inland Flyer* were all drafted into duty to get the local citizens and dignitaries to Seattle for an 11 A.M. rally and parade. Crossing the Sound, the passengers, sporting special badges for the occasion, practiced their official yell— "Bremerton, Charleston, Port Orchard, Manette; Uncle Sam's Navy Yard, Don't Forget; Hiyu Kitsap, Don't you See; We Are

Here at the A-Y-P." Rousing versions of the chant could be heard as the boats entered Seattle's harbor.

From day picnickers to tent campers, not only did the Mosquito Fleet vessels stimulate recreation by transporting urban dwellers to shoreside cottages and hotels in the more primitive areas than Seattle, they also created new communities by encouraging real estate developers to offer homes and property along the steamer routes. Warren Gazzam, known in Kitsap County as the "Colonel," was able to use his role as one of the owners of Kitsap County Transportation Company, in combination with his real estate enterprises, to fulfill his mission of developing Kitsap County "through transportation and colonization." In order to facilitate the real estate fortunes of Indianola, a small community in North Kitsap, Gazzam's KCT Co. built a 900-foot-long pier so that steamers could land.

Another developer, Ole Hansen, Seattle's flamboyant mayor from 1918–1920, preceded his political career with a crusade to populate the Olympic Peninsula through profitable real estate sales. Planned communities featuring building lots for $50 and diminutive bungalows that sold for $315 attracted hundreds of new residents.

More than one hundred years later, communities on the Kitsap Peninsula still hold out the possibility of attracting East Sound residents with the promise of better values in real estate and fast passenger-only ferries to transport them to their jobs in Seattle.

The community-building role of the Mosquito Fleet is a reminder that not all passengers were summer excursionists. The steamers were also commuter boats and as such they offered all the problems and anxieties that modern-day commuters may experience aboard ferries. In any mode of public transportation, conditions may not always be pleasant or peaceful. When engines broke down and vessels missed their runs, early commuters gnashed their teeth with the same aggravation exercised by their modern counterparts. Criticizing the quality of ferry service is a bona fide tradition on Puget Sound, stemming back to the days when Theodore Winthrop's Indian paddlers decided to nap instead of keeping momentum in the canoe.

Along with the trend towards more luxurious vessels, and their increasing role as both excursion and commuter fleet, the Mosquito vessels continued to in-

THE *VIRGINIA V*

One of the two last vessels of her type in the nation and the last surviving veteran of the steam-powered Mosquito Fleet, the *Virginia V* was built in Maplewood, South Kitsap County in 1922 by master shipwright Mathew Anderson. Captain N.G. Christensen of the West Pass Transportation Company, the vessel's owner, named all of his steamers Virginia. He referred to them by their numbers, hence the III (three), or the IV (four) or the V (five). The *V*, designed with a hull patterned after the *Virginia II*, was powered by the triple expansion reciprocating steam engine of her predecessor, the *Virginia IV*. The wood-hulled, 125-foot vessel, with a substantial 24.1-foot beam, carried 320 passengers and was assigned to the Seattle–Tacoma run. Her route took her to dozens of small communities along Colvos Passage on the west side of Vashon Island where she was a familiar figure to the residents of places such as Olalla, Clam Cove, and Maplewood until 1938.

Even after her days as Mosquito Fleet community builder, the *Virgina V* continued to serve various local communities—social ones. She carried Camp Fire girls and Boy Scouts to their summer camps, participated in the Special People's Cruise sponsored by Seattle's Seafair, and served the area through donated charity cruises.

A designated landmark for the cities of Seattle and Tacoma, the *Virginia V* was placed on the National Register of Historic Places in 1973 and also granted National Historic Landmark status in 1992. Her fate is currently in the hands of the *Virginia V* Foundation. The organization acquired the vessel in 1976 and is dedicated to restoring it to full operational condition and making her available for interpretive outreach programs throughout Puget Sound. Funded by thousands of individual donations in addition to support from the U.S. Department of Transportation, Washington State and King County, a more than $3 million renovation has been underway since 1997. If the Foundation is successful in making the *Virginia V* an operational vessel once again, residents of Puget Sound will have the opportunity to hear the famous steam whistle. Geographically it echoes over six miles. Historically it echoes across generations.

Above: The legendary Virginia V *out of the water for repairs in the 1950s. Photo by Edward Watton,* Seattle Times, *courtesy,* Virginia V Foundation/v5.2

Left: The Virginia V *in 1996 prior to restoration. Photo by Will Blethen, courtesy,* Virginia V Foundation/v5.1

The vessel in the foreground is the diesel-powered Suquamish. Her appearance differs significantly from older Mosquito Fleet boats. Courtesy, Puget Sound Maritime Historical Society, 2439 Seattle

corporate technological innovations. Triple-expansion engines achieved greater efficiency by using the same steam three times. Steam passed first through a high pressure cylinder, then continued to generate energy by passing through intermediate pressure and a low pressure cylinder. From there it moved to a condenser and returned to the boiler as water.

In 1914 the *Suquamish* became the first diesel-powered passenger vessel built in the United States. Her designers were Lee & Brinton, naval architects from Seattle. The wood-hulled, 92-foot boat carried 130 passengers and normally cruised between Seattle, Bainbridge and the town of Suquamish at a speed of 10 knots. The speed may not have been impressive, and her nickname

"Squeaky" might not be associated with a great vessel, but her 180-horsepower Nelseco (New London Ship & Engine Company) diesel engine made the *Suquamish* far less expensive to operate than the steam-powered vessels. She was welcomed as a high point and a trend setter for the Kitsap County Transportation Company. By 1925 most of the Mosquito Fleet had converted to oil as a source of fuel.

Other technological advances eventually contributed

A frequent visitor to the Puget Sound Navy Yard, the Rapid Transit carried construction materials for the facility. The name certainly has a modern ring to it. Courtesy, Puget Sound Maritime Historical Society, 2113-4 Seattle

From 1913 to 1930 the Tacoma carried passengers between Seattle, the "Queen City", and Tacoma, the "City of Destiny. Courtesy, Kitsap County Historical Society Museum Archives

to the demise of the small ferries. Because much of the business was generated by freight, the development of dedicated freight boats equipped with elevators drew revenue away from the passenger vessels.

The elevator on the Kitsap County Transportation Company's *Manitou* was a step beyond the simple cargo boom of the *Rapid Transit*, an earlier freight vessel.

The last steel-hulled Mosquito Fleet steamship built on Puget Sound saw the sun set on an era. The *Tacoma*, launched May 13, 1913, was supposed to be the first of a new breed of fast and elegant passenger ships—at least that is what her owners at Joshua Green's Inland Navigation Company thought. Instead, she was the finale. Built over the period of ten months at Robert Moran's Seattle Dry Dock and Construction Co., the *Tacoma* was designed to accommodate more than 1,000 passengers and slated to replace the *Flyer*. By routinely covering her Seattle–Tacoma route at a speed of 21 knots, and making the trip in 77 minutes, the *Tacoma* met the goals for speed, size and comfort. But these goals were changing, and by the end of the 1920s the most desired feature in a cross-Sound vessel was the ability to carry automobiles.

The Tacoma routes were first to note the societal shift toward land-based modes of transportation. There had never been much success with a steamer route between Bremerton and Tacoma, a situation that local newspapers blamed on haphazard business methods that failed to properly publicize the existence of the route or the departure and arrival times of the boats. Apart from the failure of publicity, it is likely that by the first decade of the 1900s Seattle had so firmly established itself as the terminus for Bremerton merchants and residents that Tacoma was out of the picture and would remain so until it made the bridge connection to the Kitsap Peninsula in the 1940s.

The Seattle to Tacoma boats had felt the pressure as early as 1902, when the opening of the electric interurban rail line forced the *Flyer,* and its competing boat, the *Sentinel,* to cut fares. The *Flyer* cut fares to 85 cents for a round-trip and the *Sentinel* scaled hers down to a very thrifty 40 cents. So thrifty in fact that the profits left the business and the *Sentinel* was sold to the Hansen Transportation Company in Poulsbo in 1903. Obviously, passengers continued to "Fly on the Flyer" and take the *Tacoma*, but the trends of the future were appearing. The opening of the Seattle–

Above: The Tacoma *was one of the most famous and the last of her type built on Puget Sound. This commemorative plaque is part of the exhibit at Bill Somers's maritime Museum of Puget Sound. Photo by Tom Janus, courtesy, Museum of Puget Sound*

Right: The traffic in Tacoma's harbor was never on a par with the activity in Seattle's Elliott Bay. Courtesy, Puget Sound Maritime Historical Society, 31415-1025 Seattle

Tacoma highway in 1928 celebrated one of the first four-lane highways in the nation; it also marked the beginning of the end for the steamers.

In his book, *Steamer's Wake*, author Jim Faber describes a poignant scene in December 1930 when the steamers *Tacoma* and *Indianapolis* made their last runs on the Seattle-Tacoma route. In the light of the full moon, as the two veterans passed, the *Indianapolis* blew her whistle three blasts while the passengers on the *Tacoma* stood on the deck and sang "Auld Lang Syne." It was, as they say, a moment.

In an evolutionary process, the vast fleet of jaunty steamers gave way to the lure of the automobile. Enamored with new transportation methods, the traveling public did not stop to analyze the convenience they had given up with the passenger boats. At least not until years later, when the automobile had created a Puget Sound megalopolis and spawned gridlock, was there a serious reflection on the practicality of what had been regarded as a nostalgic fascination with the steamers of the past.

The nostalgia plays out in several ways. One is the annual Mosquito Fleet Days celebration held in Port Orchard. It provides an opportunity to revisit the past aboard the floating *Carlisle II* museum. Built in 1917 and

purchased by the Horluck Transportation Company in 1936 to serve as one of the passenger boats connecting the north and south shores of Sinclair Inlet, the *Carlisle* is a fitting representative for the older Mosquito Fleet.

By the late 1970s Washington State transportation officials were publicly discussing a possible return to the Mosquito Fleet concept. Nostalgia aside, a myriad of problems are associated with creating new traffic patterns on the waters of Puget Sound. Travelers using passenger-only vessels still need places to park their cars. Fond memories of the small private and community docks that were "steamer landings" fail to consider the economic and environmental impacts of recreating those docks, not to mention possible difficulties in overcoming classic "not in my backyard" resistance from beach front property owners.

Speed is another consideration. Modern commuters are not likely to accept the slow leisurely pace and many stops of the old Mosquito Fleet routes. However, faster vessels require high performance engines that may need frequent repairs. Still, the pressure for fast, affordable, comfortable passenger-only vessels remains, and it is with some irony that the models of the past find themselves once again grouped with the ferries of the future.

In the first half of the twentieth century, Seattle's busy waterfront and its landmark 42-story skyscraper, the Smith Tower, were indicative of the former frontier town's development into a modern metropolis. Courtesy, Author's collection

Chapter 3

The Black Ball Line:
A Ferry System Emerges

The growing number of automobiles and their increasing importance as the transportation mode of choice led to a reworking of Puget Sound's marine transportation system. Throughout the 1920s the operators of the Mosquito Fleet faced the challenge of providing new types of vessels and docking facilities. No longer was it practical or necessary for boats to stop at every small community. Automobiles led to roads and the roads made it possible for passengers to drive to more centralized ferry landings. The multi-stop passenger services that had been the bastion of small steamboat operators were no longer required and routes were consolidated. Coupled with the expense of converting existing ferries into auto ferries and the investment required for new vessels, many of the transportation companies fell by the wayside, leaving a smaller roster of highly competitive groups to struggle for supremacy on the Sound's waterways.

Out of that handful of companies, two were worthy opponents—the Kitsap County Transportation Company and the Puget Sound Navigation Company (PSN). By the 1930s they had each successfully absorbed a number of other companies servicing the same routes. The one exception was the south Sound area, where ferries operated under the umbrella of the Pierce County government and generally avoided intrusion from the two large companies. From the turmoil of the Great Depression and the labor movements spawned by economic necessity, one outfit emerged as the major ferry transportation company. Puget Sound Navigation, popularly known as Black Ball Ferries, achieved dominance in 1936 and maintained a virtually unchallenged position until the State of Washington took over in 1951.

Before the ferries of the "Mosquito Fleet" were transformed into auto ferries, they did occasionally carry a few cars—as cargo. Unlike the cows and horses of earlier days, cars could not be pushed off the boat to swim ashore. However, they could be loaded via the dockside elevator, rolled onto a ferry's deck and rolled off at the other end. It worked; but as cars increased in numbers it became more expedient to adapt the vessels in order to handle the automobiles.

The first steamer to be adapted was the Puget Sound Navigation Company vessel *Whatcom,* built in 1901 in Everett, Washington, for the Seattle-Victoria route operated by the Thompson Steamboat Company. Originally named the *Majestic,* she moved to the PSN fleet in 1903 and was renamed *Whatcom.* The process used to transform the passenger vessel *Whatcom* into an auto ferry became standard procedure between 1912 and the early 1920s. The first auto ferries were all conversions. Changing the sleek lines of Mosquito Fleet vessels involved removing the superstructure above the deck and widening the hull as well as widening the bow and stern to fit the landing slips and to provide the ramp necessary for the movement of cars on and off the ferry. A new superstructure, wide and square, was added to the deck. This would be what legendary Captain Everett Coffin contemptuously called a "garage." The passenger cabin, sometimes all or part of the original vessel, the wheelhouse, and its surrounding deck (Texas deck) were placed back on top of the new superstructure. One part of the vessel not removed was the ship's power plant.

Even though early ferries were single-ended, cars could still drive off the boat's stern, but it was necessary for the boats to back into the landing slip. In other words, a ferry would head bow first into one landing slip, cars would drive on, and the ferry, upon reaching its destination, would back up to the dock so that the cars could drive off. Eventually double-ended ferries would eliminate that problem since they had propellers on each end and could easily go in either direction. In 1921 the *Whatcom*'s conversion took 40 days, cost $100,000, and included steam-driven elevators to facilitate landings at Port Orchard and other terminals that did not yet have regular ferry slips. Seattle and Bremerton had updated landings that allowed them to accommodate the new type-ferries.

The "traveling public," increasingly traveling by car as

Left: The steamship Whatcom, *shown here as a passenger vessel, was the first to undergo the complete conversion process to become an automobile ferry. Courtesy, Jefferson County Historical Society Museum, 2:154*

Opposite page, top: Early auto ferries were simple drive-through affairs capable of carrying only a few cars. Courtesy, Kitsap County Historical Society Museum Archives

Opposite page, bottom: After her conversion, the Whatcom *became the* City of Bremerton, *a full-fledged auto ferry. Courtesy, Puget Sound Maritime Historical Society, 541-8 Seattle*

The Puget, *a passenger vessel when this picture was taken in 1912, was converted to a semi-diesel auto ferry. Her pace was* too slow for the Bremerton run. *Courtesy, Jefferson County Historical Society Museum,* 2.341

well as by ferry, got its way. The *Whatcom,* no longer a passenger-only vessel, became the new *City of Bremerton,* capable of carrying 60 automobiles. Installed on the *City of Bremerton* was the chime whistle removed from the *Bailey Gatzert.* For those who appreciated the personality characteristics of individual vessels, moving the famous whistle to another vessel may have been somewhat sacrilegious.

In 1924 the *Seattle* underwent a similar conversion process and emerged ready to carry cars. The burgeoning auto traffic obviously required new fare structures. While passengers continued to pay 80 cents round-trip, car and driver fare was $2 one-way or $3.50 round-trip if the car weighed less than 3,500 pounds. Heavier cars cost their drivers fares of $2.50 or $4.50 round-trip.

One of the first ferries to undergo the change from steam to semi-diesel as part of the conversion process was the *Puget.* The new power plant was economical, but her running time on the Seattle–Bremerton run—one hour and 20 minutes—was unacceptable to commuters and the *Puget*

was moved to shorter routes. By the mid-1920s ferries were being specifically designed to carry automobiles and they were being built with diesel rather than steam engines. One of the earlier shipyards to build auto ferries was the Skansie Brothers yard in Gig Harbor. The *Wollochet* (renamed *Fox Island*), the *Defiance* and the *Skansonia* were all built by the Skansie Brothers Shipyard between 1925 and 1930.

Puget Sound ferry routes can be broken into several geographical regions, although early terminology referred only to upper and lower Sound. The modern, and for some, more easily understood breakdown refers to the upper Sound as the south Sound, an area which includes Olympia, Tacoma, Steilacoom, Gig Harbor, southern Vashon Island, Longbranch, Lakebay, and a number of small islands such as Anderson Island, Fox Island, and McNeil Island. The central Sound region encompasses Bremerton, South Kitsap County, the north end of Vashon Island, Bainbridge Island, and North Kitsap County. Across the Sound, west Seattle, Seattle, and Edmonds are in the central region. In the north, formerly lower Puget Sound, one finds ferries running to Whidbey Island, the San Juan Islands, and across the Straits of Juan de Fuca to Victoria, British Columbia. Somewhat set apart in the central area were the ferries that crossed Hood Canal, a narrow hook-shaped inlet on the west side of Kitsap County.

One other place adjacent to Puget Sound where ferries played an active role was on Lake Washington. From the earliest settlement until the completion of the second floating bridge in 1950, ferryboats served the communities east of Seattle. While they were not Puget Sound ferries in the strictest sense of the word, they were part of the culture and occasionally ventured out of the fresh water for service on the Sound. Operators such as Captain John Anderson had the entrepreneurial skills to operate on the lake and then move on to operations on the large body  of water. In 1925 Anderson became one of the owners of Kitsap County Transportation Company.

Steamboating in southern Puget Sound developed along the same lines as those in Poulsbo, with one major difference—the main destination points were Steilacoom or Tacoma. In accordance with the pattern that seemed to mark Sound transportation enterprises, one of the first south Sound businesses was operated by a set of brothers. The five Hunt brothers from Gig Harbor built or operated steamboats beginning in the late 1880s. The *Sentinel*, on the Seattle–Tacoma run, and the *Crest* were two boats built by the Hunt brothers. The *Susie*, a third boat, not only carried passengers and freight, but also hauled the bricks from Fox Island that built most of old Tacoma. When money got tight the *Susie* would also tow Tacoma's garbage out into the Puget Sound where it was dumped. Sometimes a quick load of garbage could be hauled while a group of paying excursionists were ashore for their picnic.

In 1902 the partnership of Hunt brothers broke up; Emmett Hunt continued to run the *Crest* while brother A.M. took over the *Sentinel*, a money-losing proposition that he quickly sold. A.M. Hunt joined with a new partner in the Tacoma Burton Navigation Company in 1905. That partner, Frank Bibbins, sold out in 1908 to A.R. and L.B. Hunt. The brothers, Arthur, Arda, and Lloyd regrouped, running the steamer *Crest*, followed by the *Atalanta* and the *Ariel* until 1919 when the company dissolved. In 1921 the Hunts were back with a new company, the Tacoma Ferry Co. operating the *City of Tacoma* between Tacoma, Vashon and Gig Harbor under contract for the Pierce County Commissioners.

Within three years the *City of Tacoma* was declared inadequate because her capacity of 300 passengers and

Lincoln of Kirkland *was one of the Lake Washington ferries operated by King County. Courtesy, Puget Sound Maritime Historical Society, 1429-8 Seattle*

35 automobiles was not sufficient to meet the demands of automobile travelers. Even the added presence of the ex-*Florence K*, rebuilt as the *Gloria*, did not satisfy the demand. Thus the *City of Tacoma* spent some time at Tacoma's Western Boatbuilding Co. and emerged 34-feet longer and capable of carrying 50 automobiles.

Four Yugoslavian immigrants, Gig Harbor brothers Pete, Mitchell, Andrew and Joe Skansie, founded their shipbuilding company in 1912 and produced several boats each year. Many of their boats were fishing vessels and the Skansies reportedly built the first gasoline launch for seine fishing on Puget Sound. Starting in 1922, they also built ferries, including the *Skansonia* and *Defiance*. The Skansies pioneered the use of diesel engines in ferries, and, in an era devoid of the concept of "brand names"

for boats, the Skansie name represented quality shipbuilding.

In 1926 Mitchell Skansie combined his shipbuilding talents with an early ferry company, the Washington Navigation Company. Pierce County had provided automobile ferry service to Gig Harbor since 1918. When the County could no longer afford to run ferries, contracts were let, first to Martin Petrick of Tacoma, and then to Mitchell Skansie. With the blessing of Pierce County, the Washington Navigation Company had a good share of the ferry business on the south Sound. By the 1930s the firm had several ferries running. Along with the *Skansonia* and *Defiance*, the earlier-built *Elk*, *City of Steilacoom*, and the *Fox Island* (ex-*Wollochet*) had regular routes. Besides the Gig Harbor-Point Defiance route, there were ferries between Steila-

The Atalanta, one of the fleet owned by the Hunt brothers, was built in 1913 for service on the Gig Harbor route. Courtesy, Gig Harbor Peninsula Historical Society

A closer view of passengers boarding the City of Tacoma in 1918. Courtesy, Gig Harbor Peninsula Historical Society

coom, Longbranch, Anderson and McNeil Islands. The 67-foot ferry *Elk* operated on the Steilacoom–Longbranch Island route. Another route covered Wollochet Bay and Fox Island.

The Great Depression hit Washington Navigation Company hard, and the opening of the Tacoma Narrows Bridge in 1940 all but finished the company. However, when the bridge collapsed in a spectacular fashion less than a year after it opened, the Skansies were ready to restore ferry runs across the Tacoma Narrows to Point Defiance. Having sold the *Skansonia* and the *Defiance* to the State of Washington, Mitchell Skansie and his son operated the ferries under state contract. They served Vashon Island as well as the Gig Harbor area. After 18 months the contracts came up for renewal and the Skansies lost out to a low bid from the giant Puget Sound Navigation Company. In 1948 the Skansies were again serving Vashon Island, winning a new state contract with a low bid of $2,975.

At the opposite end of Puget Sound, the San Juan Island auto ferry routes, unquestionably the most beautiful of all Puget Sound routes, were pioneered starting in 1922 by enterprising tugboat operator Captain Harry Crosby (unrelated to Bing's clan or his own partner, Roy Crosby). Harry Crosby tested his maritime business skills in several of the Sound's various regions. When small companies operating competing ferries in the San Juans began to threaten Crosby with rate wars, Puget Sound Navigation Company, easily

Right: In building ferry-boats, Mitchell Skansie pioneered the use of diesel engines. He was a great fan of the Fairbanks Morse engine shown here. Photo by Boland, courtesy, Washington State Historical Society, 16200 Tacoma, Neg. #16200

Opposite page: Early Gig Harbor waterfront site of the Skansie shipyards. Courtesy, Washington State Historical Society, Tacoma, Boland Collection

Below: Skansie shipyard workers are dwarfed by the hull of the vessel they are building. Courtesy, Washington State Historical Society, Tacoma, Boland Collection

capable of withstanding the competition and fully aware that the San Juans was a desirable route, stepped in and bought the Crosby operation. Crosby shifted his focus to the south Sound, purchasing the *Elk* from the Skansies and establishing a new route between Tacoma and Gig Harbor. The venture quickly failed because of competition from the Pierce County ferries.

Seemingly undaunted, Crosby moved the *Elk* to a Ballard-Kingston run. There he encountered the time-consuming problem of having to pass through the Lake Washington Ship canal every trip. Furthermore, Crosby found it hard to dock at the Kingston side in Kitsap County because competing interests there did not hesitate to block his access to the ferry landing. Crosby kept up the run during the summer of 1924 before he conceded to the faster Kingston-Edmonds route that was the territory of the Sound Ferry Lines, a company owned by Captain O. Joyce along with his brothers, Alfred R., Clarence J., Arthur, and Percy. Their auto ferry *Whidby* had started on the Mukilteo-Whidbey Island route in 1919 and was one of the earliest auto ferries in the north Sound region. The Joyce brothers also had the Port Gamble-Shine run on Hood Canal.

In 1925 Crosby was back in business as the Crosby Direct Ferry Lines running between Manchester on the

FERRY DOCKS

Ferry docks, like ferries, have had to change with the times and adapt to automobiles as well as meeting the traveling public's demand for comfortable waiting rooms. Built in 1882 by Scottish engineer James M. Colman, and located on the present site of Washington State Ferries' Seattle terminal, the first Colman Dock was a simple 40-foot by 60-foot wharf. It became the main facility for the Mosquito Fleet. The dock was enlarged in 1886, only to burn down in the great Seattle fire of 1889. The much larger, 92 by 100-foot, 1890 version reflected Seattle's growing importance as a transportation center for Puget Sound communities. The 1908 incarnation of Colman Dock, designed by Seattle architect Arthur Loveless, had an added air of sophistication thanks to the 72-foot high Italianate clock tower, prominent at the end of the 705-foot long wharf. It provided a distinctive landmark for boats steaming into Elliott Bay.

In April 1912 the steamer *Alameda* was heading towards that landmark with her engines mistakenly set to full speed ahead. The *Alameda* proceeded helter-skelter through the end of Colman Dock, smashing the sternwheeler *Telegraph* into the neighboring Grand Trunk Pacific Dock. The unfortunate *Telegraph* sank while the runaway *Alameda* suffered only minor damage. The other "victim"

of the accident was the clock tower found floating in the harbor the next day. When the battered dock was reconstructed, the clock tower was replaced by an even more ornate version.

Colman Dock suffered some damage again in 1914 when a spectacular fire at the neighboring Grand Trunk Dock spread. The dock, which featured a 130-foot tower, served Canadian vessels traveling to Victoria and Vancouver. The fire was a disaster in the truest sense as four Seattle firefighters lost their lives battling the flames.

Automobiles began to exert some impetus for change between 1916 and 1917 after a ramp for cars and trucks was constructed. In 1923 there were further modifi-

Above: Seen from this angle, Colman Dock's second clock tower appears to be level with Seattle's first skyscraper, Smith Tower. Photo by Asahel Curtis, courtesy, Washington State Historical Society, Tacoma, Negative #37206

Left: This photo shows Colman Dock prior to its encounter with the Alameda in 1912. The Grand Trunk Pacific Dock is on the left. Courtesy, Seattle Public Library

cations when a short slip capable of handling bow loading of cars was added to the north end of the dock.

In 1936 Colman Dock and its clock were reincarnated as an art deco styled Black Ball ferry terminal. As form follows function, this version was designed with automobiles in mind. While walk-on passengers sat above, cars and drivers were relegated into narrow, numbered loading lanes in the dimly lighted cavernous space under the terminal. One oversight that made the terminal nearly obsolete from its beginning was the narrow entryway that prevented big trucks from getting through the entrance. The problem was corrected by reconstruction work in the 1940s.

Both the art deco terminal and the Grand Trunk Dock were reduced to the status of memories, demolished in 1964 and 1965 to make way for the Washington State Ferry Terminal,

Above: One casualty of the runaway ship Alameda *in 1912 was the first Colman Dock clock tower which was found floating in Elliott Bay. Photo by Asahel Curtis, courtesy, Washington State Historical Society, Tacoma Negative #23561*

Right: A spectacular fire, started when something ignited sawdust, engulfed the Grand Trunk Pacific Dock in July 1914. Courtesy, Seattle Public Library

which opened in 1966 on the waterfront space once occupied by the two docks. While the terminal is designed to accommodate four ferries, its automobile holding space has become severely challenged in the 30 plus years since it opened.

In Bremerton the early twentieth century ferry dock was advertised as having one of the finest waiting rooms on Puget Sound. City founder and real estate mogul William Bremer, who owned the dock, built the waiting room in 1909. Today the building would be called a terminal, but the purpose was the same. While waiting for Puget Sound ferries of whatever sort, steamer or superferry, the traveling public has always desired reasonably comfortable conditions. Shelter, heat, and restrooms are basic. The building on Bremerton's wharf went beyond minimum needs. It offered flowers, fruit, cigars, candy and newspaper stands; a ticket outlet for Seattle theaters, a lunch room, and an entire second floor devoted to lockers where the navy's enlisted men could change clothes before heading over to Seattle for a little excitement. Large windows are an amenity in ferry waiting rooms, but Bremerton's had the added features of two chandeliers and shaded lights around the walls to give the appearance of warmth to the oak finished hardwood floors in the evenings.

The flags denote that this sailing of the Washington Navigation Route ferry Wollochet *is a special occasion and that the crowds are not typical ferry commuters. Courtesy, Gig Harbor Peninsula Historical Society*

A crew of Skansie shipyard workers in 1915. Courtesy, Gig Harbor Peninsula Historical Society

southern end of the Kitsap Peninsula and Alki Point south and west of Seattle. The *Elk* was also back although she was longer, had a new engine, and was now named the *Airline*. Enjoying real success for the first time, the Crosbys ordered a new ferry to be built at Seattle's Duwamish-based Marine Construction Company. At 142-feet-long and with a 65-car capacity, the *Crosline* bore an estimated price tag of $25,000. While the new ferry was under construction, Crosby relieved pressure on the *Airline* by purchasing the *Gloria* (ex-*Florence K.*) from the Hunt brothers in the south Sound. In keeping with the alphabetical and "-line" theme, the *Gloria* became the *Beeline*.

Crosby challenged both the Puget Sound Navigation Company and the Kitsap County Transportation Company with his short distance route and his lower fares for cars and drivers. KCTC, which had just started a Fauntleroy–Vashon–Harper route about five miles to the south of Crosby's route, was dismayed by Crosby's 50 cents fare. Joining with the Puget Sound Navigation Company (PSN), owner of the Navy Yard Route, KCTC filed a protest with the State Department of Public Works, a regulatory agency for ferry service. The order to Crosby to raise his fares provided some relief for the other two companies although Crosby only raised his ticket prices to 85 cents for a one-way fare and the other two companies kept theirs at a dollar. A more permanent solution

to the Crosby problem was found in 1926 when Puget Sound Navigation completed a merger with the Crosby Direct Ferry Lines. As a result, the A-B-C ferries and the route passed over to PSN which continued to operate them until 1936.

The consolidation of lines such as the Crosby enterprise was characteristic of the way ferry companies evolved on Washington's inland waters. Both Puget Sound Navigation Company and Kitsap County Transportation Company had their beginnings in the early 1900s and both were built through mergers with other transportation companies. One such merger gave PSN a president and gave Northwest its "Commodore of all Puget Sound Fleets," an honorary title bestowed on Joshua Green in 1969.

Green's own biographical account of his life, given to Gordon Newell for publication in the *H.W. McCurdy Marine History of the Pacific Northwest*, says that he was born in Jackson, Mississippi in 1869 and moved to Seattle with his parents in the 1880s. After a year on the local railroad and a year aboard the steamer *Henry Bailey* as the purser, Green convinced four friends to borrow enough capital to join him in purchasing the steamer *Fannie Lake*. Profits from that vessel went to purchase other steamers and by 1900 Green's business, the LaConner Trading and Transportation Company, was a going concern with such vessels as the *Rapid Transit* and *George E. Starr* in its fleet. In 1903 Green

While the Gig Harbor ferry Skansonia *looks ship shape, the ferry dock is another matter. Courtesy, Gig Harbor Peninsula Historical Society*

merged his holdings into Charles Peabody's Alaska Steamship's Puget Sound Navigation Company. In the restructuring, Green took over as PSN president while Peabody moved up to chairman of the board. Under Green's tenure the company was known briefly as Inland Navigation Company. Furthermore, PSN had not yet acquired its alternate name of Black Ball Ferries and its house flag was not a black ball but rather a red star on a white diamond centered on a blue field. Until 1926, it was the standard flown from all Puget Sound Navigation vessels.

Three of Puget Sound Navigation's early vessels, the *Indianapolis*, *Iroquois*, and *Chippewa*, were Great Lakes steamers purchased in 1905–1906. The *Indianapolis* had been built for the Indiana Transportation Company to run between Michigan City and Chicago, but she proved inadequate to handle the crowds and was sold to PSN in 1905. The *Iroquois* and *Chippewa* were both coal-burning passenger-steamers for the Arnold Line of Mackinac Island until they were found to be too big and too expensive to operate. One at a time, starting with the *Indianapolis*, they made the long trip from the East Coast by way of the Great Lakes, the Saint Lawrence River, down the Atlantic Coast to the

Straits of Magellan and then up the Pacific Coast to Puget Sound. Of the trio, the *Chippewa* had the most difficult voyage, encountering nine days of bad weather at the tip of South America. The trip that had taken the *Indianapolis* 51 days took half-again as long for the *Chippewa*.

Despite her difficulties in reaching Puget Sound, the *Chippewa* had a long and successful career on the inland seas. After serving on the Victoria, Bellingham, and Tacoma routes, she was drafted as a training ship in World War I. In 1926 she underwent a conversion that made her—with a capacity of 90 cars and 2,000 passengers—the largest auto ferry on Puget Sound. The change in size slowed her speed somewhat but the *Chippewa* was a mainstay on the Navy Yard Route. In 1932 her steam engines were replaced with diesel. The lighter power plant resulted in a 2-3 knots increase in speed. She remained on the Seattle–Bremerton run through the 1950s and was serving as a reserve boat in 1964 when her car deck was ruled too tight for the large fin-featured cars of the time. The *Chippewa* was sold to California owners and left Puget Sound, although she is still fondly remembered by many Bremerton-based residents of the baby-boom generation.

Left: Commemorative plaque at Seattle waterfront. Photo by Tom Janus

Below: The Skansie-built ferry Elk, shown here at Longbranch, was renamed the Airline after her sale to entrepreneur Harry Crosby. Courtesy, Gig Harbor Peninsula Historical Society

Opposite page: The launching of the ferry Crosline in 1925. Courtesy, Puget Sound Maritime Historical Society, 680-8 Seattle

THE LACONNER TRADING AND TRANSPORTATION COMPANY'S BOATS PLYING BETWEEN SEATTLE, PUGET SOUND NAVY YARD AND OTHER PORT ORCHARD POINTS.

Left: A 1901 agreement between Joshua Green and H.B. Kennedy put the LaConner Trading & Transportation Company on the Port Orchard Route. Courtesy, Kitsap County Historical Society Museum Archives

Below: The lunch counter on the Chippewa was a favorite place for riders on the Seattle-Bremerton route. Courtesy, Puget Sound Maritime Historical Society, 526-32 Seattle

The third steamer, *Iroquois,* made trips from the Great Lakes twice— the first time in 1906. She returned to the Great Lakes in 1920, a trip made easier by the six-year-old Panama Canal. Seven years later she was reclaimed by PSN and returned to Puget Sound for transformation into a night boat and service on the Seattle–Port Townsend–Port Angeles–Victoria run. She continued in that role until replaced by the newly built *Chinook* in 1947. The *Iroquois* was then reconfigured as a freight boat, working in that capacity until 1972 when she made the voyage that is often the last for former Puget Sound ferries. She was taken to Alaska for use as a crab processor. In 1984, after 83 years of useful and varied service, the *Iroquois* was taken to deep water and sunk.

While Puget Sound Navigation Company prospered and grew under Joshua Green's leadership, he remained first and foremost a steamboat man, keeping away from the automo-

bile ferry era. Although he continued to declare that his 40 years in Puget Sound steamboating had been the happiest of his life, he resigned from PSN in 1927 in order to devote himself to banking interests. As president of the People's National Bank, Green was a powerful mover and shaker in the Puget Sound economy and a much beloved figure in Seattle society. In 1966 he was on hand to dedicate the $35,000 fountain he had donated to dress up Seattle's new Washington State Ferry Terminal. After vociferously announcing his love for Seattle's "dear old waterfront" Green added that the fountain was not spouting as high as he would have liked but that maybe it would get better with practice. At his last birthday party in 1974 Green's cake bore a drawing of the Puget Sound sternwheeler *Fanny Lake* and the notation, "Joshua Green, still on deck at 105." He died in 1975, just four weeks after the death of Laura "Missy" Green, his 101-year-old wife of 73 years.

After Green's departure from PSN in 1927, the company eventually fell under the leadership of Charles Peabody's son, Captain Alexander Marshall Peabody. The Peabody family's maritime tradition stretched back to 1816 when

Above: The Chippewa *underwent a series of conversions. Courtesy, Puget Sound Maritime Historical Society, 526-40 Seattle*

Right: Seen here in a 1930 conversion, the Chippewa *emerged as a diesel powered vessel. Courtesy, Puget Sound Maritime Historical Society, 526-125 Seattle*

the Black Ball Line, a fleet of Atlantic clipper ships, was founded by Captain Charles H. Marshall. His brother, ship's captain Alexander Marshall, was Charles Peabody's grandfather. When Charles first organized Alaska Steamship Company in 1894, his ships adopted the Black Ball house flag that had graced the family's earlier Atlantic fleet. The flag stayed with Alaska Steamship Company after Charles sold the firm. In 1928, his son Alexander Peabody, as the new head of Puget Sound Navigation Company, was able to get permission from Alaska Steamship to reclaim the flag's image for PSN. The black ball on a red field replaced Joshua Green's red, white, and blue flag. The change was symbolic of the new era. Captain Alexander Peabody's nearly 25 years in charge saw the emergence of the Black Ball Ferries as synonymous with Puget Sound Navigation Company and the continued consolidation of independent companies into what some considered a Puget Sound monopoly. By the late 1920s the Black Ball Ferries had emerged as a force to be reckoned with.

The competing power, Kitsap County Transportation Company stemmed from Warren Gazzam's consolidation

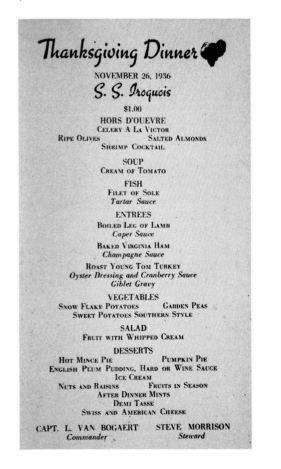

of the pioneer steamboating companies operating in the North Kitsap area. Starting in 1905, KCTC eventually either acquired or eliminated from business the Moe Brothers, Hansen Transportation Company, the Liberty Bay Company, and the Poulsbo Transportation Company. Colonel Gazzam, as he was known in Kitsap County, was one of Joshua Green's most bitter rivals. Between 1903 and 1923 Puget Sound Navigation and Kitsap County Transportation Company competed ruthlessly. Green's company, enhanced by the former Great Lakes steamers, had the bigger vessels. Gazzam relied on smaller and faster vessels and on technological innovation. The first diesel-powered passenger vessel, Gazzam's 92-foot *Suquamish* launched in 1914, was an example of one-upmanship.

While there was a spirited rivalry between Puget Sound Navigation and the White Collar Line, as KCTC was commonly called, there were also unfortunate accidents. In December 1910, in the midst of a thick fog, the White

Collar steamer *Kitsap* left her Seattle pier bound for Poulsbo. She had only been underway a few minutes when she ran down and sank a launch named the *Columbia*, killing one man aboard. After a 25 minute delay while she returned to the dock with the *Columbia*'s rescued captain, the *Kitsap* started out again. On her second foray into Elliott Bay, the *Kitsap* was mowed down by PSN's *Indianapolis*. While it sank, her passengers and crew were safely transferred over to the *Indianapolis*.

In 1917 Gazzam stepped down as president of Kitsap County Transportation Company. The ferry company he had pieced together was a thriving business when he left. The new owners, Lyman Hinckley, Philip MacBride, and George Russell, had been operating the Kingston Transportation Company. Not only did they acquire a well-established business, they were also able to retain the veteran boat operators, Alf Hostmark and the Hansen brothers, as part of the company. When Lyman Hinckley died in December 1924, Captain John Anderson,

veteran of Lake Washington ferries, bought controlling interest and became KCTC president.

The White Collar Line was operating four ferries and three passenger steamers in 1935. The auto ferry routes included Ballard–Suquamish, Fauntleroy-Vashon-Harper (South Kitsap), Fletcher Bay–Brownsville (Bainbridge Island's west side to a spot north of Bremerton), and Port Blakely–Seattle.

The passenger steamer *Hyak*, a great favorite in North Kitsap, made two round-trips a day from Poulsbo to Seattle with 10 stops—Scandia, Pearson, Lemolo, Virginia, Keyport, Seabold, Suquamish, Indianola, Manitou, and Ferncliff. The

HORLUCK TRANSPORTATION

One of the few small companies not absorbed by Puget Sound Navigation Company is Horluck Transportation Company in Kitsap County. A surviving remnant from the Mosquito Fleet days, the small but long-lived enterprise has operated passenger-only ferries in Sinclair Inlet and Port Orchard Bay since 1925. In the first years of the Bremerton Navy Yard's operation, employees who lived in Port Orchard, across Sinclair Inlet from their jobs, rowed to work, or traveled on the assorted vessels of early transportation businesses. In 1925, two men, Penze and Horluck, incorporated Horluck Transportation as a local ferry service. Four years later, Willis Nearhoff, former operator of a Whidbey Island ferry company forced out of that area by the expansive Puget Sound Navigation Company, purchased Horluck. Nearhoff kept the company name of founder George Horluck who left ferries in favor of the ice cream business. At the time of the purchase, Horluck had boats running to Keyport, Poulsbo, Annapolis, Port Orchard and Bremerton. For a time they also ran between Bremerton and Bainbridge Island's Point White.

During World War II Horluck ferries carried 16,000 passengers daily for a dime fare each way. Modeled after the "nickel snatcher" nickname for San Francisco ferries, the Horluck fleet became commonly known as "dime snatchers" or "puddle jumpers," a reference to the short distance across Sinclair Inlet. One of the Horluck boats, the *Carlisle II*, acquired in 1934, was until recently the oldest continually operating ferry vessel on Puget Sound. She is now a floating museum. In 1946 the company created a subsidiary, Port Orchard Marine Railway, as a maintenance and repair facility for the ferries. The Horluck ferries *Spirit of '76* and

Mary Lieseke in 1976, a savvy business-woman and well-known figure on Sinclair Inlet. She and her husband Fritz took over the Horluck Company in 1934 when Mary's father Willis Nearhoff died. Courtesy, Port Orchard Independent

Eagle were finished at the facility. The company's other vessels were the *Thurow*, *Retsil*, and *Carlisle*.

After owner Mary Lieseke's death in 1991 at the age of 84, the company continued under son Al Lieseke and Willis Nearhoff Jr. until 1995 when the line was purchased by Seattle businessman Hilton Smith. Not only does the Horluck name remain after all these years but the memory of Mary Lieseke is still present on Sinclair Inlet with the addition to the fleet of the *Mary L*. Besides acquiring the newly built *Mary L.*, Hilton Smith's first five years as Horluck's owner were marked by frustrated efforts to expand the potential of private enterprise in providing ferry service on Puget Sound. State regulation of ferry routes as well as ferry service, once non-existent, is now firmly entrenched in Puget Sound waters, making it difficult for the private sector to institute new services.

Boat maintenance for Horluck was done at the company-owned Port Orchard Marine Railway. Courtesy, Kitsap County Historical Society Museum Archives

steamers *Winslow* and *Manitou* served Bainbridge Island with stops at Creosote, Wing Point, Hawley, Eagledale, and Winslow. The *Manitou's* route included Rolling Bay, Yeomalt, Ferncliff, Manitou Beach and Manitou Park.

Kitsap County Transportation subsidiaries added three freight boats and three passenger steamers to the fleet. The Washington Route's *Commander* on the Bremerton–Seattle run was the only "opposition" boat to successfully challenge the predominant PSN-owned Navy Yard Route. The *Atalanta*, formerly a Hunt Brothers boat operating in the south Sound, connected Seattle with the east side of Whidbey Island. She was part of the subsidiary Whidby Island Transportation Company. Kitsap County Transportation Company's freight and reserve boats included the *Verona*, *Suquamish*, *Speeder*, and *F.G. Reeve*.

With the exception of the *Commander*, KCTC vessels did not directly compete with those of Black Ball and, once the two systems firmly established themselves, there was a certain understanding between the companies that guaranteed orderly ferry service. The status quo was upset by the Great Depression of the 1930s that caused the same economic downturn in the Northwest as it did in the rest of the country. It was fertile ground for union organizing and ferry workers eagerly signed up in the hope of attaining the level of wages that prevailed on San Francisco Bay ferries. Initially, Black Ball President Alexander Peabody simply ignored the unions, not recognizing them until 1933. Thereafter, strikes every two years during the 1930s created the beginnings of union contracts that would ultimately guarantee fair wages in the industry.

In November 1935 the ferry-based unions struck Kitsap County Transportation Company. Captain Peabody later recounted that he had first tried to avert the strike because he knew it would ruin the opposing company, and then had offered help to KCTC by sharing any windfall that Black Ball Ferries might receive as a result of increased revenue while KCTC's boats were tied up. Kitsap County Transportation Company responded with an offer to sell-out. By that time Black Ball had also been struck, and most ferry service on Puget Sound halted for what would be a 33 day work stoppage. Black Ball weathered the strike and was able to acquire Kitsap County Transportation Company in the process by agreeing to assume $140,000 in liabilities.

Peabody believed that the financial difficulties KCTC had experienced stemmed from changes wrought by time. The days of the passenger steamer stopping at every community landing had passed in favor of automobile ferries and consolidated routes. Peabody set about reshaping

In 1939 the Hyak *was dismantled by the Seattle Iron & Metals Corp; the hull was abandoned in the Duwamish River. Courtesy, Puget Sound Maritime Historical Society, 1188-16 Seattle*

Formerly the General Frisbie of San Francisco, the Commander went into service on the Seattle-Bremerton run in 1930. She carried 750 passengers and 12 cars. One way fare for a car and driver was $1.00. Courtesy, Puget Sound Maritime Historical Society, 623.13 Seattle

Puget Sound ferry service. Some vessels, the *Commander*, *F.G. Reeve* and *Atalanta* never resumed service after the strike. Some of the boat stops such as Eagledale and Port Blakely on Bainbridge Island were phased out more gradually since state approval was necessary before service to remote routes could totally cease. Seattle-Tacoma passenger service ceased in 1930 and the Seattle-Anacortes-Bellingham route was abandoned in 1935. Other discontinued routes included Edmonds-Port Ludlow, Edmonds-Port Townsend, Everett-Langley (Whidbey Island), and Seattle-Manchester.

Another private ferry operator who eventually sold out to Black Ball and Captain Peabody, although under more friendly circumstances, was Berte Olson. As the first female auto ferry operator on Puget Sound, Norwegian-born Berte was sometimes compared to the character "Tugboat Annie." Over the years she enjoyed friendship and help from Alexander Peabody.

In the early 1920s Berte and her husband, Agaton Olson, operated ferries between Whidbey and Camano Islands as well as between Whidbey Island and the mainland town of Anacortes. In keeping with Northwest style,

the name of the company was the Olson Bros. Thanks to help from Peabody, Berte, who split the ferry assets with her husband in the early 1930s, acquired a boat named the *Central II* and, along with her other boats, was able to maintain the Whidbey routes. Agaton Olson and his brother moved to the other end of Puget Sound, operating ferries between Steilacoom, McNeil Island, and Anderson Island.

When the 1935 Deception Pass bridge connected Whidbey Island with a route to Anacortes, Berte Olson's ferry business suffered a financial blow. Peabody again helped out, this time with a ferry route between Port Gamble and Shine on Hood Canal. Berte moved her operations and her ferry *Acorn* along with the Black Ball boat *Clatawa* to Port Gamble and set up shop as the Olympic Navigation Company in 1936.

Within three years she had expanded the service to include a Hood Canal crossing between Seabeck on the Kitsap side and Brinnon on the Jefferson County side, a route originally served by the ferryboat *Pioneer*. Although Berte Olson may have been compared to Tugboat Annie, one of her employees, Earl Ferguson, a deckhand on the *Acorn,* recalls that Berte Olson was very much a stylish lady, as well as a competent and well-liked business-woman.

When it became evident that new ferry and bridge combinations would open the route to the Olympic Peninsula as a tourist destination, Alexander Peabody stepped in again—this time with a friendly purchase offer. In 1950, Peabody bought the route franchise and pre-pared for larger auto ferries to handle the anticipated tourist onslaught. In June 1950, Peabody and the newly-retired Berte Olson were both aboard the ferry *Vashon* for her inaugural run on the Hood Canal crossing be-tween Black Ball's new landings at Lofall and South Point. The route would remain a vital link until the completion of the Hood Canal Floating Bridge in 1961 and would again become important as part of the state-operated ferry system after a windstorm destroyed the bridge in 1979.

Once Black Ball had obtained a near monopoly status on the Sound, the company had to increase the number of vessels in its fleet to meet the demands for ferry service. Puget Sound Navy Yard's defense build-up before World War II and the shortage of housing in Bremerton resulted in more commuters traveling from Seattle to Bremerton. That,

plus increased populations in the areas outside of Seattle, required more ferries. Ferry construction on Puget Sound had ceased after 1930 for two reasons. One was the lack of capital caused by the economic collapse that spawned the Great Depression. The other was the availability of San Francisco ferries. Bridge-building in the Bay area had rendered that once vast ferry fleet redundant. Conse-quently, San Francisco ferry companies offered a source of existing vessels. A number of these ferries made their way north into Puget Sound.

Peabody was able to make a bulk purchase of six wooden-hulled diesel-electric ferries from the Southern Pacific-Golden Gate Ferries. One ferry, the *Golden West,* was immediately sold to California interests. The remaining five "Golden" vessels were towed up the coast to Puget Sound beginning in November 1937. Despite bad weather, all but one of the ferries successfully made the voyage. The lone casualty was the *Golden Bear,* her superstructure flat-tened by waves off the Oregon coast. The hull stayed afloat and it was announced that the vessel would be rebuilt. A closer scrutiny revealed the full extent of the damage, including a twisted hull. The *Golden Bear* became a cement barge and then a breakwater. Her four sister ships fared better— rechristened with Indian names, the *Golden State, Golden Poppy, Golden Shore,* and *Golden Age* joined the

Looking somewhat like a toy boat, the ferry Clatawa *served the Hood Canal crossing between Brinnon and Seabeck in the 1930s. Courtesy, Jefferson County Historical Society Museum, 8:141*

Puget Sound Navigation fleet as the *Kehloken*, *Chetzemoka*, *Elwha*, and *Klahanie*, respectively.

Another six ferries, steel-hulled diesel electrics, were purchased in 1940 at a total cost of $300,001—the extra dollar being part of bidding strategy. That price is mentioned in a quote from Alex Peabody printed in Graham Schrader's *Black Ball Line* (Edmonds Printing Company, 1980). It should also be noted that in *Ferryboats: A Legend on Puget Sound*, authors Mary Kline and George Bayless peg the purchase price at $330,001. The *Santa Rosa*, built in 1927, had run between San Francisco and Sausalito. In Puget Sound she became the *Enetai*. The *Lake Tahoe*, also built in 1927, was renamed the *Illahee*. The *Stockton* became the *Klickitat*; the *Mendocino* became the *Nisqually*; and the *Redwood Empire* became the *Quinault*. The *Fresno*, another 1927 boat, had been on the San Francisco-Oakland run where one of her honorary duties included a trip for President Herbert Hoover. She continued her career in Puget Sound as the *Willapa*.

Three steam ferries made up Peabody's penultimate purchase of California ferries. The *Napa Valley* became the *Mahalat* on the Bremerton run. The *Shasta* and the *San Mateo* were also transplanted and, although they were used mostly as extra boats, they became local favorites, retaining their California names.

The last California ferry to travel north in the 1940s was the *City of Sacramento*, arriving in 1944. When Black Ball Ferries left Puget Sound in 1951, the *City of Sacramento* moved north again. Rebuilt and renamed *Kahloke*, she was part of Peabody's British Columbia operation.

With the help of the California ferries, Black Ball provided stellar service for the war effort on Puget Sound. By 1942 its 23 vessels had the capacity to carry some 22,500 cars and 315,000 passengers daily. Fifteen different routes and 452 sailings each day is evidence of the Herculean task. In cooperating with the needs of the U.S. Government to provide war workers, Peabody also agreed to reduce ferry fares by 10 percent. Riders on the Bremerton run saw their commuter book per trip cost drop from 22.5 cents to 20 cents.

Black Ball's postwar plans included a spectacular new vessel for a new era. The motor ferry *Chinook* slid down Todd Shipyard's Seattle launchways in April 1947. Slated to be the successor to the aging *Iroquois* on the Seattle-Victoria run, the *Chinook* had all the elegance that the traveling public had been deprived of during the war. Her salon, coffee shop, and dining room, decorated by Fredrick and Nelson, designers from Seattle's premier department store, were more in the tradition of ocean liners than ferryboats. News of the *Chinook* caused resentment among Puget Sound commuters faced with higher fares in order to balance Black Ball's company books. She was the first American postwar vessel built entirely with private financing. The $2,500,000 ferry seemed like a luxury in more ways than one. At 318-feet long she had room for 100 cars and a matching 100 staterooms with room for 208 people or a total ferry capacity of 1000 people. Wartime technology benefited the *Chinook* with radar and ship-to-shore telephones.

Although a costly investment, the *Chinook* was a success, carrying more than 195,000 passengers in her first year of operation. Black Ball's outreach to tourist bureaus, automobile clubs, and tour organizers all over the United States not only attracted travelers but helped to promote Puget Sound's image as the "Evergreen Playground." The company's promotional strategy has been continued by Washington State Ferries, making the ferry system the state's largest tourist attraction.

From a myriad of small independent ferry companies operating in the first decades of the century, Puget Sound

Navigation had helped foster the change from passenger-only steamers to auto ferries. By 1936 it had consolidated, centralized, and absorbed routes and companies, achieving dominance of Puget Sound ferries. Under Alexander Peabody's leadership, the company adopted its popular nickname Black Ball Ferries and emerged at the end of World War II positioned to assume its place as the Sound's ferry monopoly.

The former California ferry City of Sacramento *continued her northward migration, becoming the Black Ball's British Columbia registered ferry* Kahloke. *Courtesy, Puget Sound Maritime Historical Society, 5200-1 Seattle*

Stream-lined and rounded, the art-deco ferry Kalakala is instantly recognizable because of her unique one-of-a-kind design. Courtesy, Author's collection

Chapter 4

Kalakala:
A Class of Her Own

In the Chinook Indian language her name meant "Flying Bird," although local commuters were more apt to call her the "Galloping Ghost of the Seattle Coast," the "Silver Slug," or a host of other unflattering nicknames. Whatever the label, the *Kalakala* remains the most famous ferry to have sailed in Puget Sound waters. In a fleet where ferries are grouped by class, she was the only vessel in her class—one of a kind. Years before the Space Needle graced Seattle's skyline, the *Kalakala* was the symbol most often pictured on the city's postcards.

The shiny streamlined ferry was originally a more traditional vessel, built in Oakland for San Francisco's Key Transit System. In 1927, the *Peralta*, as she was then called, and her sister ship, the *Yerba Buena*, were passenger-only ferries. At 256 feet long, they were among the largest ferryboats on the West Coast and they were the last steam ferries built on San Francisco Bay. Like other Key System ferries, the *Peralta* and *Yerba Buena* sported bright orange and white paint with cream colored stripes. Their luxurious interiors featured murals of San Francisco. The vessels themselves were constructed of steel and touted as unsinkable and fireproof. In contrast, their mahogany pilothouses added a touch of old-fashioned elegance reminiscent of wooden sailing ships.

Bad luck plagued the *Peralta* during the six years she spent on the Oakland–San Francisco run. In the first year she gained notoriety through several expensive dock-ramming incidents. Then, in February 1928, as the typically overloaded Friday night 5:15 commuter run approached the Oakland terminal, a freak accident occurred. A series of small waves washed across the open bow where passengers, eager to be first off the vessel, crowded together. Suddenly, the ferry's bow dipped

This particular model of the Kalakala *was a big hit when the ferry was first launched on Puget Sound in 1935. Photo by Asahel Curtis, courtesy, Washington State Historical Society, Neg. #61088 Tacoma*

forward and downward; a giant wave surged across the ferry's lower deck. In the words of an eyewitness, passengers on the lower deck were "washed off like flies." Rescue efforts were hindered by the panic of other passengers who believed the ferry was sinking. Nearby, the passing ferry *Hayward* was also slow in efforts to aid *Peralta* victims. Passengers aboard the *Hayward* claimed that it took the crew approximately eight minutes to get life boats in the water. Furthermore, as witnesses later testified, at least one crew member apparently did not know how to row. The most effective rescue actions were credited to naval personnel stationed on Goat Island (now called Yerba Buena Island) some 300 to 400 yards away. Their boats were the first to reach the scene and begin pulling victims out of the cold San Francisco Bay waters.

One of the survivors, a 17-year-old art student named Peggy Naylor, described how she was standing by a rail as it was swept away and how she was suddenly under water. "It seemed as though I was never going to come up," she said. She finally managed to get her hat and coat off and began swimming away from the ferry. She continued to swim until rescued by one of the *Hayward's*

lifeboats. Like the other survivors thrown into the chilly San Francisco Bay waters, Naylor owed her life to the fact that she was a strong swimmer.

Goat Island personnel estimated they had seen at least 60 persons go into the water. The actual number of victims varied with each newspaper account, although the official count of rescued passengers was 17 and the number of missing was placed at five, three men and two women. In a tally of Bay ferry disasters, only the 1859 boiler explosion on the *Contra Costa*, in which six people perished, had been worse.

Amazingly, after the incident, the *Peralta* made another round trip to San Francisco. Returning to Oakland again, the ferry was placed under police guard. Later she was moved to the Moore drydocks, where she had originally been built, for inspection and repairs.

Initially the accident was blamed on improper use of the *Peralta's* two 30-ton ballast tanks, located on each end of the ferry. When filled with salt water they were designed to keep the vessel trim (or level) as she was approaching or leaving a dock. When passengers moved to the bow of the ferry in order to disembark, the aft ballast tank would be filled with water to compensate for increased weight on the forward end. Early speculation was that the *Peralta* crew members had mistakenly filled the forward ballast tank instead of the aft tank. Combined with the weight of the passengers on the forward deck, such a mistake would have caused the bow to dip significantly. Testimony revealed that ferry engineers did not know how to operate the tanks.

Ironically, while the official report cleared the crew of wrongdoing, the investigating commission also stated that despite the absence of proof, they believed misuse of the ballast tanks was the most likely cause of the accident. However, the weight of the crowded foredeck, the swell of the passing steamer *Hayward*, and an existing riptide could also have accounted for the dipping bow. The Key System Transit Company (Key Route) labeled the accident an "act of God." In any case, the ballast tanks were never used again and wary ferry commuters adopted the habit of avoiding the *Peralta*. It was recalled that the *Peralta* had gotten hung up on the building ways during her launching; in the lore of the sea that meant that she was a jinxed ship.

The tragedy also aided the arguments of San Francisco's pro-bridge faction. Within days of the accident, the city's board of supervisors adopted a resolution asking Congress not to "perpetuate indefinitely the menace to human life" stemming from San Francisco's "ferry-crowded" bay. Concern for the safety of human life demanded a bridge, said the board of supervisors as they asked Congress to overrule the Navy's objections to an Oakland–San Francisco span and to grant the bridge permit. Within five years, San Francisco had its bridges and began to rid itself of its ferries.

In May 1933 the *Peralta's* career in San Francisco came to a fiery end. The supposedly fireproof and unsinkable ferry was moored at the Key System's Oakland ferry terminal when the terminal was engulfed in a spectacular fire. As the fire spread to the ferry, the *Peralta's* steel structure funneled the flames, increasing their intensity. Three men trapped in the burning terminal jumped to the *Peralta*, cut her mooring lines and drifted with her into the bay where they were rescued by a tugboat. By morning all that was left of the *Peralta* above the waterline was a grotesque and twisted mass of steel. Below the waterline, the hull remained intact. The *Peralta* had not been fireproof, but at least she did not sink.

Like the mountain behind her, the Kalakala *was a head-turner from the start. The* Saturday Evening Post *called her the biggest ferry story since Noah. Courtesy, Puget Sound Maritime Historical Society, 1298-5 Seattle*

Four months after the fire, Captain Alex Peabody bought the remains of the *Peralta* for Seattle's Black Ball Line for a mere $18,000. She was the first of 15 San Francisco ferries to be moved north to Puget Sound. Towed up the coast by the tug *Creole*, the *Peralta* settled in at Lake Washington Shipyards at Houghton, Washington for renovation and restoration.

Like the mythical Phoenix, the *Peralta* was about to emerge from the ashes in spectacular fashion. In a conversion from steam to diesel power, she received a 10-cylinder, two-cycle, 3,000-horse power Busch-Sulzer diesel engine. The largest of its type to have been installed in a ferry, the new engine was designed to move the ferry along at a speed of 18 knots. Likewise, the supersensitive Hyde electric-hydraulic steering gear was the fastest steering device available. Her superstructure was the first to be "electro-welded," meaning that no rivets were used. Her nine watertight bulkheads attracted the attention of shipbuilders in England, France, Holland and Germany. In 1954 she was the first commercial vessel to carry a radar system, as denoted by the 001 on her Federal Communications Commission license. The redesigned single-ended vessel could carry

2,000 passengers and somewhere between 90 and 110 automobiles (sources vary on the point). One thing missing from the new ferry—the ballast tanks that had earmarked the *Peralta*.

It was the new superstructure, however, that captured imaginations. Constructed mostly of steel, 97.75 percent to be exact, the shiny silver-painted superstructure could only be described as futuristic and, hopefully, fireproof. The absence of external decks and the streamlined contour supposedly cut wind resistance by 10 percent, but the shape was actually adopted more for its dramatic effect. From a distance the new ferry was supposed to resemble a giant airplane skimming across the water, although critics commented that she looked like a pregnant whale. The *Seattle Times* called her the "strangest looking vessel that ever turned a wheel in Elliott Bay..." For many years the exact source of the *Kalakala*'s design was unknown although there were a number of theories. It was speculated that the unique streamlined design may have been the work of off-the-clock Boeing engineers who favored the airplane mode, or it may have been the inspiration of famous industrial designer Norman Bel Geddes, who supposedly drafted plans for a streamlined

The fast steamer Tacoma *(shown here on another occasion) accompanied the* Kalakala *on her maiden run and was forced to slow her pace to match the ferry's 15 knots. Courtesy, Special Collections Division, University of Washington Libraries Neg. # 18581*

ocean liner in 1932. Even Mrs. Peabody, the Captain's mother, claimed credit for the design.

In 1999 while preparing for a museum exhibit titled "A Ferry Tale: The *Kalakala* Comes Home," the staff at Seattle's Museum of History and Industry discovered a five-foot balsa wood model of the ferry. They believe that the *Kalakala*'s designer was a man named Louis Proctor. A Boeing model-maker, Proctor had been laid off from his job in 1934. After Peabody hired him to create a model that would capture imaginations, Proctor spent six months crafting the likeness of what would become the *Kalakala*. Subsequently, Proctor returned to Boeing, retiring in 1948, and moving to California where he became a foremost builder of radio-controlled model airplanes.

Whatever the genesis of the idea, there is no doubt that Captain Peabody personally supervised every aspect of the ferry's appearance, sometimes to the detriment of its operational features. The framing enhanced the architectural effect of the ferry but it also caused the vessel to vibrate so badly that windows broke and coffee sloshed out of cups as passengers tried to drink. Also, the winged appearance of the bridge enhanced the "Flying Bird" name, but it made it impossible for the captain to get a clear view of the dock while landing. At least one former captain has declared "I didn't like that boat; no one did." A deckhand, stationed above where he could actually see the dock, had to radio directions to the captain. The visibility factor may explain some of the subsequent hard landings as the ferry bashed into various terminals.

In 1935, after 19 months of remodeling, the new ferry, christened with an Indian name as was customary in the Black Ball Line, emerged from the Lake Washington Shipyards as the *Kalakala*. The name required an advertising campaign to instruct ferry users in the proper pronuncia-

tion, which was kah-LOCK-ah-la. The most common mispronunciations include kah-LACK-ah-la or even kala-kala. An intentional play on the name came from commuters who preferred to call the shaking and shuddering vessel the "Kelunkala."

The *Kalakala*'s debut was accompanied by a blitz of national publicity. In the dreary years of the Depression, her shiny streamlined look may have had an extra impact as a vision for a new and better era. Movie-goers across America saw the *Kalakala* in newsreel footage. This was not merely a ferry but a symbol of progress and, possibly, hope. Not surprisingly, in all the publicity little was said about the *Kalakala*'s earlier history.

The "world's first streamlined ferry," as her publicists dubbed her, missed her scheduled July 1, 1935, inaugural

Almost immediately the Kalakala *became the popular postcard to mark a visit to Seattle. Courtesy, author's collection*

run on the Seattle–Bremerton route. Bremerton officials who made their way to Seattle expecting to return in triumph aboard the *Kalakala* found that the trip had been canceled because work on the ferry was not finished. Bremerton's mayor was left in the position of being "all dressed up and having nowhere to go."

The next day, Tuesday, July 2, the *Kalakala* made her first trip to Bremerton. She was accompanied on the maiden run by the ferry *Tacoma*. The *Tacoma's* Captain Everett Coffin had been instructed that his vessel was not to pass the *Kalakala*. While this was proper decorum, it also concealed the fact that the *Kalakala*, which was touted for her 18 knot speed, could in truth do only 15 knots. The *Tacoma*, on the other hand, as pointed out by Jim Faber in his book *Steamer's Wake*, had been judged by Lloyd's of London as the "world's fastest single screw steamer." As the *Tacoma* made the return trip to Seattle unaccompanied, a frustrated Captain Coffin, calling for full speed, set an all-time record.

Meanwhile, the *Kalakala* was greeted in Bremerton by an invited and cheering crowd of 2,000. They immedi-

ately boarded the vessel and had to content themselves with looking around while a problem with the steering gear was resolved. Two hours later, the *Kalaklala* departed for a special cruise. She returned in the early evening so that children could have their turn on the new ferry. For the rest of the evening the *Kalakala* remained docked in Bremerton for the viewing pleasure of the general public. For those not inclined to view, two orchestras provided onboard music for dancing until midnight.

Local newspaper reports, if not the public, marveled over the brown and white color scheme of the downstairs lounge and the blue and red color scheme of the upstairs. Other notables were the corduroy-upholstered chairs, the red-leather seats of the double-horseshoe lunch counter, and the gay red curtains. A partially covered upper deck featured wicker chairs and tables set against green enameled walls hung with creme and green drapes. It was a cacophony of color even though Captain Peabody's mother had spent weeks selecting the draperies and upholstery for the chairs so that there would be no outrage of color harmony. The chairs were

Kalakala food was cooked to order and served by waitresses who were careful to only half fill the coffee cups. Courtesy, Puget Sound Maritime Historical Society, 1298-94 Seattle

The Kalakala's double horseshoe lunch counter was the only one of its kind on a Puget Sound ferry. Courtesy, Puget Sound Maritime Historical Society, 1298-19 Seattle

not only attractive, each also contained a special case in which rested a regulation life jacket.

In contrast to present-day ferry food—pre-packaged, microwaved, and served cafeteria style—the Kalakala's double-horseshoe lunch counter offered china plates and cups, waitresses and cooks, not to mention 15 cent hamburgers and a ham, egg, and coffee breakfast for 55 cents. To allow the five cent coffee enough room to slosh around while the ferry was underway, it was only served half a cup at a time; a special lip on the counter's edge kept the china from rattling off onto the floor. For those desiring something stronger than coffee, the price of a bottle of beer was 25 cents.

The state-of-the-art galley not only served the Kalakala's passengers, it also served as a central kitchen for other ferryboats. Food prepared aboard the Kalakala was packaged and served to the rest of the fleet.

Like the Peralta, the Kalakala's interior included art. A large marine painting done in a brilliant blue and framed in silver depicting the Black Ball heritage, graced the wall. The area below the main deck could best be described as male territory. A tap room and men's lounge adjoined a shower/locker area where shipyard workers could freshen up after a day's work. Upstairs, the ladies had their own more sedate lounge with a seating capacity of 100.

Each day the Kalakala made six round-trips to Bremerton. For many years the fare was 45 cents each way and $1.10 for car and driver. On summer evenings she cruised around Elliott Bay with passengers who paid $1.00 to dance to the live music of the Flying Bird Orchestra under the direction of Joe Bowen. For a time the music was shared with Northwest residents listening at home on their radios. The cruises had to follow authorized Black Ball routes but there were a variety of possibilities. They could travel around Vashon Island or cruise to Bainbridge Island, Bremerton, or Tacoma. These special evenings set the Kalakala apart from other Puget Sound ferries that merely provided transportation from one place to another.

Another thing that distinguished the Kalakala was her safety record, or lack thereof. The Kalakala's first captain, Wallace Mangan, former captain on the H.B. Kennedy and several other Puget Sound Navigation Company vessels, had spent 33 years at the helm without a single mishap. His record ended with the Kalakala, a vessel that could not seem to shake the old Peralta jinx.

In one of the incidents, confused whistle signals led to a crash of ferries in November 1936. It was a clear day as the ferries Chippewa and Kalakala approached each other in Rich Passage. By blowing two whistles the Chippewa signaled the intention to pass starboard to

starboard. Instead of agreeing with two whistles of her own, the *Kalakala* replied with one blast which meant that she also was moving towards starboard. As the ferries drew closer, the *Kalakala* signaled danger with four short blasts. The *Chippewa's* three answering blasts meant that her engines were full speed astern. If ferry whistles could sound frantic, these must have. The ships collided almost head-on. The *Kalakala* received dents in her superstructure, broken windows and a damaged pilot house. The more seriously damaged *Chippewa* suffered a 40 foot gash at the car deck level. Five automobiles were demolished.

In September 1938, the *Kalakala* crashed into Seattle's Colman Dock with no apparent damage. However, as passengers disembarked on an elevated loading platform, the platform shot upward 10 or 12 feet into the air and then collapsed onto the main deck of the wharf. Ten catapulted passengers suffered a variety of injuries. Black Ball Line officials attributed the accident to a strong cross-current. Captain Mangan blamed the forward concentration of weight caused by 300 shipyard workers eager to disembark which was enough to cause the

aft propeller to tilt and lose thrust. Anyone with knowledge of the *Peralta's* troubles may have considered the incident as a slight version of déjà vu.

The *Kalakala* also earned the distinction of being probably the only ferry ever to sink railroad cars. The cars were aboard a barge on their way to Puget Sound Navy Yard in August 1943 when the *Kalakala* plowed into the barge and dumped two boxcars into Puget Sound.

Along with the dock bashings, which became almost routine, and the collisions, there were the groundings. In 1945 an 8:15 a.m. run from Bremerton went out of control when an auxiliary engine supplying all the electrical power failed. With no engines and no steering, the helpless *Kalakala* plowed onto southern Bainbridge Island's Pleasant Beach and grounded herself in 10 feet of water. One commuter reported seeing six-foot-tall passengers wresting life preservers from other, smaller passengers. Within an hour the ferry's 350 passengers were transferred to another ferry while two Navy tugs tried unsuccessfully to refloat the beached "Flying Bird." Freed by the incoming tide, the *Kalakala* reached Seattle at noon, underwent inspection, and was back on schedule to Bremerton by

12:30. She made an unplanned landing on Bainbridge Island again in June 1951 and ran aground in Rich Passage in 1953.

While ferry groundings are frightening for the people on the vessel, they are equally terrifying for shore residents who are accustomed to the routine engine noises of the passing boats. Imagine hearing a sharp variation in the noise, going to the window and seeing through the fog a fully-lighted ferry heading straight for the beach. The grating and crunching sounds of a grounding ferry are part of Puget Sound ferry lore for some waterfront dwellers.

Ferries and bridges came together in July 1940 when the *Kalakala*, as flagship for the Black Ball Ferries, participated in the grand opening of the Tacoma Narrows Bridge. The bridge replaced the ferry route that had connected Gig Harbor with Tacoma for the preceding 21 years. About 1,000 passengers traveled aboard the *Kalakala* as she made the last symbolic crossing between Tacoma and Gig Harbor with the added flourish of passing underneath the new bridge. Ironically, in one of the Northwest's most famous disasters, the bridge, nicknamed "Galloping Gertie," collapsed into the Narrows four months after this opening celebration. Ferry service was quickly restored

and remained in place until a new Tacoma Narrows bridge was built in 1949.

During World War II, the *Kalakala* was the workhorse of the Black Ball fleet. The ferry that had started as a vision of a new high-tech and shiny future became a major transportation link in the war effort. Each day 5,000 shipyard workers, along with 500–1000 navy personnel, made the trip from Seattle to Bremerton and back again. By 1945 the ferries *Kalakala, Chippewa, Willapa,* and *Enetai* were making a total of 38 round-trips a day with departures every 15–25 minutes. Enroute, the ferries had to pause while two barges opened the gates which allowed vessels to pass through the steel cable submarine nets that protected Bremerton's Rich Passage and the Navy Yard.

The trips were not without problems. Passengers had to check in all cameras and binoculars since the route afforded an excellent view of the ships moored at the Navy Yard piers. Regular commuters had other difficulties. Just boarding the 5 p.m. ferry out of Bremerton posed hazards. Police had to perform crowd control duties after several workers suffered injuries in the nightly rush. Aboard the boats, passengers complained of foul language, gambling, drunkenness, property damage and

Right: When the Kalakala's *first captain, Wallace Mangan retired in 1941, Captain Louis Van Bogaert, pictured here, took command. Courtesy, Puget Sound Maritime Historical Society, 1298-67 Seattle*

Opposite page: In addition to her regular ferry service, the Kalakala *moonlighted" with special evening dance cruises. Courtesy, Author's collection*

Above: The Kalakala's round portholes were a tourist favorite. This photo was taken around 1949 on a trip to Victoria, British Columbia. Courtesy, Gail Goodrick

Below: Looking very much like something from a Buck Rogers episode, the Kalakala noses her way into Victoria harbor. Courtesy, Ralph White Collection, Kitsap Regional Library, Bremerton

fire hazards. Vandalism, a common occurrence and a costly problem for the Black Ball Line, consisted mostly of slashed upholstery, broken chairs, seats set on fire, and cork life rings and hemp rope thrown overboard, scarce materials in wartime.

One vandal found warming his hands over a blazing seat may have simply been trying to get warm. Wartime women shipyard workers making their daily commute on the early morning Kalakala run from Seattle complained to navy officials that there was no heat in the ladies' cabin. Earlier complaints to ferry officials had accomplished nothing. The women claimed that they knew heat was available because in the summer it was turned on and left on all day. Meanwhile, the chilly cabin was blamed for severe colds, employee absences, and the resignations of a large number of female shipyard employees. Because of the labor shortage and the critical needs of war production, the loss of the women workers was a problem. Pressured by the navy, the Black Ball officials explained that the heat had been turned off because of complaints about it being too hot. They promised to rectify the situation, but weeks later the women were still writing to Navy officials about the cold Kalakala.

Once beer became suspect as the underlying cause for some of the vandalism, all beer sales aboard ferries were stopped. The lack of beer, removing the tempting chairs and replacing them with benches, and adding the presence of Coast Guard patrolmen succeeded in drastically reducing the vandalism and in giving the once elegant ferry a more suitable wartime utilitarian look.

"Floppers," people who slept stretched-out on ferry seats, were another problem. By taking up more than their share of space, the floppers forced other passengers to stand for the whole hour's ride between Seattle and Bremerton. Shore patrolmen were able to move through the Kalakala and force sleeping sailors to sit upright. Prone civilians, however, continued their slumber since the Shore Patrol had no authority over them. Evidently, even a local editorial labeling floppers as "hogs" guilty of greed and discourtesy was not enough to get them in the upright position.

Occasionally the Kalakala left the Seattle–Bremerton run for service in other waters. She ran from Seattle to Victoria, British Columbia for a couple of summers in the 1940s and from Port Angles to Victoria during summers in

Bremerton's waterfront is identified by one the world's largest hammerhead cranes. The view from the passing ferries into the east end of the naval shipyard was a concern of wartime security measures. Courtesy, Author's collection

the later 1950s. The ferry, which shook so badly in the sheltered inland waters of Puget Sound, actually did better in the open waters of the Strait of Juan de Fuca because she was able to maintain her engines at a uniform speed.

In 1949 the ferry actually managed to go *through* a dock. In what was described as a "freak" crash the *Kalakala's* engines failed to reverse as she approached Seattle's Colman Dock. Under the best of conditions, ferry landings are described as a controlled crash. This one was uncontrolled. As office employees on the dock ran frantically away from what they thought was a major earthquake, the *Kalakala* chewed her way through the landing and headed towards Alaskan Way and Seattle's single skyscraper, the Smith Tower. It was called "going uptown," and the ferry nearly made the trip. Surprisingly the damage to the *Kalakala*, a gaping hole in her port bow, was temporarily repaired in a matter of hours so that the ferry could continue her runs. The lack of serious damage to the ship was a consistent feature of her escapades. She seemed to be able to ram, butt, and hit the beaches with a minimum of destruction to herself, although docks certainly took a beating.

At least one human tragedy beset the boat when a deckhand named Nels Forfang was thrown from the ferry and presumed drowned. On a windy January 1947 night, Forfang was on the car deck opening the large doors at the *Kalakala's* bow. The doors, which swung outward, were usually opened at the end of a run. Just as the man was performing the task, the wind caught the door, swinging it wide open and throwing him into the water. The bow doors were finally removed in the mid-1960s to facilitate faster loading of automobiles.

For the majority of time throughout the 1950s and the early 1960s the *Kalakala* continued service on the Seattle–Bremerton run. She was an oddity and people either loved or hated her. Despite efforts to remedy the vibration problem, it was never solved. It has been more than 30 years since the *Kalakala's* last run, but ask any former passenger and they may still complain about the fact that it was impossible to write even a note while the ferry was in motion. The incessant shimmy would not let pen meet paper. One commuter called it a "traveling earthquake."

However, at least one Iowa tourist visiting the area in 1947 reported to relatives back home on the obligatory postcard bearing a picture of the *Kalakala*. The card, written aboard the ferry, says "This ferry boat runs so smooth you hardly know you are moving." Anyone familiar with the *Kalakala* might conclude that the card was written before the ferry actually left the dock.

Couples met on the *Kalakala*, and first dates were that much more memorable if they happened on the streamlined ferry. Bremerton high school seniors skipped a day of school and partied aboard the *Kalakala* for their "Senior Sneak." Babies were born on board when the hour trip just wasn't enough time to reach the hospital—perhaps because the ferry's vibrations led to premature

contractions, as one Kalakala baby alumnus speculated. True, babies are also occasionally born on other Washington State Ferries (a ferry captain's nightmare), but there is a distinctive difference in the folklore of being born aboard "a ferry" and being born on the Kalakala. She was the one unforgettable ferry, although one of her former captains noted that there was a reason why the Kalakala was the only one of her kind ever built—one was enough.

In 1962 Seattle hosted Century 21, the World's Fair. Along with the exposition came the Space Needle, a distinctive 605-foot tower that instantly identified the Seattle skyline. In the era of the sixties and in the shadow of the Space Needle, the Kalakala was becoming outdated. The large diesel engine, burning 300,000 gallons of fuel every seven days of operation, became increasingly expensive to operate. Furthermore, cars had taken on larger proportions, reducing the carrying capacity of the old auto ferry. Newer, larger, and more fuel efficient "superferries" were on the drawing boards at the Washington State Ferry System and the Kalakala's days were numbered.

In what might be considered a parting shot, the Kalakala did manage to ram the Washington State Ferry System's brand new $3 million Seattle Ferry Terminal even

before its formal dedication. The February 21, 1966 collision with the Terminal's south landing slip did not seriously damage the ferry, but it did put the slip out of commission for two months. Less than three weeks after disabling the south slip, the Kalakala bashed into the north landing slip. Fortunately the damage was slight and the slip remained operational.

The fall of 1967 marked the end of the Kalakala's career as a Puget Sound ferry. She had dominated the Seattle-Bremerton run for most of her 32 years. Using log book information, one of her captains, Louis Van Bogaert, estimated that the streamlined ferry made 47,700 round-trips to Bremerton and traveled a total of 1,411,532 nautical miles. Recent estimates on the number of passengers carried total around 30 million.

Sold for somewhere in the neighborhood of $100,000 in 1967, the Kalakala was towed to Alaska for use as a floating crab-processing plant. After several years of working around Dutch Harbor in the Aleutian Islands, she was sold to a Kodiak firm. Partially buried in mud on a Kodiak beach and renamed the Gibson Cove, her streamlined art deco contours and aluminum paint were still recognizable through the rust when Seattle sculptor Peter Bevis first saw her in 1984. Bevis returned in 1988 for a closer

Top: From this angle the Kalakala *did somewhat resemble a pregnant whale.* Courtesy, Puget Sound Maritime Historical Society, 1298 Seattle

Bottom: Beached, and used as a seafood processing plant, the Kalakala *was a sad sight when Peter Bevis embarked on his quest to bring her back to Seattle.* Courtesy, The Kalakala Foundation

look, and his vision was the beginning of a decade-long struggle to bring the *Kalakala* back to Puget Sound.

Bevis harbors a sense of community and believes that the *Kalakala* is a symbol of Seattle's past and a way to bring the community together around a cultural artifact. With that in mind he founded the Kalakala Foundation, a nonprofit organization dedicated to the preservation, restoration, and return of the *Kalakala*. After he acquired the former ferry from the city of Kodiak for virtually nothing, a small army of Foundation volunteers went to work to stop the deterioration of the vessel. Over a period of years they fought the rust spawned by Kodiak rain while they painted, sealed, welded, and hauled out 230 tons of piping and equipment associated with the ship's days as a processing plant. Additional tons of concrete that had been poured into the ferry had to be blasted out.

Battling the Alaskan winters and the ravages of time was only part of the task. The city of Kodiak was anxious to get rid of the vessel in order to more profitably use the beach where she rested. A letter writing campaign from art deco societies around the world bought the ship some time while the foundation worked to raise the funds to refloat her and bring her home.

As part of the fundraising campaign, the Kalakala Foundation sold posters of the former ferry. For $19.35 (to mark the 1935 debut of the *Kalakala*), purchasers had

their choice of three designs. Featuring pictures of the famous ferry and sporting such slogans as "She Magically Whisked People to Mars (Okay, Bremerton)," "The Ship That Launched a Thousand Electric Shavers," or "She Enhanced Sailors, Mesmerized Fishermen and Baffled Seagulls," the posters have been popular nationwide. With the help of grants, corporate sponsorships, memberships, leasing arrangements, licensing agreements, and a million dollars from Bevis himself, the *Kalakala* was freed from her muddy berth in June 1998.

Minus her engines, the choices for getting the *Kalakala* back to Puget Sound were simple—either barging or towing. When Seattle-based Dahl Tug and Barge offered the services of its tug, the *Neptune*, in October, the only remaining obstacle was weather. Blessed by a Russian Orthodox priest, the *Kalakala* set off on a 16-day, 1,500 mile voyage which included moving between two fall storms in the Gulf of Alaska and rocking through 12 and 15-foot swells near the Barren Islands. The *Neptune* and her Captain, Odd Johnsen, safely shepherded the 63-year-old ferry into Seattle's Elliott Bay.

Accompanied by harbor seals, a flotilla of sailboats, fishing boats, luxury cruisers, tour boats, and small aluminum boats, some sporting banners with "Welcome Home" and "Thank you Peter" messages, and by fireboats shooting the traditional water stream tribute, the *Kalakala* returned to a welcoming throng of over 500 cheering and hooting people. They lined up on Pier 66 to celebrate the homecoming of a cultural icon. One bystander compared it to imagining that the Space Needle had been gone for 30 years and then had suddenly reappeared as part of the skyline.

Local dignitaries, an orchestra, vocalists, and swing dancers contributed to the festive mood. It was a day to come together as a community and remember the past in a thoroughly nostalgic fashion. A weary and dazed Peter Bevis seemed overwhelmed by the attention of supporters who hailed him as a hero. Several years earlier, Seattle's local public television station had aired a documentary about the *Kalakala* and the foundation's efforts to liberate the ship from the Alaskan mud. The 1995 film, recounting *Kalakala* history and whimsically titled "Things That Aren't Here Any More," was, by 1998, wrong about one thing. The *Kalakala* was back.

Throughout the ceremony the star and main focus of

SHE ENCHANTED SAILORS, MESMERIZED FISHERMEN AND BAFFLED SEAGULLS.

SAVE *the* KALAKALA

She's an art deco masterpiece who finds herself stranded on a beach in Alaska. Won't you help bring her back home? Call the Kalakala Foundation at (206)632-0540.

Above: One of the three Kalakala Foundation posters that were such a hit with the vessel's fans. Courtesy, The Kalakala Foundation

Opposite page: Peter Bevis, the driving force behind the movement to return the Kalakala to Puget Sound. Courtesy, Kalakala Foundation,

attention was the *Kalakala*. It was she, after all, that people had come to see. With her once shiny hull peeling and dulled and her windows broken or boarded up, the *Kalakala* could have been a sad sight. Instead, through the cloudy overcast November afternoon, shafts of breaking sunlight illuminated the ferry and recalled for an instant the glimmering "Flying Bird." Washington's newest ferry, the 470-foot *Tacoma*, a Jumbo Mark II class boat, dwarfed the *Kalakala* as the two passed in Elliott Bay. Yet, like every other ferry that afternoon, the *Tacoma* blew a special whistle blast to salute the historic old ferry; she truly was one of a kind.

Despite her somewhat decrepit state the *Kalakala* became a tourist site after her return to Seattle. For several months she was moored next to a maritime museum on Seattle's Elliott Bay, not far from the current ferry terminal. Gawkers paid for guided tours and a chance to board the classic ferry. Gaps in the floor made the tour off-limits for children under 12, and the bobbing action of the lightened and therefore extra-buoyant boat was enough to cause the Coast Guard to halt tours altogether in rough weather. For those who remembered her glory days, the tour was a ghostly experience—the cold empty ferry stripped of her interior furnishings, creaking and groaning in the wake of passing ships. There are, however, hints of the bygone elegance and glimpses of the former magic that ear-

marked the *Kalakala*. The curved interior sides, the grand staircase, and the curved wrought ironwork are enough to stir the imagination.

Once the subject of innumerable postcards, the *Kalakala* is again appearing in national media. Her refloating in Kodiak was documented in dramatic photos published in the major weekly news magazines. A May 1999 *Newsweek Magazine* book review of a novel by Seattle author Neal Stephenson featured a photograph of Stephenson. In the background and unmentioned was the *Kalakala*, immediately recognizable to those who know her and probably a bit of a mystery for those who might wonder about the significance of the odd looking boat.

An interesting biological sidelight of the *Kalakala*'s move from Alaska turned out to be a new strain of microbe found aboard the ferry. Prior to her departure from Alaska, it was necessary to remove the oily water from the *Kalakala*'s tanks and bilge. Martin Environmental Technologies (MET) of Edmonds, Washington, stepped in with donated technical assistance and a product called BOE 505 that blends nine kinds of oil-eating microbes. The bugs went to work performing their bioremediation tasks, and, by the time the *Kalakala* left Alaska, she was oil-free. During the tow to Seattle, some residual oil from the *Kalakala*'s pipes was released back into the bilge. In the process of testing the bilge water, a new strain of oil-eating bacteria was discovered in her hull. The appearance of the new microbe, tentatively named *pseudomonas Kalakala 98*, caused some excitement in the field of oil-spill cleanup technology because of the possibility that the new bug might prove stronger in saltwater than the current forms of bioremediation bacteria.

As with other ongoing efforts to save historic vessels on Puget Sound—the steamboat *Virginia V*, the schooner *Wawona*, and the lightship *Swiftsure*—the future of the *Kalakala* could be in doubt. At least it would be, had she not been lucky enough to have Peter Bevis as her patron saint. Bevis is a man intolerant of negativity who is consumed with the goal of seeing the *Kalakala* refurbished, all 30,000 square feet of useable space, housing everything from a museum and a conference center, to shops and restaurants. Although his philosophy is "take everything one step—in this case, one bucket of rust—at a time," Bevis can also take giant steps. Along with the other dedicated volunteers of the Kalakala Foundation, and the monetary support of the individuals and communities in Puget Sound, Bevis seems dedicated to restoring the *Kalakala* and giving her a permanent place somewhere on the waters of Puget Sound where future generations can experience her magic without the shimmy and shake.

Included in the state purchase of ferries was the Crosline, built in 1925. Courtesy, Puget Sound Maritime Historical Society, 680.5 Seattle

Chapter 5

Washington State Takes Over

It was a four-year-long bitter and sometimes ugly struggle involving private enterprise, specifically the Puget Sound Navigation Company, the state of Washington through the terms of two governors, the legislature, the superior and state supreme courts, the labor organizations, Seattle's elite leadership, and, in the middle and every bit a player, the traveling public and businesses that depended on freight transported by ferry. At the end of the fight, in June 1951, the nation's largest privately-owned ferry system became the largest publicly-owned system. The state of Washington was in the ferry business or, as the state's literature phrased it: "Washington State Ferries—Owned by the 2,378,963 people of Washington."

Out of the ferry business, at least on Puget Sound, was Captain Alex Peabody, president of the Puget Sound Navigation Company. The charming but stubborn Peabody was frequently the center of controversy, butting heads with labor, with state authorities, and with critical consumers. In waging battle to save his company Peabody championed free enterprise, representing stockholders who expected him to preserve their investment and make a profit. He was also acting out of personal pride and the maritime traditions of the Peabody family. The Puget Sound Navigation Company derived from the enterprise founded in 1900 by Peabody's father, Charles Peabody. The signature flag featuring a black ball on a red background gave the company its common nomenclature—the Black Ball Line. PSN, Puget Sound Navigation Company, and Black Ball all referred to the company built and operated by the Peabodys. In the relative wilds of the Pacific Northwest the prestigious company qualified the Peabodys as Seattle's version of Captains of Industry.

Having moved successfully from Mosquito Fleet days to the beginning of auto ferries, Puget Sound Navigation managed until about 1930 to stay ahead of the transportation revolution caused by cars. At that point, auto traffic began to strain the capacity of the ferry line. Highway construction to the north and south of Seattle made the ferry runs on that side of Puget Sound obsolete. However, the need for auto ferries running east-west from Seattle to the Kitsap Peninsula, Bainbridge and Vashon Islands kept increasing.

Faced with a growing need and unable to initiate a construction program that would provide enough ferries in a short amount of time, Peabody received a major windfall with the 17 ferries he purchased from San Francisco between 1937 and 1942 at a fraction of what it would have cost to build new ones. The expanded fleet was crucial in carrying the traffic that World War II brought to the war production areas on Puget Sound.

During the war, ferries between Seattle and Bremerton ran on the hour, 24 hours a day. It was a high-water mark for the commuting employees of Puget Sound Navy Yard and the citizens of Bremerton. Never before, or since, had service been so conveniently scheduled. Furthermore, consumer complaints were minimized by the general spirit of sacrifice that prevailed on the home front. War workers also benefited from lower ferry rates. Peabody, whose revenues were rising, voluntarily agreed to fare reductions subject to yearly review. Reductions on the Seattle–Bremerton run eventually amounted to 30 percent.

Shortly after the war ended, the relationship between Black Ball and the public began to unravel. The abrupt halt of defense industries had an immediate impact on ferry traffic, ferry schedules and ferry revenues. Postwar consumers who had spent their savings on new cars were eager to get out and see new sights. They wanted the same convenient ferry schedules and rates they had enjoyed during the war. They also wanted clean, modern vessels. Their expectations were clearly not in line with what Peabody could, or would, deliver.

Concerned with company finances, Peabody made cuts in service in May 1946. The public was indignant. In December 1946, he announced that the company would apply to the State Department of Transportation for a rate increase to cover wage hikes. Four days later he declared that Puget Sound Navigation would reinstate pre-war fares

Although he was most often described as charming, Captain Alexander Peabody could do battle with the best when it came to business matters. Courtesy, Ralph White Collection, Kitsap Regional Library, Bremerton

effective January 1, 1947. This second move, tied to the wartime agreement reducing rates, did not require permission from the state. The public was becoming increasingly unhappy with everything having to do with ferries and Peabody found himself a frequent apologist at various Chamber of Commerce meetings around the Sound.

As a company providing public transportation, PSN operated under a franchise granted by the state of Washington. The state involvement gave the public a place to focus their complaints and a person, Governor Mon C. Wallgren, to complain to. As a Democrat and proud New Deal liberal, Wallgren seemed a likely choice to place public needs above a private company that was being characterized as greedy and profit-driven. The governor listened but did not take any particular action. He may have been hoping that the issue was a temporary one that would diminish on its own. Logically, he may have realized that demands for increased service and low fares were simply not reasonable.

While Wallgren faced the public, Alex Peabody faced his unionized employees. The new year ushered in contract talks will all three of the labor unions representing ferry workers positioning themselves for a strike vote. The Inland Boatmen wanted a $36.00 per month pay raise, bringing a deckhand's salary to a total of $198.50. In hourly terms the increase meant that a basic wage of 78 cents would be raised to $1.14. Workers also wanted their workweek reduced from 48 hours to 40 hours. The other two unions, the Masters, Mates, and Pilots Association, and the Marine Engineers Beneficial Association, wanted similar adjustments in wages and hours.

On New Year's Day, 1947, one ferry rate increase went into effect. A little more than a week later the Inland Boatmen's Union rejected Black Ball's contract offer which included a 10 percent wage increase. Along with its rejection of the offer, the union served notice that it would strike. Black Ball settled.

In conjunction with accepting the union demands, Black Ball also submitted its application to the state asking permission to increase fares by another 30 percent. The return to prewar fares plus the requested increase meant that ferry fares would rise by a total of 60 percent. On the Seattle-Bremerton route, the heaviest commuter run, one-way fares would go from 52 cents to 68 cents for walk-on passengers and from $1.19 to $1.55 for car and driver. Travelers from Vashon Island to Seattle would face an increased ticket price of 26 cents rather than the 20 cents they had previously paid. Automobile fares went from 50 cents to 91 cents.

To the undoubted dismay of ferry riders, the State Transportation Director, Paul Revelle, temporarily approved the Black Ball request pending a complete study of the company's finances. Although it could charge the extra 30 percent beginning February 15, the ferry company faced the prospect of having to refund monies to commuters if the state ultimately decided that the 30 percent increase was too high. As a guarantee of this refund, Black Ball was required to post a bond and issue refund coupons to ferry riders who could then get their money back if the rate hike was ultimately rejected.

This seemingly reverse order of dealing with the increase, i.e. granting it and then investigating the need for it, aroused the suspicions of some critics that the Transportation Department had made a secret bargain not in the best interest of ferry riders. Public confidence in Paul Revelle diminished somewhat. In reality, Puget Sound Navigation Company officials had already provided the state with convincing evidence that company finances necessitated the fare increase if the company was to continue to operate on Puget Sound. Making the increase temporary was just the state's way of acknowledging PSN's pressing need without neglecting the state's duty to conduct its own analysis of the ferry company's books. The requirement of ferry refund coupons was another protective measure the state took on behalf of ferry users.

The ferry-riding public did not wait until February 15 to have its opinion heard. Referring to the fare increase as "suicide" and declaring that Puget Sound's island communities would be reduced to summer vacation spots, the Vashon Island Chamber of Commerce took steps to rally opposition to the rate hike. A mass meeting of approximately 600 island residents raised tempers as well as an initial $1,500 for what became the "ferry fight" fund.

On February 11 the Vashon group sponsored a meeting of Sound area civic groups. Alexander Peabody was invited to explain his position. Gamely, the ferry boss accepted the invitation and told the group that his company was losing as much as $125,000 a month. The unsympathetic audience was not convinced. They believed that Peabody could provide better service at lower cost simply by trying harder. Furthermore, they assumed that since the company had made healthy profits during the war there was no reason that it could not absorb financial losses in the postwar era.

When the members of Olympic Peninsula civic groups organized their cars into a caravan and headed off for the state capitol in Olympia to plead their cause, their only success was in fueling the public imagination. Clubs and organizations ranging from the Veterans of Foreign Wars to the local Chambers of Commerce united over the "ferry problem." The *Bremerton Sun* newspaper and the Bremerton Junior Chamber of Commerce co-sponsored a letter writing contest on the topic of "How Lower Ferry Rates Would Benefit Bremerton and Kitsap County." The purpose of the contest, according to its organizers, was to stimulate public thinking. It may have also been a way for Bremerton businessmen to refute the persistent rumor that they actually favored higher fares as a means to keep local business just that—local. The mere fact that the Jaycees had to offer $50 to answer that question should have been a matter for concern. Whatever the benefits of lower ferry rates might have been, Kitsap residents did not get to experience them—the rates went up as scheduled on February 15.

The public protest moved to the state legislature, flooding lawmakers with demands for relief. As a new player in the drama, the legislature assumed the role of investigating the actions taken by Revelle and the State Department of Transportation. Was the fare increase justified or had "deals" been made? Determined to find out, the legislature promptly set up committees to study the situation.

Ultimately, public dissent coalesced under the leadership of lawyers on Vashon Island with the formation of the Northwest Washington Community Council or NWCC. Their initial strategy was to place a bill before the Washington State Legislature authorizing the State Department of Transportation to purchase vessels and operate a ferry system.

The Washington State Legislature has been, and continues to be, characterized by the geographical division of the state into two distinct regions. Split by the Cascade Mountains, the state has a desert-like eastern portion that relies on agriculture for its economic base. The part of Washington west of the Cascades is smaller in area and is home to Puget Sound and its bordering urban industrialized areas. In many ways the two halves of the state have little in common. Consequently the farmers in Eastern Washington and their elected representatives were not inclined to be moved by any impending ferry crisis. They were, however, concerned by any legislative action that would put all of Washington's citizens and taxpayers in the position of having to subsidize the purchase and operation of a ferry system. In all likelihood any subsidizing monies would have been taken from the state's gasoline tax. These were revenues which otherwise would have gone for road construction, something near and dear to the hearts of citizens east of the Cascades. Therefore, it was not surprising that these political forces did not favor a state takeover of the ferries.

They did, however, agree to a compromise bill authorizing the creation of special districts to operate ferries. The legislation, which passed in February 1947, gave Puget Sound residents some leeway in making their own arrangements with Black Ball, thus escaping state conflict with the company, or in setting up their own alternative solutions. In addition, the State's House of Representatives also recommended that the State Highway director conduct a feasibility study for state operation of ferries on those routes where rates were perceived as inequitable.

Vashon Island residents seized the opportunity to create their own ferry district, gathering enough signatures to authorize an election on the issue in September 1947. Northwest elections are often influenced by the rain that can keep voters away from the polls. The September one was no exception, but the 316 votes for, as opposed to 38 against, were enough to establish the Vashon-Maury Island ferry district.

The legislature's actions may have fueled the activities of the NWCC. The coalition had achieved some state action and had successfully focused attention on the ferry problem, even if Eastern Washington representatives chose not to take a strong stand on the issue. There were, however, internal problems with the NWCC that kept it from being a stronger advocate. Part of the difficulty was the structure of the organization. Some of the component groups of the alliance had a higher visibility than the NWCC and tended to overshadow the leadership

One of the ferries purchased in California, the Golden Bear *suffered major damage in a storm off the Oregon coast. She continued under tow to Puget Sound where it was determined she was beyond repair. Courtesy, Puget Sound Maritime Historical Society, 1030-3 Seattle*

of the coalition. And, while the NWCC was united in its desire to solve the ferry problem, it really did not have a single solution to offer. Ideas ran the gamut from increasing state regulation of the Black Ball Line to eliminating the ferries entirely—replacing them with bridges.

Meanwhile, March 1947 brought the threatened strike by the Marine Engineers Beneficial Association. With 70 engineers off the job, the strike left the Black Ball ferries at the dock and 10,000 commuters on dry land. On Puget Sound, where the water is the most efficient and sometimes the only highway, a ferry strike is truly something to fear. The Kitsap Peninsula offered one sure means of escape via the narrow neck of geography that joins it to the mainland near Shelton. Another route, connecting Bremerton to Tacoma via the Tacoma Narrows, was available, however, because the connecting ferries had been operated by the state since the collapse of the famous "Galloping Gertie" bridge. Extra buses were pressed into service on that route. Island residents had fewer options—all boat-related.

With what Northwesterners like to think of as typical aplomb, they coped. An excursion vessel chartered by Bremerton's minor league baseball team, the Bluejackets, carried sports fans to the state basketball tournament in Seattle. All 650 Puget Sound naval shipyard workers living in Seattle were transported to their Bremerton jobs aboard navy LSTs, the Landing Ship Tanks of World War II fame. The Bremerton–Seattle Airlines quickly filled the waiting list for its one plane, an eight-passenger float aircraft. Two other airlines offered flights from Kitsap County to Boeing field in Seattle. The U.S. mail to Bremerton took a new route through Tacoma but continued to be delivered. Island residents hired whatever would float, used their own pleasure craft, and generally managed to get around. Vashon Island commuters were so pleased with their emergency transportation, a 125-passenger dine and cruise boat named the *White Swan* (Bremerton newspaper called it the *M.S. Silver Swan*), they wondered why they couldn't have such a vessel all the time. The biggest problem was the delivery of freight which suddenly became more expensive to haul to the Kitsap Peninsula and nearly impossible to get to the islands.

The walkout was in its fifth day when Governor Wallgren called the various parties into his Olympia office for some closed-door discussions, the first of many such meetings in the years to come. Peabody held firm for the 48-hour week but agreed to a 23.8 percent pay increase.

The strike fueled public discontent. Labor demands had been met, but the traveling public was still paying fares that were 60 percent above the 1946 rates. Furthermore, Peabody had failed to abide by the original provisions of the conditional rate increase. Puget Sound Navigation Co. had not reserved enough funds to repay ferryboat passengers should the rate increase be proven unjustified. Neither had the company posted a bond guaranteeing the ability to make the refunds if so ordered. At a show cause hearing in June, 1947, Peabody explained that the company revenues had not been reserved because they were needed to keep the company operating from day to day. Failure to post the bond had simply been a misunderstanding, he said. Public hearings on the rate increases were held two days later on June 4, 1947. It was a triangular affair held in Seattle's City Hall with Peabody and company accountants on one side, accountants for the Department of Transportation on another side, and lawyers representing the NWCC on behalf of the public on yet another side. Black Ball had graciously offered to give free passage to Bainbridge Islanders who wished to attend the hearing. People gladly took the trip to Seattle but for some reason many did not make it to the hearing.

Peabody, never one to be intimidated, may have hurt his case somewhat by declaring on the witness stand that the Puget Sound Navigation Company was considering another 10 percent fare increase. While he was obvi-

Below: Renamed the Illahee, *former California ferry* Lake Tahoe *performed marathon duties transporting workers during World War II. Courtesy, Puget Sound Maritime Historical Society, 1030-4 Seattle*

*Opposite page: Another California transplant, the ex-*Napa Valley, *renamed* Malahat, *lost her upper works in a mysterious fire at her Bremerton berth in 1943. Courtesy, Ralph White Collection, Kitsap Regional Library, Bremerton*

ously trying to stress the company's financial needs, the statement did not endear him to the consumer groups.

Accountant Stewart Kreiger presented a 253-page financial report, painstakingly explained in his testimony. His most pertinent points were that PSN's net earnings had dropped in 1946 and that six of the company's 12 ferry routes were losing money. And, though impossible to predict future patterns of ferry travel on Puget Sound, clearly the existing ferryboats were not going to suffice. Most had been built prior to World War I and could not easily accommodate any auto larger than a Model A Ford. Modern cars took up so much room that, on a fully loaded ferry, car passengers were trapped in their vehicles for the duration of the ride unless they could manage to squeeze through their doors which could only open 12-14 inches.

Lawyers for the NWCC, aided by their own accountant and rate authority, Ray Allen, did not buy Krieger's logic, nor his charts and figures. They represented a public who wanted only one outcome to the hearings—lower fares. One of the public voices belonged to Thomas Revelle, Transportation Director Paul Revelle's brother. The Vashon Island real estate broker testified that island prop-

erty values had already declined owing to the paralyzing effect of higher transportation costs. Black Ball's rates, according to the NWCC, as quoted in the June 5, 1947 *Vashon Island News Record* were "unfair, not reasonable, and inimical to the best interests of the State as well as of the area served." The NWCC had earlier released a statement pointing out that casual ferry users on summer trips were forced to turn back from ferry docks because, to their embarrassment, they found they could not afford the fares.

The final decision on the validity of the rate hikes was left to Paul Revelle. It would have been difficult not to bow before public opinion. In what he probably considered a compromise, Revelle rolled back the fare increase to 10 percent and ordered the ferry company to make $652,000 in refunds to passengers holding the coupons that had been issued since February's 30 percent increase.

The Northwest Washington Community Council claimed credit for having achieved the 20 percent reduction in rates. In the pages of the *Vashon Island News Record* which billed itself appropriately as "An Island Paper for Island People," the Vashon Island Chamber of Commerce claimed credit for having created the NWCC. Vashon citizens had contributed generously to what they called the "Ferry Fight Fund." One of their fundraising tactics was to ask island commuters to donate their ferry refund coupons to the fund. The argument was that, had not the Vashon group spent money on lawyers and accountants, the fight would have been lost, refunds non-existent, and the coupons worthless; as it turned out, the coupons *were* worthless since Black Ball never refunded any of the fare monies.

The public was generally satisfied with the ruling. Peabody, on the other hand, was surprised, and not pleasantly. Not only was he convinced that the numbers supported the company's claims, he also believed that customers had used political pressure to influence the state agency and that he was being unjustly burdened with a fare schedule designed to drive the Puget Sound Navigation Company out of business. Peabody was probably right. While Bremerton businessmen openly called for a state takeover of the ferries, the feisty Black Ball captain fought back.

Throughout July 1947 the ferry company moved the battlefield to the courts. A pair of writs filed in Thurston

County Superior Court were designed to trigger a new review of the evidence (i.e. financial statements) and to stop enforcement of Revelle's order to rollback the fares.

Vashon Islanders countered by filing a writ which would have stopped Black Ball from collecting higher fares. When Black Ball threatened to tie up the ferries if the writ was granted, the NWCC stepped into the picture with a resolution to the State Toll Bridge Authority calling for state operation of the ferries in the case of a shutdown and demanding that the state explore the possibility of purchasing the ferry system.

The war of the writs went in favor of Peabody and the Puget Sound Navigation Company. The company did concede that, contrary to the earlier threat, the ferries would continue to operate while the courts reviewed the evidence. For its part, the NWCC continued to put pressure on Governor Wallgren who publicly admitted that the state might be forced to go into the ferry business.

By this time, August 1947, it was obvious to even the casual Puget Sound observer that the ferry situation had reached crisis proportions. Individuals and organizations in leadership positions far above the level of the NWCC began to apply their talents to solving the problem. Their common territories were most often Seattle's exclusive Rainier Club, the Chamber of Commerce, the Municipal League, or the Central Labor Council. Their members included the top echelons of the city's largest manufacturing and retail businesses, labor unions, politicians, social movers and shakers. The information and ideas flowing through these groups as they discussed the ferry dilemma found its way into print in the *Seattle Times*. Associate Editor Ross Cunningham, himself a Seattle insider, gave the public the bad news that no matter who controlled the ferry system—Black Ball or the State of Washington—higher fares were unavoidable. Higher operating costs and decreased traffic reflected the simple economic reality.

Captain Peabody was pleased to see that Cunningham agreed with his position. The two men had discussed the issues and Cunningham was able to isolate the facts from the public's version of economic truths. As the representative of the public, the NWCC, on the other hand, still clung to its view of commuters held hostage by an exploitative monopoly.

Depending on the point of view, Black Ball's decision

Washington Governor Mon C. Wallgren found he could not avoid the "ferry problem." Courtesy, Washington State Historical Society, Neg. # Wal 14 Tacoma

to take one of the ferries off the Bremerton-Seattle run, thus reducing it to two boats, was either bowing to economic realities or putting more pressure on the "hostages." An impartial observer probably would have characterized the move as a political mistake which hurt the company more than the loss of revenue.

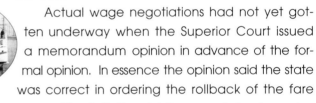

In January 1948 the New Year began with the question of rates still working its way through the processes of the Superior Court. The Inland Boatman's Union and the Marine Engineers Beneficial Association (MEBA) prepared to start contract negotiations with Black Ball. Peabody, typically aggressive, sent both unions a letter requesting that, in the interest of allowing the company to continue to operate, their members accept wage cuts and added hours. One might have expected an explosive response from the unions in their rejection of Peabody's suggested terms. Both labor groups did categorically reject the idea of wage cuts, but issued statements basically sympathetic to the company. Peabody had gotten a "helluva bum deal from the state," commented the business agent of the Inland Boatman's Union. The MEBA representative agreed that Peabody's claims of financial duress were accurate, yet responded that it was not the unions' responsibility to make up the shortfall—the state

had erred, he said, in allowing only a 10 percent fare increase.

Actual wage negotiations had not yet gotten underway when the Superior Court issued a memorandum opinion in advance of the formal opinion. In essence the opinion said the state was correct in ordering the rollback of the fare increase. Black Ball, said the court, had used a skewed depreciation allowance to show the need for the 30 percent increase. Instead of basing its depreciation figures on the cost of the ferries, Black Ball had used a figure reflecting the cost of replacing the ferries. Keeping in mind that the ferry fleet was aging and getting more outdated with each change in automobile sizes, it should have been obvious that the new ferries could not be acquired for the same dollar figures that had prevailed in the 1930s. The court decision seemed to stem from some twisted logic. It was, however, a logic shared by the NWCC, which was fully satisfied with the decision.

In response to the court's memorandum, Peabody notified Governor Wallgren that Black Ball's projections showed a $1,000,000 deficit in 1948. Therefore, the state should be prepared to lease the ferry operations and infrastructure under terms that would guarantee the company a reasonable return on its property. The alternative was abandonment of all ferry service. In calling Peabody's statement "silly," Wallgren commented that if the state had wanted the ferry system on a temporary basis "...we would have taken them over during the war when they were making money." On its own, the governor's remark seemed, like all the other evidence, to support Peabody's position.

Paul Revelle was more concerned about what he perceived as a threat from Peabody to stop ferry operations. He calmed public fears by asserting that a public utility could not abandon service without permission from the state. The State Director of Highways, Clarence Shain, was less sure of that position. Black Ball was, after all, a private company and it was questionable whether the state had the power to force a company to operate against its will.

The "will" of the company, as indicated by a stockholder vote, was to stop operations at midnight Sunday, February 29, 1948. The deadline brought a cold dose of reality to the situation and initiated a series of last-minute remedial efforts from every direction. The state resorted to legal means, convinced that any tie-up would be illegal and that, if necessary, they could condemn the property. Friends of Peabody, aided by other prominent businessmen who shared the same view of protecting free enterprise against "creeping socialism," tried a gentler approach, suggesting that Peabody postpone the action or meet with community leaders who would then sit down with the governor. In response, Peabody was pleasant, reasonable, and firm.

Other mediation efforts came from the state legislature. Jack Rogers, chairman of the Interim Committee studying the problem and a reasonable, charming, and intelligent man in his own right, offered to mediate between Black Ball and the Department of Transportation. No one seemed inclined to listen.

The battle had become personal, thus diminishing the role of compromise and common sense. Paul Revelle, proud of his work, believed he had been fair, even-handed, and totally impartial in his review of ferry finances. He was therefore personally offended by Captain Peabody's characterization of him and his department's performance as "bureaucratic bungling" in Olympia carried out by "proponents of creeping socialism." Wallgren sympathized with his department head but was also annoyed

Retain This Receipt - It May Be Valuable

In accordance with orders of the State Department of Transportation the rates charged by the Puget Sound Navigation Company and now in effect are temporary, and if found excessive after investigation and public hearing by the Department of Transportation of Washington, this evidence of purchase may be used in establishing refund claims.

Puget Sound Navigation Co.

N⁰ 208400

President

FULL FARE PASSENGER • ROUND TRIP

Route Bainbridge

Void After December 31, 1947

because the whole problem was like a hurricane headed directly toward his office. If the focus shifted in his direction, as it would, he would be required to provide the final solution, no matter what the outcome. In a choice between public interest and private enterprise he was going to lose potential votes. Wallgren was furious with Peabody for holding "... a knife at the state's throat."

In the charged atmosphere the NWCC became somewhat demure. Having pushed the whole issue to the crisis level, the group was now uncertain about what it really wanted. Some commuters swore to swim to work rather than capitulate to Black Ball. The group members who wanted Peabody's company out of Puget Sound did not necessarily want state-owned ferries. Nor, as was quickly becoming the case, did they want the issue to become a political football. This was ironic, since all of the NWCC's earlier actions had moved the problem in a political direction.

On Black Ball's side, 540 company employees weighed in with a petition to the state's attorney general asking that the rate order be removed and expressing their belief that the 30 percent increase was justified. This was on February 24, five days before the scheduled tie-up.

While the attorney general petitioned for a temporary restraining order to stop the ferry shutdown, the Director of Highways assured Bremerton commuters not to worry; the state was looking into the acquisition of its own ferries. Since there were no state ferries, crews, or operating authority in sight, commuters placed their bets on the court system to keep the Black Ball ferries on the water.

This time the Thurston County Superior Court ruled

against the attorney general and for Black Ball. The court memorandum stated that while a public service corporation could not abandon operations without showing just cause, neither could it be forced to operate at a financial loss. Black Ball had effectively shown that it faced such financial difficulties—that it could not operate at all.

Having won somewhat of a Pyrrhic victory, Captain Peabody announced that much to his regret the company would discontinue operations. He placed blame on "the utter collapse of the regulatory functions of the Department of Transportation" and reminded everyone that the court's ruling indicated that rates fixed by the Department of Transportation left the company unable to operate except at a tremendous loss.

With the political football definitely in play and elections only eight months away, Wallgren went on record. He was now committed to state ownership of the ferries as the only way to get "reasonable transportation." He promised not only to get rid of the monopoly but to "clean it up once and for all." All he asked was that the public have patience and be willing to endure some inconveniences.

The term "inconvenience" was accurate enough for commuters but much more was at stake for Puget Sound business interests. Interruption in cross-Sound transport jeopardized the economic survival of some companies who depended on ferries to move their freight trucks. These interests managed to arrange a last-minute, presumably closed-door meeting between Peabody and his top advisors on one side and Governor Wallgren, Paul Revelle, and their advisors on the other. Although really too late for compromise, Wallgren did offer to start over with a new temporary 30 percent fare increase and a new state study of Black Ball's financial statements. Two years of arguments could be rehashed in a civil manner but the

process did nothing to establish common ground where it simply did not exist. Peabody was through dealing with Revelle and the Transportation Department. The Captain and his group left Olympia and arrived back in Seattle in time for him to personally give the order to tie-up the 16 ferries.

The tie-up order created an eerie scene on the Seattle waterfront. Ferry boats—which had always seemed to represent constant motion in their comings and goings—now sat dark and abandoned in their moorings. The Black Ball terminal, normally a bustling place with thousands of commuters passing through each day, took on a ghostly atmosphere, a cavernous empty space filled with shadows.

A year after the labor issue had temporarily stopped the ferries, commuters found themselves beached once again. Where the 1947 action had stranded 10,000 commuters, now according to newspapers there were 115,000 commuters reportedly trapped on the Olympic and Kitsap Peninsulas. Since that represented the area's entire population and certainly not everyone commuted, one can assume that either the newspapers slipped up on the numbers, were trying to blow the crisis further out of proportion, or regarded everyone on the two peninsulas as being trapped even if they did not use ferry services. Whatever the numbers, it was a major headache for those who did commute or who depended on the ferries to deliver their goods and transport their products.

The navy stepped in to take care of its civilian and military personnel. Of all the commuting groups, they had the easiest time. The existing emergency plan was quickly activated, providing transportation to and from Seattle via LST. On the Seattle side, station wagons raced up and down the waterfront route carrying workers from their normal pier to the emergency transports at Pier 91, a mile away. It was a little chilly on the craft's tank deck where 700 chairs had been arranged for passengers, but despite cold hands they were generally a cheerful group and the navy won high praise for its efforts. Passengers continued to be happy with the service even when, two days later in the middle of dense fog, the LST ran aground on its way to Bremerton. A pair of navy tugs were sent to rescue the stranded vessel and escort it to the Bremerton shipyard. Workers were two hours late for their jobs but in good spirits. Since their pay was not docked for lateness the only thing they lost were the portions of their lunches that had been eaten prematurely while they were stranded.

Besides the LST problem, the navy had to send out another tug to rescue the 50-foot motor launch used to transport workers from Bainbridge Island to Bremerton's navy yard. That vessel lost her bearings in the fog, then anchored next to a buoy light and hailed a passing motorist on the shore who obligingly telephoned the shipyard with news of the vessel's dilemma. The navy had no reason to be embarrassed. Fog in Bremerton's Rich Passage can be so thick that it's impossible to see more than a few feet. Experienced ferry captains, guiding vessels equipped with modern radar, have been known to run aground in such conditions.

In the absence of ferry service, commuters who lived in Bremerton and worked in Seattle had a more difficult route. Horluck, the small ferry company that normally provided transport from a tiny spot called Annapolis across the inlet from Bremerton, was able to patch together a route whereby commuters traveled on a Horluck ferry from Bremerton to Annapolis, transferred to a bus which took them to the South Kitsap dock at Manchester where they boarded another Horluck passenger ferry which took them to Seattle. The total cost of the trip was 85 cents—15 cents for the Annapolis crossing, 20 cents for the bus, and 50 cents for the ferry to Seattle. As creatures of habit, the commuters had to cope with strange boats, strange docks, longer commute times, and the fact that the 85 cents was 17 cents more than the "unreasonable" fare charged by Black Ball.

Other commuters had to resort to equally expensive options. On Bainbridge Island, where private excursion boats were pressed into service, the fare to Seattle was 75 cents one-way compared to Black Ball's 46 cents. In the Suquamish and Indianola area it cost $1.25 to get to Seattle instead of the 52 cents for normal ferry service. The only route which kept a price even close to Black Ball was the Kingston-Edmonds run, which increased by a mere nickel. One commuter group actually reaped dividends from the situation. Shipyard workers and navy personnel got free passage, perhaps explaining why they were so content to ride on the drafty LST.

Vashon Island was less impacted. Thanks to their foresight in forming the Vashon–Maury Island Ferry District No.

1, Vashon citizens were able to operate the former Lake Washington auto ferry, the Lincoln, at lower fares than those charged by PSN. That does not mean, however, that Island residents were not equally angry with the Puget Sound Navigation Company. Local author Betty MacDonald, famous for her novel The Egg and I, used her radio program to lambast Captain Alexander Peabody in The Bad Egg and I. In another incident, a ferry tollbooth missing from the PSN dock on Vashon was found floating in Puget Sound. One report claimed that after Black Ball restored service, Vashon Islanders armed with clubs stationed themselves at the dock to fend off the ferry Illahee which was temporarily filling in for the Lincoln at the request of ferry district commissioners.

Inspired by the self-sufficiency demonstrated by the Vashon Island people, the citizens of Bainbridge Island started to circulate their own petitions for a ferry district. Although the Island's newspaper, the Bainbridge Review, compared the petition drive to the Boy Scouts' "be prepared" principle, it was hard to ignore the fact that the Bainbridge petition move started after Black Ball had docked the ferries and ceased services to the island. If the idea was to be prepared, the folks on Bainbridge Island were a little late.

If the state could not force Peabody to operate the ferries, Revelle could at least open the field for other firms to fill the transportation void. On March 1, he canceled the Puget Sound Navigation Company's operating certificates, thus paving the way for other companies that may have had ferry boats ready to operate on Puget Sound. No company stepped forward, although the NWCC did seek Coast Guard approval to run six former submarine chasers, berthed in Seattle, on the Seattle-Bremerton run. Fitted with airliner seats, each boat could supposedly carry 150 passengers and travel at speeds of 21-knots. They could not, however, solve the problem of transporting automobiles across Puget Sound.

In another effort to provide some kind of ferry service, Wallgren tried to gain possession of the old San Francisco ferry Hayward. The veteran vessel was in Seattle along with three other Bay area ferries slated for scrapping. The Hayward was the only one of the group still intact enough to be resurrected for use. In his short-lived effort to bring the ferry online, Wallgren neglected to say how he would solve the problem of terminal facilities. All docks, terminals, and access roads were owned by Black Ball.

Peabody provided an alternative by declaring a willingness to sell the Black Ball ferries. However, without waiting to see if an agreeable purchase arrangement could be reached, Kitsap County commissioners issued statements threatening to condemn the ferries and their docks. State law did indeed permit such action by the counties or by the Toll Bridge Authority, according to state Attorney General Smith Troy. No matter who initiated the action, it was obvious that ultimately the state would have to pay the ferry company for the condemned ferries and their facilities. Also, any condemnation action would have to work its way through the court system, a process further complicated by the fact that Puget Sound Navigation Company was incorporated in Nevada. Involving the federal courts meant that condemnation proceedings could easily take years.

Meanwhile, Alexander Peabody, famous for his chutzpah, filed an application with the State Department of Transportation headed, of course, by Paul Revelle. The Captain's application sought to divide his holdings into two companies, Puget Sound Navigation Co. which would handle routes within the State of Washington, and the International Corp. which would operate between Seattle and Victoria, B.C. Peabody also asked that his operating certificates be reinstated and the company be allowed to reinstate the 30 percent fare increase which had been in place plus an additional 30 percent which

would constitute the minimum fares for a period of a year. Someone on the state's side proficient in mathematics quickly pointed out that the second 30 percent increase, added to the first, would represent a total 69 percent increase. In denying the application, Revelle complained that Peabody was trying to turn public sentiment against *his* department and the state administration. Nevertheless, he invited Peabody to submit another application, providing that it did not try to dictate rates.

As governor and future candidate for re-election, Mon Wallgren could not afford to sit in Olympia and do nothing. Through Highway Director Clarence Shain, he investigated the possibility of purchasing ferries from the San Francisco Bay area. He then asked the State Toll Bridge Authority to

This navy LST (Landing Ship Tank) was used to transport shipyard workers to Bremerton during the strikes and ferry tie-ups. Courtesy, Puget Sound Maritime Historical Society, 3773 Seattle

contact Peabody about the possibility of buying eight of PSN's 16 intrastate ferries. The state, said Wallgren, could operate the ferries more efficiently than the company. The previous day the governor had proposed tying Bainbridge Island to the mainland Kitsap Peninsula via a toll bridge across Agate Pass. A temporary Bailey Bridge—the type used by American forces during World War II—would be followed by a permanent structure. The Bailey bridge, which could be constructed in 30 days, was a lifetime to commuters. Wallgren announced that work on the bridge would start "within a week." By the fourth day of the tie-up the governor was growing ever more vague, announcing that he and Paul Revelle had been looking at several vessels that he did not identify which could be used in the emergency. Separate from the governor's proposals, Kitsap County, now joined by a reluctant Snohomish County, proceeded with the idea of condemning the property owned by Puget Sound Navigation Company. Somewhat important to the whole argument, according to a news report in the *Bremerton Sun* on March 4, 1948, King, Island, Jefferson, and Skagit Counties all opposed condemnation proceedings "on the grounds that residents of their counties were unwilling to see the state enter the ferry business." Regardless of what King and Snohomish Counties wanted, it was possible that Kitsap's condemnation proceedings could extend to those counties, all tied together by the ferry routes.

By the fifth day of the Black Ball tie-up, most participants had shifted gears yet again. Wallgren and the state of Washington were negotiating with Henry Kaiser to build six or eight new steel ferries at a cost of $5 or $6 millions. Gone was the talk of Bailey bridges and offers to buy Peabody's ferries. Peabody had refused to sell to the state. Condemnation of the fleet had been rejected because of the potential length of time involved and the sudden discovery that the Black Ball fleet was old and needed to be replaced at some point. Even more interesting was Highway Director Shain's assessment that ferries which the state operated across the Tacoma Narrows generally lost money and, while it would be nice if they could break even, they were not really expected to make a profit. In other words, operating costs exceeded income—an argument that Peabody and the Puget Sound Navigation Company had been making all along.

Lack of agreement between the state government and the ferry company did not preclude the county governments from working on a solution. Peabody may have been too annoyed to talk to the men in Olympia but he was willing to listen to his cronies in King County. And King County was willing to lease the Black Ball ferries—complete with the 30 percent fare increase Peabody wanted. Some of the conditional language in the agreement, in addition to allowing cancellation of the entire contract at any time by either party, called for reviews of ferry finances and possible adjustments to the rates. The contract was enough to get most of the ferries back on the water on March 9. However, the Kingston-Edmonds run remained off-line another three months because governing bodies in Kitsap and Snohomish Counties would not make a charter arrangement with Black Ball. In June, Kingston Port Commissioners gave in and negotiated a charter.

Bypassing state control also gave Wallgren time and room to maneuver toward a firmer and better conceived

Although the Hiyu was built in 1967, the design is similar to ferries the state was considering building in 1948. Courtesy, Kitsap Regional Library, 1-14-00(7) Bremerton

state position. His public brainstorming, i.e., the Bailey bridges, had not enhanced his image. As a Democrat he had to be painfully aware that the powers in King County government who had successfully put the ferries back into motion were Republicans.

In an effort to convince voters that he was in charge and did have a plan, Governor Wallgren took several positive steps. Responsibility for any state ferry system was formally delegated to the Toll Bridge Authority rather than to the Highway Department. The move seemed to insure

that the gas tax revenue administered by the Highway Department would not find its way into the cost of operating ferries. Furthermore, as a quasi-state agency the Toll Bridge Authority was experienced in moving traffic across water, even if it was via bridges. The TBA began with a proposal to build 10 new ferries at a cost of $8 million.

In the interest of developing a comprehensive long-term plan for efficient operation of whatever ferry system the state might build, Washington State contracted with a Chicago-based transportation consulting firm. The Gilman study became the object most representative of the hoped-for ferry panacea. Governor Wallgren predicted that as soon as results of the study were available, the state could have three boats operating within eight or nine months, possibly 10. Even more impressive was his conjecture that the proposed state system could operate at fares lower than the 1946 level and still yield a net revenue of $1 million per year. Wallgren was either the eternal optimist or a man grasping at any solution.

The Gilman Report, although finished by June 1948, and heralded as the "only existing impartial survey of Puget Sound ferry operations," was held back under a previous dictate that no report be issued until after the November elections. If the idea was to keep the report out of politics, or politics out of the report, it generally failed since the public demand to know the contents of the report made it a political issue anyway.

A summary of the report's contents sent to Alexander Peabody and promptly released to the *Seattle Times* indicated that if the state pursued Wallgren's plan of operating new vessels, the cost would be greater than the cost of operating the existing Black Ball ferries. The governor, claiming that the Gilman Report contained a variety of miscalculations, briefly proceeded with plans to build a state owned fleet of 12 ferries. In the Governor's favor was Gilman's assessment that the state could feasibly operate a ferry system.

Architect's drawings, representing one type of ferry the state was considering, showed a vessel with mostly open car decks. Capable of carrying only 60 cars and 100 passengers, the ferry was no improvement over the Black Ball vessels. Significantly, the architect's somewhat plain and simple ferry did not include a restaurant, a must for longer ferry routes.

In a genial mood, Captain Alexander Peabody (second from right) is shown here with ferry Captain Louis Van Bogaert on the far right. The other two men are unidentified. Courtesy, Puget Sound Maritime Historical Society, 1298-61 Seattle

As the summer progressed, it was obvious that problems existed with the charter arrangement between King County and Black Ball. The NWCC had remained quiet about the fares agreed to in the contract. In April the group's president, Kenneth Price, had written a letter advocating state ownership of the ferries and comparing the situation to renting versus buying a house. Without using the terms, Price essentially said that paying fares to Peabody was like rent—never to be seen again. By contrast, fares paid under state ownership were described as the equivalent to building equity in the system. Once the purchase debt had been satisfied, commuters could enjoy lower fares.

New leadership in the NWCC finally accepted the realities of Peabody's financial situation and backed away from the state ownership position. Commuters, however, remained irate over the cost of their daily ferry ride. In May 1948, they formed a new group calling itself the Puget Sound Ferry Users' Association (PSFUA). The split into the NWCC and the PSFUA represented two different viewpoints, the former desiring stronger regulation of Black Ball, and the latter more radical position, advocating state ownership. Nor did the PSFUA particularly care about the details of state ownership. They labeled

any discussion of routes and terminals as mere engineering problems. What the PSFUA wanted was low-cost, uninterrupted ferry service.

In June the King County commissioners, overwhelmed by angry ferry users, demanded a 40 percent rate reduction. Peabody, not given to idle threats, declared his intention to shut down the ferries on July 6. This time the two sides were able to compromise despite voices in the PSFUA who favored letting Peabody quit. The ferries kept running and King County achieved a 10 percent reduction in auto/driver fares for a one-month trial period. The county commissioners justifiably felt they had made the greater compromise and vowed to seek further rate reductions. In the meantime the hope was that a trial reduction would lead to increased auto traffic which would lead to more revenue and thus allow further reductions in fares.

When his own efforts indicated that building ferries was too expensive, Wallgren bowed to economic reality. Shifting gears one more time, he began negotiations to purchase the existing ferries. With the help of a public endorsement from the PSUA, Wallgren finally seemed to have a direction. The PSFUA had made its position clear, and the Governor was able to follow the same line. The plan called for a self-supporting ferry system operated by the State Toll Bridge Authority. All existing Puget Sound ferry routes would remain and only one bridge would be built, the one connecting Bainbridge Island to the Kitsap Peninsula. Taxpayers would not have to shoulder the financial burden for the system and ferry riders would pay reasonable fares.

Although Peabody maintained that he would not sell the ferries to the state of Washington, some of the company's stockholders were willing to accept offers. The negotiations yielded an agreement, subject to stockholder approval. While the feisty Captain Peabody would have preferred to go on fighting, he followed Black Ball stockholders in voting to sell the company's 21 vessels, docks, and facilities to the state of Washington. A September 18, 1948, *Business Week* article featured a photo of a grim Peabody captioned "Ferryboat Operator Gives In." Washington State planned to meet the $5,975,000 purchase price by issuing bonds worth $8.5 million. Bundled into the bond issue was $1.5 million for the Agate Pass bridge to Bainbridge Island.

The bridge itself was another bone of contention between Peabody and the state. Believing that opening a highway access across the Kitsap Peninsula would ultimately create a gateway to the larger and more isolated Olympic Peninsula, Peabody had commissioned his own engineering studies for a Bainbridge link. He correctly assumed that increasing the flow of traffic via the bridge could result in consolidated ferry routes (three or four instead of seven), lower ferry operating costs, and subsequently lower ferry fares. Seeing the bridge as a long-term solution, Peabody was prepared to use his own resources to build it. The state, however, denied him permission. Now, with Peabody out of the picture and the state ready to enter the ferry business, Wallgren was taking action to build the bridge. Facing an election in November 1948, he also promised ferry users that there would be rate reductions totaling "hundreds of thousands of dollars a year."

While the governor, the PSFUA, Black Ball, and the average ferry rider may have felt that the issue was solved,

state Republicans and the state court system were not yet finished. At the urging of a GOP gubernatorial candidate, Arthur Langlie, the three-member subcommittee on the Legislative Transportation Committee announced its intention to investigate the ferry deal. There were, Wallgren critics hinted, back room deals that made the whole ferry purchase, at least the price, look suspicious. The subcommittee undoubtedly added to the aura of suspicion when it issued subpoenas to Governor Wallgren, Alex Peabody, and members of the Toll Bridge Authority.

A defensive and undoubtedly angry Wallgren defied the subpoena and denounced the legislative move as pure politics. He assured voters that the ferry system would be a "gift" to the state, allowing Washington to move forward in fully developing its economic potential. In using the term gift, Wallgren meant that the purchase price on the

Above: One of the classic ferries of the late 1920s, the Mount Vernon *was the first of the Black Ball fleet to run between Port Townsend and Keystone. Photo by Joe Williamson, courtesy, Ralph White Collection, Kitsap Regional Library, Bremerton*

ferries would come from private investors and the subsequent payments on the loans would come out of ferry fares. On an even brighter note, thousands of those fares would be paid by out-of-state tourists. Thus, by Wallgren's logic the ferries would require no subsidies or support from state coffers.

The Northwest Washington Community Council joined Wallgren in condemning the actions of the legislative subcommittee. NWCC president Kenneth Price refuted charges of secret deals by revealing that the ferry group had on several occasions invited the members of the subcommittee to attend their meetings. Furthermore, said Price, the NWCC and other interested parties had been kept informed of each step in the process leading up to the state's purchase of the ferries. In Price's opinion, the legislative subcommittee was launching an investigation purely for political purposes.

For its part, the court had been asked to rule on the legality of the ferry purchase. The move was in the nature of a formality, securing the State Supreme Court's blessing in order to forestall any negative legal action from those opposed to the sale. The court ruled that the question had been premature. When the State Toll Bridge Authority was fully prepared to secure the $10,500,000 bond issue, it again asked the state court to rule on the legality of the question. This time the State Supreme Court ruled that the state of Washington did not have the authority to purchase a ferry system through the sale of bonds.

Had Wallgren survived the 1948 election and remained governor, he may have been able to pick up the ball again and craft a new agreement. But negotiations now rested with Washington's newly-elected and former (1940–1944) governor, Arthur Langlie. Like Wallgren, Langlie was committed to the idea of state ownership of the ferries but he had characterized Wallgren as "blundering and gullible" and Peabody as a robber baron. Langlie preferred the condemnation process for securing the ferries. For Peabody, it was not a good place to start talks. The Captain marshalled his strength for another battle.

Langlie, an experienced executive, wasted no time when the state legislature convened in January, 1949. He oversaw the introduction of a bill that would clearly grant the state the right to establish and conduct ferry operations. He also traded support with Black Ball's unionized

employees. In exchange for union support of the ferry enabling act, the governor gave his blessing to a bill that allowed workers in a state ferry system the right to retain union membership and bargain collectively. Coming from a business-oriented Republican governor, the agreement with labor was surprising but effective. Both bills made their way through the legislative process and were signed by Langlie on March 12, 1949.

Peabody responded on three fronts. He offered the King County Commissioners a 20 year lease continuing the current ferry operations. The NWCC moderates, working with Peabody, proposed that Black Ball continue to operate the ferries under contract to the State Toll Bridge Authority (TBA) and that operations, rates, and wages be set and monitored by various bodies including the Gilman company and a permanent advisory board. To further appease commuters, at least those residing on Bainbridge Island, Peabody held out the hope of all-night ferry service between Winslow (on Bainbridge) and Seattle. He also proposed using faster ferries to make the trip a 32 minute commute and promised to build a new terminal building in Winslow.

Langlie wasted no time in rejecting the NWCC proposals for contracting the ferry service to the state. Claiming that the public had lost confidence in Captain Peabody's operation of the ferry system, Langlie, backed by the PSFUA, announced his intentions to forge ahead with state acquisition of the ferry system.

Peabody won a heartening if not useful victory when the State Supreme Court refused to affirm the Superior Court decision which had upheld the Department of Transportation's rate reduction order. Unfortunately Black Ball's problems had moved so far beyond the rate controversy that Peabody's only choice appeared to be selling his operation to the state. He won a reprieve for the second half of 1949. Langlie became ill, and significant ferry negotiations stalled. Peabody saw the governor's absence as a chance to continue his struggle to keep the company private. His stockholders, however, saw the opportunity to intensify their efforts of selling to the state.

Talks with the TBA broke off when Black Ball refused to accept the bottom line—that the Langlie administration would not pay the price agreed to by the Wallgren admin-istration. Politically, Langlie was in a corner. After denouncing the Wallgren deal as a giveaway of state funds, he could hardly offer the same deal. In order to emphasize that the state could get ferries elsewhere, the TBA bought the four ferries and facilities owned by the Vashon Maury Island Ferry District in the fall of 1949. It appeared that the state was trying to undermine Peabody one ferry route at a time. However, the renewal of operating agreements between Black Ball and King County in January 1950 seemed to dispel that rumor.

Black Ball's finances were secure enough that the company felt no need to accept the state's $3,332,000 offer. Peabody denounced the price as an attempt to acquire the system at less than fair value. He also refused the next offer of $4,983,000. Langlie tried to bypass Peabody by appealing directly to individual stockholders, offering to buy their shares at par value—a move that would have resulted in a total cost of $3,900,000.

The state tried other ways to put pressure on Peabody. Black Ball's plans for improved service across Hood Canal, a vital link between the Olympic and Kitsap Peninsulas, were hampered when the state blocked the acquisition of tidelands for a Black Ball dock at Lofall. The facility site had to be moved 200 yards to privately-

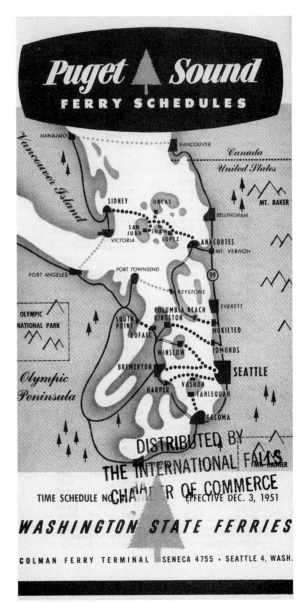

owned tidelands. Plans were also hampered by the state's refusal to complete 600-feet of road linking the state highway to the ferry company's dock at South Point. Failing to gain a purchase option on the docks, the state wanted the right to use the docks in case Black Ball stopped providing service across the canal. Rather than trade that guarantee for a road, Peabody had the road built at company expense.

Once again the picture of cross-Sound bridges entered the dialogue. Langlie stated that he was looking beyond the ferry boats and envisioning a Puget Sound area economy based on a series of bridges that would eventually provide free 24-hour access to all areas of the Sound. He used as models New York and San Francisco, where bridges had largely replaced ferries. Peabody agreed that bridges were technically possible and were part of the future of Puget Sound. His only argument was that it would be a decade or so before the volume of traffic made the bridges an economic feasibility. In the interim, ferries were crucial and he still intended to be in control of the ferry system.

In an effort to break the impasse, Langlie went back to the courts. In July 1950 the state Supreme Court ruled that the Public Service Commission had always had jurisdiction over Black Ball rates and schedules. Peabody argued that the lease arrangement with King County took precedence, but for all intents the battle was over. All that remained was some kind of agreement on a price.

On December 30, 1950, Governor Langlie announced that for a price of $4,900,000, the state had purchased all equipment and facilities used in Black Ball's domestic operations. The company retained the *Chinook* and several smaller vessels for its Canadian operations. Because of the agreement with King County, Black Ball would continue to operate ferries on Puget Sound until May 31, 1951. The company was freed from any requirement to make fare refunds.

An editorial in the June 1, 1951, *Bremerton Sun* newspaper called the purchase an "historic event" that was "sickening" to believers in private enterprise and smaller government. But, the editorial claimed, public temper and the company's refusal to be regulated had necessitated the change. It was now up to the state to resist local political pressures, do away with money-losing

routes, and build a comprehensive transportation system that blended highways, bridges, and ferries. And, now that the fight over the ferries was over, the editorial was able to praise Alexander Peabody as a rugged individualist and champion of free enterprise who had stood his ground against bitter criticism, including that from the *Bremerton Sun*, and government pressure far longer than most men would.

A further vindication of Peabody came from the Public Service Commission. As heir to the Transportation Department's function in the area of determining rates, the commission had re-examined the original ferry rate hike issue. With two weeks to go until the state takeover of the ferries, the commission issued an order reversing Paul Revelle's 1947 decision to roll back the 30 percent rate to 10 percent. A second look at the figures had shown that Peabody had been right all along. The Public Services Commission also relieved the company of any responsibility for refunding monies to ferry users. Like the rate increase, the refund had already been rendered a moot issue by the ferry purchase agreement which had canceled the refund. While the majority of ferry stories had occupied page one space in Kitsap county newspapers for years, the story about the Public Service Commission ruling appeared on page 14. The belated victory and the small attention it received could only have added to Peabody's bitterness.

In May the Washington Toll Bridge Authority issued bonds in the amount of $6,800,000 to pay Black Ball and to rehabilitate its vessels and docks. Washington State citizens found themselves ready to take ownership of 19 ferries and 20 terminals.

The actual transfer was a quiet anticlimax to the years of acrimony that had preceded it. Governor Langlie spoke at a noon luncheon in Seattle and then boarded the ferry to Bainbridge Island where he followed the so-called gateway route across the Agate Pass bridge to

the grave of Chief Seattle. It was a fitting pilgrimage if one remembers that canoes were truly the first of the Puget Sound ferries. From Poulsbo the governor traveled to Bremerton for a reception at the local Elks Temple and then back on the ferry for the return trip to Seattle. Langlie's schedule called for returning to Seattle aboard the 4:55 p.m. run.

Ferry fares and schedules remained the same. The only visible change upon state takeover was the re-painting of the boats. The familiar Black Ball symbol disappeared from the stacks of the vessels, replaced by the green color traditionally associated with the Evergreen state. The audio change may have been more poignant. The traditional whistle blast of the Black Ball ferries—the one long and two short blasts that had echoed over Puget Sound for the first half of the century—were replaced by the one long and one short blast of the new Evergreen Fleet.

The Illahee *became one of the mainstays of the new Washington State Ferry System. Courtesy, Puget Sound Maritime Historical Society, 3148-21 Seattle*

Prior to the opening of the Hood Canal Floating Bridge in 1961, ferries ran between Lofall on the Kitsap side and South Point on the Jefferson County side. Courtesy, Ralph White Collection, Kitsap Regional Library, Bremerton, WA

Chapter 6

The Evergreen Fleet

Washington State entered the ferry business with a confident outlook. Commuters had been freed from the stranglehold of Black Ball, Puget Sound voters were happy, and the ferry system would be run efficiently and in the public interest. In acquiring an already existing system—its terminals, boats, and employees—all the state had to do was keep things running, at least until the ferries could be replaced by an anticipated system of cross-Sound bridges. The job was more difficult than state officials could have imagined; politics became an integral part of ferry operations and each decade brought its own set of ferry crises.

It seemed only appropriate that the most famous ferry in the new Washington State fleet should be the first to misbehave. Less than a month after the state takeover, the *Kalakala* lost power and went dead in the water off Bainbridge Island. There were only 100 people on board the late night run to Bremerton; they napped, or gathered in the coffee shop while the ferry gently drifted onto the beach at Point White. They also helped with joking suggestions for the subsequent towing operations which involved two navy tugs from Bremerton, a commercial tug, two Coast Guard cutters and four patrol vessels. The situation was not as desperate as the influx of rescue vessels might have indicated. The ferry was easily freed and docked in Bremerton at 2:00 a.m. instead of the scheduled midnight arrival time. It was a gentle introduction to the ferry business.

The first decision of the new state management had been to abandon Black Ball's traditional docking signal. The order rankled old-time ferry captains, some of whom had taken decades to perfect their individual whistle style. On his last trip before retirement in 1957, Captain Louis Van Bogaert acted on the universal fantasy of people on their last day on the job—he did things his way and docked the *Chippewa* using the outlawed Black Ball signal. It apparently reopened the issue and inspired the Puget Sound Maritime Historical Society to do some lobbying. On May 24, 1958, the familiar long toot followed by two short toots once again became the standard on Puget Sound ferries.

In another conscious effort to make its own imprint on the new ferry system, the state also decided to discontinue Black Ball publicist William Thorniley's practice of giving new vessels names chosen from Chinook jargon. The state argued that the names were too hard to pronounce and that they were confusing. They may have had a point about the confusion. In the midst of ferries generally named with Northwest words, names like Iroquois and Chippewa did indeed raise questions. Furthermore, the current ferry system operators report that tourists will sometimes ask ticket sellers questions along the lines of "When does the ferry *Spokane* arrive in Spokane?" However, the confusion there lies not in naming the ferry after an Indian tribe but in naming it after a city.

The changes in the ferry naming policy went largely unnoticed when the first new state ferry, *Evergreen State*, was launched. It was, after all, a bit of boosterism much like the 1889 sternwheeler *State of Washington* had been. But, when names for the next two ferries were announced, Bill Thorniley sprang into action. The proposed *Vacation State* and *Washington State* were just too much. Thorniley was aided by a flood of letters to newspapers protesting the new names and demanding a return to the old custom. Responding to the crisis, Governor Langlie appointed a nine-member commission and charged them with the task of selecting ferry names. To the relief of Thorniley and his supporters the first names were *Tillikum*, meaning "friendly people," and *Klahowya*, meaning "greetings."

The whistle signal and the ferry names were the least serious problems faced by ferry system head Floyd Mc-Dowell, Jr. in the first years of ferry operation. Clauses in the 1951 purchase agreement had stipulated that the Bremerton-Point White (Bainbridge Island) run and the Indianola-Suquamish-Seattle run would be discontinued after the state takeover. For the first time in more than 50 years the citizens of Indianola and Suquamish found themselves without direct ferry service. They would have to travel north to Kingston and across the Sound to Edmonds, or cross the toll bridge at Agate Pass and take the ferry from Winslow.

Left: Along with the Indianola–Suquamish runs, the state also discontinued service between Bremerton and Point White on Bainbridge Island. Before the Agate Pass Bridge was built, Kitsap County's library bookmobile had to travel via ferry to reach Bainbridge Island. Courtesy, Kitsap Regional Library, 1-14-00(14) Bremerton, WA

Opposite page: While Seattle is the main terminus for ferries, smaller landings like the 1950s version shown here are still representative of life on Puget Sound. Courtesy, Ralph White Collection, Kitsap Regional Library, Bremerton, WA.

The state's position was that the ferry route had not been profitable and that it was the state's job to provide not only the best and fastest service on Puget Sound, but the cheapest as well.

North Kitsap residents reacted to the loss of their ferry with outrage. They predicted a general exodus of the area's population, claiming people would be forced to abandon their homes and friends and take up residence in places where they could earn a living. The pleas went unheeded, the runs were abandoned, and there was no noticeable population exodus. Commuters chose one of the other two routes and continued to get to their jobs on the Seattle side of the Sound.

Puget Sound ferries tend to work in tandem with bridges; Hood Canal Floating Bridge and the Agate Pass bridge made up part of a highway corridor that funneled traffic from the Olympic and Kitsap Peninsulas through Bainbridge or Kingston and across to Seattle via ferry. The hope, however, was always that bridges would provide the traffic path all the way to Seattle. After all, bridges had

replaced the San Francisco ferries and once they were built bridges offered a far cheaper alternative to operating aging vessels and maintaining terminal facilities. It was assumed when the state purchased the ferry system that it would be a temporary measure until the inevitable bridges were built.

Nearly every decade after 1950 had advocates of various bridge plans. As early as 1957 a *Bainbridge Review* editorial noted that "if all the surveys on that pie-in-the-sky bridge were placed end-to-end, they'd make a nice start on the span." Sometimes the plans were simply repeats of earlier ideas. One of the earliest, most radical, and most laughed at plan called for running concrete tubes under Puget Sound between Bainbridge Island and Seattle. Two separate underwater tubes, one for eastbound and the other for westbound traffic was perhaps too big a concept for the average Northwest resident to grasp in 1950. Puget Sound was for fishing, boating, and taking a cold swim, not driving under. Today, with the Chunnel connecting Britain and France, the plan is not so

laughable; but given the current knowledge of earthquake fault lines in the vicinity of Bainbridge Island, the tubes may not have been a good idea.

Another plan, offered by Ralph Purvis, a Democratic state senator from Bremerton, received more serious attention and occasionally resurfaces in some form or other as a new idea. He proposed consolidating the Bremerton and Bainbridge Island routes into a single route leaving from Winslow. Those travelers leaving from Bremerton would have easy access to the island terminal via a bridge between Bainbridge Island and Brownsville, a small community four miles north of Bremerton. Many Bainbridge residents, not yet having developed their "no bridge" stance, supported the Purvis idea. The combination bridge-ferry route, called a travel "desire-line," represented a cheaper alternative, at $14 million, to another plan for a pair of cross-Sound bridges that would have used Vashon Island to link the Kitsap Peninsula to West Seattle at a projected cost of $154 million.

The Vashon bridge concept had been debated for several years and by more than one session of the state legislature. Most of its support came from South Kitsap, while much of the opposition originated on Bainbridge Island and in North Kitsap. Bainbridge made its voice heard loud and clear in a 1957 survey which indicated that 86 percent of the Islanders did not want to trade

their ferries for a bridge, particularly a bridge at Vashon. In three and one-half inch high red letters the December 26, 1957, *Bainbridge Review* declared "We Want Our Ferries!" In nearby Poulsbo, city officials passed a resolution opposing any cross-Sound bridge at Vashon Island unless the continuation of the Bainbridge ferry was guaranteed. Such a bridge was of "little or no assistance" to the inhabitants of North Kitsap, especially if it meant discontinuing the Winslow–Seattle run, a move that would cause severe damage to the economy of North Kitsap and Bainbridge Island. The Poulsbo resolution was just one of many that came from all areas including the powerful Municipal League of Seattle. The residents of Vashon were considerably more direct in their opposition—unofficially, they threatened to blow up any bridge reaching their island. While many Sound residents think of the Sound as a barrier that must be traversed, island residents from the San Juans in the north to Vashon in the south have increasingly come to think of the waters as a protective moat guarding their way of life.

Some of the general opposition to bridges arose from postwar fears. In the case of war and enemy air raids, ferries were numerous moving targets, superior to bridges where one good air strike could disrupt the whole system. Luckily for those in opposition, it did not take a war to quash

Opposite page: Many Vashon Island residents value their isolation. This ferry terminal and one other are the main ways on and off the island. There is no bridge. Courtesy, Ralph White Collection, Kitsap Regional Library, Bremerton, WA

Right: W.C. Nickum and Sons, Seattle-based naval architects, designed the first ferry built by the State of Washington. Courtesy, Puget Sound Maritime Historical Society, 8182 Seattle

Below: A former Maryland ferry joined the Washington State fleet as the Rhododendron. Courtesy, Kitsap Regional Library, Bremerton, WA

the project. The Vashon bridge proposals failed several times in the state's biennial legislative sessions. The Purvis plan was left "on the back burner" although the governor had the authority to resurrect it for study at any time. The Sequim Chamber of Commerce saw the failure of the Vashon bridge plan as an opportunity to voice support for another bridge, this one located between President's Point on the North Kitsap peninsula and Richmond Beach on the Seattle side. The Number Four bridge, as it had been proposed, would cut travel time from Port Angeles to Seattle down to about 75 miles and would provide a gateway route for tourists to reach Olympic National Park.

If bridging the Sound did not seem to be on the immediate horizon, the ferry fleet needed some attention. In 1953 the state bought two steel, diesel ferries from the state of Maryland, where another bridge had somehow been built. The *Governor O'Connor* and the *Governor Nice* were towed the 6,000 miles down from the East Coast and through the Panama Canal and up to Puget Sound. After several weeks of refurbishing, they emerged as the *Rhododendron* and the *Olympic*.

COMMUTING

Not all experiences on the Evergreen Fleet are tied to finances, labor, or politics. There are other issues such as ferry safety and commuter etiquette.

One of the natural hazards offered by Puget Sound's geologic activity is the possibility of a tsunami or tidal wave that could accompany a major earthquake. Such an event in the Seattle area would wreak disaster in the city's waterfront district. Ferryboat passengers would inevitably be among the casualties. While this is a genuine danger, it is also a worst-case-scenario fit for Hollywood. It is not one that regular ferryboat patrons give much thought to.

The day-to-day risks of riding a ferry are more likely to involve breakdowns in the middle of a crossing, which are rare, and running aground, which is equally rare. On those scattered occasions when ferries do run aground, the public response is apt to be a mixture of anger and humor. On a foggy morning in April 1981 the superferry *Walla Walla*, carrying an early morning load of commuters from Bainbridge Island, came to an abrupt stop when the ferry ran aground on a sandbar on Bainbridge's Wing Point in Eagle Harbor. As if trying to hide the error, the ferry's engines reversed in a vain attempt to back off the sandbar. Seven minutes passed before the passengers heard a blaring intercom announcement of free coffee. Astute Bainbridge Island commuters interpreted that to mean that they were stuck—a fact confirmed by a voice on the intercom 20 minutes later. The hours passed; the *Walla Walla* wallowed in the mud and the passengers drank all the coffee. A rumor circulated that if they were still stuck at the noon hour, free beer would be available. Meanwhile, the ferry system used tugs in an effort to dislodge the *Walla Walla* from its resting place. Onlookers crowding onshore and news media planes and helicopters circling above watched and recorded the unsuccessful rescue effort.

Unable to get the ferry off the sandbar, officials opted for getting the passengers off the ferry. They brought in a rescue barge so that the 648 stranded commuters could abandon ship. After all the passengers were on the barge, they belatedly fitted themselves with life jackets found piled near the barge's loading ramp. They reached shore about 11 a.m., well in advance of the rumored free beer deadline.

Subsequent newspaper accounts reported that one man objected to leaving his Mercedes car behind while he boarded the barge. Reluctant to hand his keys over to the ferry's second mate, the passenger was quoted as saying "It really seems stupid to me that the people who can't drive this ferry can drive my car."

Ironically, the ferry system spokeswoman whose duties included explaining these events to the public via the media was herself stranded on the ferry. In the best tradition of public relations as she dashed from the rescue barge Alice Collingwood told waiting press that "it was real neat" and that most people felt it was "kind of an adventure".

Diligent efforts and high tide finally freed the *Walla Walla*. She reached the Winslow dock around 7:00 p.m. Waiting at the dock, in the wind and rain, were the hundreds of people who had been separated from their cars earlier in the day. The collective good humor had somewhat soured by this time and eroded even further when car owners were told that ferry workers would drive the cars off the *Walla Walla* and park them in a nearby lot for retrieval. Faced with an impatient and ugly-dispositioned crowd, ferry officials relented and allowed drivers to board the ferry and drive their own cars off.

Within days Bainbridge Islanders regained their sense of humor and enjoyed a flurry of bumper stickers and T-shirts declaring "I Wallowed on the Walla-Walla." Commuters on the 7:50 run the day after the grounding received shipwreck certificates declaring them to be "official survivors." As one island resident summed it up, "you wouldn't live here if the boats gave you a pain in the (rear end)."

Longtime ferryboat Captain Robert Engstrom noted that years earlier he, too, had run a superferry aground in nearly the same spot on Bainbridge Island. That place was nearly

the front yard of Washington States's powerful Senator Warren Magnuson. The ferries had been one of the Senator's pet projects , funded in part by federal dollars, so Engstrom recognized the irony quirk of fate grounding the ferry near Magnuson's Bainbridge residence. Unlike the *Walla Walla* grounding, Engstrom's "oops" with the *Elwha* had occurred at 3:00 a.m. and an incoming tide freed the boat in about an hour. Passengers in the 1960s, especially those at that hour, were a little less irate than 1980s commuters.

The *Elwha* was famous for her flirtations with rocks, sandbars, and shorelines. She ran aground coming into Kingston on the Saturday of Memorial Day weekend in 1975. Low water levels just wouldn't accommodate the superferry when she attempted to dock. Not only did she fail to make the dock, but her stationary hulk blocked access for the other incoming ferries. Refloated on the returning tide, the *Elwha*, still in sight of the Kingston dock but unable to navigate the low water level, had to go to Winslow on Bainbridge Island to unload the automobile passengers. Foot passengers with cars waiting for them in Kingston were forced to make another trip to Edmonds, their point of origin, so that they could try for Kingston again on a smaller ferry unhampered by the low water. As the ferry employee in the ticket booth described the scene, it was "a bit on the hectic side."

One of the delayed passengers was a bridegroom who had gone to Edmonds to pick up the wedding cake for his scheduled 1:00 p.m. wedding in Indianola, a neighboring community to Kingston. When he finally reached Kingston, cake in hand, not only was he a little frantic, he was also a little late for his wedding.

Most of what constitutes ferry etiquetted derives from established routines. Tourists aboard Washington State Ferries obviously do not have a routine and are therefore not expected to do much beyond enjoy the ride and the beautiful scenery. Commuters, on the other hand, have habits that they develop over the years, such as sleeping on the bench seats. Not just sitting with head bowed and eyes shut as someone who might be seen sleeping on a New York subway or a Chicago train at rush hour,

Above: Some things about commuting never change whether it is marching off a Horluck ferry in Bremerton or marching onto a fast passenger ferry in Seattle. Courtesy, Kitsap County Historical Society

Opposite page: It is not uncommon for Northwest musicians to entertain ferry passengers. Here, David Michael is an added treat on the Port Townsend-Keystone run. Photo by Tom Janus

these commuters stretch out full length and catch an hour's sleep.

The other commuter habit is the ritual adoption of a personal seat. Pity the poor tourist who sits in the habitual spot of a commuter and must endure the grim glares without even knowing what the problem is. Commuters get so attached to their territory on a ferry that it is said ferryboat captains occasionally like to reverse the direction of a boat, causing commuters to load from the unaccustomed end, totally disorientating them as they seek out their customary spots. But in spite of all this, ferryboat riders are the people who really make the ferry system work; without them, what would be the point?

When no more ferries could be purchased, the state launched its own building program. Along with the acquisition of Puget Sound Navigation came three diesel-electric engines that Captain Peabody had purchased as war surplus. The state was able to use the engines in three ferries, the first ever designed and built for the Washington State Ferry System. The Evergreen State class was designed by W.C. Nickum and Sons of Seattle and built by another local company, Puget Sound Bridge and Dry Dock. The 310-foot *Evergreen State* could carry 100 cars and 1,000 passengers. She started on the Seattle–Winslow run in 1954 and was followed by the *Klahowya* in 1958 and the *Tillikum* in 1959. New ferries on Puget Sound always generate excitement. The *Evergreen State* was no exception and each of the towns on the ferry routes wanted a boat like her. There was room to get out of one's car on the car deck and the passenger cabins featured air-conditioning, vinyl flooring, wide seats, and picture windows.

In its first decade of operation, the state, which had at one time declared that it would reduce ferry fares,

was forced to raise them by amounts that ranged from 17 to 32 percent because of the addition of federal taxes. Increased operating costs, plus the need to retro-actively include ferry employees into the state retirement system as per a 1957 wage stabilization law, created a financial hole which the ferry system needed to fill. Consequently, in 1959 a one-way passenger ticket went from 55 cents to 72 cents and auto fares rose from $1.65 to $1.82. One immediate, if naïve, response from local leaders in Kitsap County was to suggest that ferries officially be made part of the state highway system and that all fares be eliminated.

The "traveling public," especially those traveling from Bremerton, launched the first of a series of complaints that would continue to the present day. While nothing, with the exception of higher fares, had come to the Bremerton run, the Winslow run had received new ferries, new docking facilities, and increased service. Propaganda flyers handed to Bremerton commuters in June 1959 called all ferry patrons "second-class citizens" and Bremerton ferry riders "third-class citizens" of the state, a sentiment generally understood, and possibly shared,

Top: All Puget Sound auto ferries feature bench seats and large windows. This is the interior of the Evergreen State. Courtesy, Puget Sound Maritime Historical Society, 5324-47 Seattle

Bottom: The galley and eating area on the Evergreen State were up to the modern standards of 1954. Note the fire axe mounted on the wall. Courtesy, Puget Sound Maritime Historical Society, 5324-50 Seattle

Opposite page: Launched in 1954, the Evergreen State was Washington's first new ferry. Courtesy, Puget Sound Maritime Historical Society, 5324-52 Seattle

by today's Bremerton commuters. The animosity over perceived inequalities of ferry service has marked the relationship between the citizens of Bremerton and Bainbridge ever since. It is not always apparent to tourists, but Puget Sound residents take their ferries very seriously and will generally do vocal battle to make sure that their communities get served. Even as Bremertonians were complaining about their level of service, the South Kitsap Chamber of Commerce petitioned the state for 24-hour ferry service on the Southworth–Vashon–Fauntleroy route.

The 1960s got off to a bumpy start as the Puget Sound Ferry Users' Association once again became active over the issue of ferry fares. Design flaws in the state's Hood Canal Floating Bridge had led to costly repairs that drew funding away from ferries and necessitated higher ticket prices. Arguments that the ferry system should be treated as part of the state highway system

seemed to shift when it came to subsidizing a bridge that truly was part of the highway system.

At the same time that West Sound residents were growing increasingly unhappy over the cost of their ferries they were also making plans to tout them. In 1960 a local booster organization sought to rename the Bainbridge–North Kitsap area as Ferryland U.S.A. They claimed to have signs ready to post on the borders of the new region. While some publicity appeared in the form of popular tourist articles about "Ferryland," and the term occasionally still appears in writing, the renaming idea, if it ever was serious, thankfully died a natural death.

Some 16 years later, another forgettable publicity campaign sought to attract commuters for an Around the World Via Washington State Ferry Register. For a $6.50 registration fee, commuters who had logged enough ferry miles to equate with circumnavigating the globe could be placed

Left: Many Black Ball employees stayed with the ferries after the state takeover in 1951. Captain Arnold "Spike" Eikum headed the Washington State Ferries from 1966 until early 1970s. Courtesy, Puget Sound Maritime Historical Society, 3148-31 Seattle

Above: While the State of Washington was adding ferries to the fleet, it was also subtracting them. In 1975 the Chetzemoka was sold to California owners. On her way south she was wrecked off the Washington coast. Courtesy, Author's collection

Aerial view of the Washington State Ferry terminal in Seattle. Courtesy, Ralph White Collection, Kitsap Regional Library, Bremerton, WA

on a register and receive a brass pin with their register number on the back. The only interesting thing about the promotion was calculating how long it would take a commuter on various runs, making 10 trips a week, to qualify as having circumnavigated the globe. For those on the Bremerton–Seattle run it only took two years and eight months of commuting. The Bainbridge run would take four years and ten months, which was close to the Southworth commuters' four years and one month and the Vashon Islanders' four years and seven months. To meet the requirement, a Kingston–Edmonds commuter would have to spend eight years and one month crossing the Sound. The register did not become part of ferry commuter tradition.

The rest of the 1960s saw enough improvements and expansion in the ferry system to calm the fears of those who may have been worried about the bridge-building plans.

In 1964 the state opened its own ferry repair and maintenance facility at Eagle Harbor on Bainbridge Island. If anything breaks on a ferry or at a terminal, the Eagle Harbor shipyard handles the problem. Currently at Eagle Harbor there are eight shops staffed by 105 employees: shipwrights, boilermakers, shore gang, pipe, sheet metal, electric, machine, and insulation workers.

The focus is on maintenance and repairs, which in 1999 averaged about 2,000 work orders. Major overhauls and renovations are handled in the area's larger commercial shipyards.

A new $3 million ferry terminal, a light and airy building in comparison to the dark cavernous feeling of the previous Black Ball facility, graced Seattle's waterfront by 1966. The terminal's three slips and 24 lanes reflected the continuing growth of cross-Sound auto traffic in and out of Seattle. Along with the terminal, four new ferries were scheduled to be built by the end of the decade. The state's spending of $22 million on the new vessels gave further evidence that there'd be no bridges in the near future.

The new ferries, in typical sixties nomenclature, were "superferries" and, at 382-feet long, represented the largest ferries yet to be seen on Puget Sound—longer than a football field and as tall as a six-story building. While average consumers most often think of ferries in terms of passenger and auto space, the superferries addressed a problem which deeply concerned freight traffic. The 16-foot deck clearance made it possible for modern commercial trucks to travel on ferries. With funding help from the federal government under the 1964 Urban Mass Transportation Act, the ferries *Hyak, Kaleetan, Yakima,* and *Elwha* were scheduled for service in 1967 and 1968. Like the Evergreen State class, they had been designed by W.C. Nickum and Sons, although the superferries were built by National Steel & Shipbuilding Company of San Diego.

In the wake of the superferries and a step ahead of the economic downturn of the mid-1970s came the jumbo ferries, built at Seattle's Todd Shipyards and bearing price tags of around $9 million each. These vessels were 440-feet long and carried 206 automobiles and 2,000 passengers. Their speed, 20 knots, was the only thing that had not changed from the Mosquito Fleet days of the *Tacoma* and *H.B. Kennedy*.

Designers Philip Spaulding, Inc. and Burhans Design Associates of Seattle incorporated a variety of style inno-

vations into the new ferries. The exhausting study of the new features was compared to the studies made on each system of the Apollo spacecraft. The difference was that the ferries were evaluating carpet, seating arrangements, and panel designs. The goal was economy and the endproduct reflected that.

Bainbridge Island commuters are a literate group; they also have their own concept of "good taste." When the new jumbo ferry *Spokane* was placed on their run early in 1973, they unleashed their considerable talents in a series of letters to the local *Bainbridge Review* newspaper. One Bainbridge resident compared the new

Spokane to walking into a beauty parlor in Phoenix, the point being that there is no thrill in beauty parlors. The writer expressed a desire to see the *Spokane* assigned to another route on Puget Sound because, as a design professional, she found the boat embarrassing and preferred not to confront it too often. All who suggested that the boat be transferred to the San Juans were gracious enough to add apologies to the people there. The problems with the vessel, according to her critics, were its bad colors, lack of richness and honesty in interior style, and poor seating. The seating was at least distinguished for its consistency—there was not a single comfortable seat aboard the boat. The piped-in music drew particular criticism from commuters who claimed that their civil rights to silence were being violated. Even the ferry's horn did not escape scrutiny—it was deemed discordant. Only the carpeting was praised and that was because it was anticipated that the floor covering would deaden the sounds of running and screaming children. Included in the ferry's smoking area were the restaurant and all of the tables. Non-smokers were forced to petition in order to secure some space in which to do paperwork, a common activity for commuters. With congratulations for things *Spokane* designers had done right, the

Above: The Vashon *was the last wood-hulled vessel in the Washington State ferry fleet. Courtesy, Kitsap Regional Library, Bremerton, WA*

Opposite page, top: Vents on older ferry boats can look like sousaphones to an imaginative child. Courtesy, Author's collection

Opposite page, bottom: The interior of the jumbo ferries drew a lot of criticism from Bainbridge Island commuters. Courtesy, Ralph White Collection, Kitsap Regional Library, Bremerton, WA

comment was that it floated, its engines seemed to work, and it was better than the New York subway. So much for the Apollo moon landing-type studies.

Along with the new jumbo ferries came yet the next set of bridge plans. As with the other bridge studies, the 1970s version offered different alternatives. One mirrored the earlier Purvis plan, calling for a bridge between Bremerton and Bainbridge Island and a consolidation of the auto ferries into a single Winlsow–Seattle route. Bremerton foot passengers would still have access to passenger-only ferries. The other alternative featured a bridge across Rich Passage and a consolidated auto ferry terminal on the South Kitsap side at Clam Bay. Passenger-only ferries would continue to serve Bainbridge and Bremerton but automobile traffic would have to travel to Clam Bay to catch a ferry. For Bainbridge residents it was an extra three and a half miles across a possible toll bridge. Bremerton drivers would have to travel an extra 20 miles through Port Orchard to reach the ferry terminal. No one, with the possible exception of South Kitsap residents, liked the plan and even those in South Kitsap had concerns over the increased traffic a ferry terminal would engender.

At the end of the 1970s there were no bridge plans on the horizon; in fact, the state was minus a bridge when a portion of the Hood Canal Floating Bridge sank in 1979 during a February storm. After a year of trying to substitute a barge and tug arrangement to move people and cars across the canal, the ferries *Quinault* and *Tillikum* began to run between Lofall in Kitsap County and South Point on the Jefferson County side.

One tradition on the state ferry system was shattered in 1973 when the first woman deckhand picked up a mop. The state's Human Rights Commission had suggested to ferry officials that it was about time they abandon the system's all-male hiring policy. Two years after the first female deckhand came the first female oiler. As part of the engine room crew, oilers monitor operating equipment and assist with its maintenance.

The 1970s were defined by oil shortages and runaway inflation. Everything suffered, ferry schedules as well as ferry revenues. Not since the days of

the *Kalakala's* famous taproom had ferries served beer, but the state highway commissioners overseeing ferry finances in 1974 came to the conclusion that beer sales might be an asset to a ferry system awash in red ink. For those worried about intoxicated ferry travelers, the state added a safeguard—the price of a cup of beer would be 75 cents. Commuters used to sneaking their own beer aboard the ferry were unimpressed. Beer sales were initiated without much comment and have since been expanded to include wine. Purchasing alcohol, or drinking on ferries, for that matter, is not really part of the ferry culture which tends more towards steaming cups of coffee.

While state officials did not actually expect beer sales to attract ferry riders, they did hope that aggressive marketing might. During their off-peak runs ferries needed more riders and the strategy called for emphasizing the destinations as well as the trip itself. Ferries began to house racks of colorful brochures informing tourists and locals about events, sights, restaurants, and accommodations. At least one ferry user suggested other strategies that were never adopted, such as opening up the engine room for tours during the voyage, placing historical exhibits on the boats so they would be like moving museums, and adding docents who could give lectures on the local marine life. Those ideas, while interesting, overlook the fact that Washington State Ferries are public transportation used by commuters and not solely by tourists. And, while they are one of the

state's biggest tourist attractions, WSF is fully aware that Puget Sound ferry commuters are its top priority.

A change occurred in 1977 that had far ranging implications for ferry management. That year the Toll Bridge Authority was abolished and ferries passed to the authority of the Transportation Commission. Commission members are appointed by the governor for six year terms. Although the Washington State Department of Transportation runs the Washington State Ferry System, policy is set in the Transportation Commission.

The use of federal funding to help build new ferries was so enticing, the 1977 Legislature considered new and creative avenues for ferry travel. For seven weeks the ferry system used a Boeing Jetfoil to test the waters of cost versus revenue. If the test was any indication—$235,000 collected in fares from 61,000 passengers versus $425,000 in operating costs—the answer was clear. Even if the federal government paid the entire cost of the vessels, the state could probably not afford to run them unless fares were significantly higher. While the test proved that Boeing Jetfoils were not likely to join the WSF fleet, ferry officials came away with a belief that fast passenger-only vessels would work for Puget Sound commuters. All the state needed were the right boats.

One bright spot was the decision to renovate rather than discard four veteran steel-electric ferries. The *Quinault, Nisqually, Illahee,* and *Klickitat* were all deemed worthy of keeping thanks to a study done by the Bremerton engineering firm of Art Anderson and

Despite their early problems, Issaquah class ferries have been a mainstay of the Bremerton run. Photo by Tom Janus

The *Sealth, an Issaquah class ferry, is seen here being nudged along by tugs. Courtesy, Ralph White Collection, Kitsap Regional Library, Bremerton, WA*

Associates. The state Transportation Commission gave the go-ahead to the firm to complete the design work that would keep the ferries, originally built in 1927, in service until the end of the century. In modernizing the ferries the state was able to keep some of the most charming examples of Puget Sound ferry heritage on the waters where the public could enjoy them.

Although the jetfoil proved unsuitable, the federal government was prepared to help fund six new conventional ferries smaller in size than superferries and intended for shorter routes such as the Kingston–Edmonds run or the Columbia Beach–Mukilteo run on Whidbey Island. The project was controversial from the start as WSF awarded the largest contract in state history to a little known Seattle firm, Marine Power and Equipment Co. A legislative add-on provided Washington firms with a six percent preferential margin in bidding. The edge was enough to eliminate a New Orleans firm and to negate a $14 million federal subsidy. The loss of the federal funds on top of the $105.8 million contract was, of course, a blow to taxpayers.

As construction on the vessels started, marine experts questioned the work done by Marine Power. The welding process drew attention because it seemed brittle and there was even more concern when it was revealed that one of the state officials in charge of the project did not even know if Marine Power was taking x-rays of its welds, a common procedure used to verify

their strength. Furthermore, 15 percent of the way into the project there were still no designs for electrical or mechanical systems. Concerned observers privately expressed the belief that the extra costs would amount to another 40 percent over the initial contract.

Experts were right to be worried about the operational features of the Issaquah ferries. As the rumors circulating through the ferry system started to make their way out into the public sector, ferry employees received a management memorandum telling them that "criticism of the new vessel will not be tolerated." It was impossible to hide the flaws in the Isssaquah class boats. All had numerous deficiencies, serious enough to cause the boats to be withdrawn from service. Computerized control systems were so erratic that in some instances the boats literally could not be steered. Twice, ferries backed out of the docks while cars were loading and in one case dumped a car into Puget Sound. Even after the problems were corrected the Coast Guard continued to require an extra engineer aboard each of the vessels, a move which made the small Issaquah ferries more expensive to operate than the larger superferries.

Aside from the mechanical problems and the general quality of the boats—they were nicknamed the "Citrus class"—there were legal and political problems. A special *Seattle Post-Intelligencer* report on the state ferry system written by Duff Wilson and published January 8,

1986, recapped the issues. A state legislator, who rode on one the ferries and declared that corruption had to be involved somewhere in order for the state to end up with such a vessel, was sued for defamation by the builder. Although evidence did seem to indicate a series of dubious ties between state legislators and Marine Power officials, a grand jury investigation into the matter never returned a single indictment. A state senate report called for an investigation into the way in which Marine Power had won most of its contract disputes with the state. The rulings in favor of the company had run contrary to expert advice, technical expertise, and the state's own interests. Something seemed wrong with the process.

In 1982 state Transportation Secretary Duane Berentson rejected a legislative inquiry, preferring to get at the facts via a lawsuit against the builders. For its part, Marine Power was already suing the state for costs it said were never paid. The suits were settled in 1985 but many questions remained unanswered. One fact never revealed was how much profit Marine Power made on the ferry contract. Estimates placed it at 29 percent when normal profit on a state contract was 10 percent. The terms of the lawsuit settlement were revealed and indicated that the state's victory was a costly one. Washington State paid Marine Power $1 million and Marine Power promised to pay the state $8.5 million over a 10-

year period starting in 1991. Thanks to the deferred payments, by 2001 Marine Power would end up paying the equivalent of $3.5 million in 1985 dollars. That meant a net gain of only $2.5 million for taxpayers after the $6.4 million in trial costs.

Not only had Washington taxpayers been victimized, faith in the Washington State Ferry System had been lost and it would be a long time before ferry users forgot the mistakes of the Issaquah class boats. Citizen animosity towards ferry management was equally matched by animosity towards ferry workers. Strong unions had won high salaries for ferry jobs, salaries the general public perceived as exorbitant. When the Inland Boatmen's Union went on strike in April 1980 and tied up ferries for 12 days in order to win a 9 percent wage increase, 33,000 commuters had had enough. While the union and the state claimed that the strike settlement had been a classic win-win situation, ferry commuters felt very much like losers.

New ferry user groups formed and used new tactics. The Washington State Ferry Consumers Union united with the goals of preventing disruption in ferry service, keeping service at the lowest possible cost and insuring and improving the quality of service. The Puget Sound Ferry (or Transportation) Coalition relied on lobbying to get their message to the state legislature. Other citizens who chose to speak through local Ferry Advisory Boards wondered if their comments ever reached Olympia. Ferries were thoroughly enmeshed in politics and the outlook was not good.

Meanwhile, the strikes continued. A 12-hour wildcat strike by marine engineers in April 1981 left consumers and politicians feeling angry enough to pass legislation that would have stripped ferry unions of salary and pension bargaining rights. Members of the Marine Engineers Beneficial Association countered with another wildcat walkout, this one starting May 19, 1981, and lasting three days. The walkout ended when Washington Governor John Spellman agreed to establish a blue-ribbon commission to investigate the ferry system and to try and rework the new law.

The ferries kept running during a July 1981 strike but there was no fresh coffee or snacks as employees of Saga, the ferry system's food concessionaire, walked off their jobs. The food-workers strike was the first of its kind in ferry history. To prove that West Sound residents still had a sense of humor, Kingston's Fourth of July parade featured a float designed in the likeness of a ferryboat bearing the name "Wegocha" and accompanied by marchers portrayed as strikers.

In August 1981 the governor's 14-member blue-ribbon commission approved new legislation which proposed tough anti-strike penalties and a binding arbitration law that would restore the ferry unions' right to negotiate. Ferry consumers, who began to speculate that the labor disputes and lawsuits against Marine Power were a diversionary tactic to keep scrutiny away from ferry system management, asked Governor Spellman to reconvene the commission in December for the purpose of investigating ferry management.

Increased fares, decreasing passenger loads, strikes, boats with poor interior design, and boats that could not steer their way out of the surrounding scandal were all part and parcel of the 1980s. The ferry

system which had been losing money during the 1970s was a financial morass ten years later. State action to increase the ferry subsidy level from 25 percent to 40 percent prevented fare hikes that would have totaled 92 percent in a 25-month period, but the overall funding problem remained largely unsolved.

With a contrariness typical of human nature, ferry riders —who had a generation earlier celebrated the state takeover of the ferries as an escape from the much maligned Captain Alexander Peabody and Puget Sound Navigation Company—began to call for a return to the good old days when Black Ball provided good service, low fares, delicious food service and a comfortable boat.

In 1966, Seattle's $3 million ferry terminal was seen as a sign of commitment to the future of ferries on Puget Sound. Courtesy, Ralph White Collection, Kitsap Regional Library, Bremerton, WA

Chapter 7

Art And The Ferry

Artists will often create works that utilize themes or scenes from their natural surroundings. This has been so since the earliest voyages of discovery and exploration to the Northwest coast. Scientists who could observe and record, and artists who could sketch or draw, accompanied captain and crew on their sailings. Russian, French, Spanish, English and American artists left their record from trips made to this region in the seventeenth century through the Charles Wilkes expedition in the first half of the nineteenth century. Wilkes himself left drawings from his exploratory mission, much as his predecessors did on George Vancouver's missions.

When the journals of George Vancouver were published after his death, they included drawings and sketches that were remade into engravings for the work. Sketches of the new lands he visited, drawings of friend and foe, renderings of the native peoples, the forts and communities, the ships and slices of daily life have all become part of the region's historical record. The works reside in museums and libraries, and have been reproduced in art and history books.

At a later date, with the advent of photography, photos were added to the record. While early artists made drawings of their ships and Indian canoes, many of which were made into engravings for publication, photographs later provided the bulk of the documentation of the steamers and ferry-boats of the nineteenth century.

It's been often said, in different ways, that art has no boundaries and the expansive edges of this definition may be seen in the ferryboat material one encounters in galleries, museums, boutiques, antique shops and the grand emporiums on or near the Seattle waterfront that deal in souvenirs, knickknacks, kitsch and nickel-and-dime items that might be collectible in some future time, and displayed in some museum dedicated to forgotten flotsam.

Clinton Ferry Dock watercolor shows the South Whidbey Island connection to the mainland at Mukilteo. Courtesy, Larry Mason

The Grand Room of the Kalakala. Courtesy, John Ohanessian

The ferryboat is an icon, a symbol and representation of life in and around Puget Sound. As such it is visually omnipresent in our daily lives, and the very commonness of ferry images makes it easy to overlook, to blank out of consciousness. Still, the images surround us. In the galleries, annual art exhibitions, and arts & crafts fairs, there will always be artists who use life on the waterways as subject material. It would be difficult not to find ferry material for show or sale.

Carey Floyd and Carl Bivens are two young artists from Port Orchard Both Attended the Art Institute of Seattle. Collaborating with the co-author, they created a series of photo-collages on their Macs. Working from roughs, photos, illustrations, clippings, and brainstorming sessions, their keyboard mastery produced unique images.

Opposite page, bottom: Fish Bowl Collage, second in the series. Courtesy, CFCB/Janus

Above: Seattle Collage, fourth in the series. Courtesy, CFCB/Janus

Right: Seagull Collage, first of a series of four. Courtesy, CFCB/Janus

Washington State Ferry in the Snow is done in soft pastel, ink and paint. The designer, raised in

Southeast Alaska, now lives in Port Orchard. Courtesy, Catherine Valley

Bremerton Ferry is an oil (48"x64") that hung at Collective Visions Gallery

in Bremerton. Courtesy, Ken van der Does

147

This painting of the Kalakala at her current home on Lake Union was past of the Trapeze Gallery exhibit at MOHAI in Seattle. Courtesy, Dave McGranaghan

Elton Bennett serigraphs depict the Pacific Northwest coastal environment. He grew up in Hoquiam in the Gray's Harbor region of the Washington coast, where mill work, fishing and dredging are common occupations and the pursuit of art was not encouraged.

Mr. Bennett's only formal training consisted of a single year at Washington State University at Pullman in 1927. He chose silkscreen printing for his medium because it allowed so many possibilities for manipulating compositions. These works have steadily gained recognition over the years. The artist's tragic death in 1974 in an airplane crash has meant a substantial increase in their value. Shown left is his work entitled Ferry. Courtesy, Murray Meld, and the Estate of Elton Bennett

Described as "near Tacoma," the Museum of Puget Sound is located on Stretch Island in Mason County and its neighborhood is surrounded by inlets and passages, dozens of sea fingers that are part of the southern end of Puget Sound. The drive from Tacoma would be anyone's perfect country drive for a weekend afternoon. Its rooms are crowded with artifacts; models, framed pictures, posters, nameplates from boats, chairs and steering wheels. There is not much empty space on the walls or in the aisles. Now retired, Bill Somers began working on the Mosquito Fleet boats at age 18. He and his wife opened the Museum in 1986 with ferry ephemera they collected for many years.

Right: This model of Seattle's Colman Dock was built by two high school seniors from Tacoma, Willard Johnson and Carl Anderson. The model was stored in a parent's attic, and was slated for the trash when the space was to be converted to rooms for rent during World War II. Bill Somers had first seen the model at an exhibition, and when he learned of its impending fate, he contacted the builders and bought the piece in 1943. The model is now housed at the Museum of Puget Sound. Photo by Tom Janus, courtesy, Museum of Puget Sound

Left: "Floatsum" greets visitors at the Museum of Puget Sound entrance. Photo by Tom Janus, courtesy, Museum of Puget Sound

The use of the 35 mm camera exploded during the WW II era, and photojournalism became the hot glamour industry and a burgeoning art.

Photographers, in capturing their surroundings, in using the camera to record history and extract essences of time and place, have looked to the landscape. In the Puget Sound, half of the landscape is water. Local photographers continue this tradition, whether they are photojournalists working for newspapers or periodicals, covering ferry issues or illustrating articles; fine art and commercial photographers using maritime themes in their art; students working on portfolios; or tourists making snapshots for their album.

Opposite page, top: Pierce
County operates ferries
from Steilacoom (near
Tacoma) to Ketron Island
and Anderson Island.
Photo by Steven J. Brown

Ferry Quinault at Keystone.
Photo by Tom Janus

Above: The Victoria Express
makes the trip from Port
Angeles to Victoria's Inner
Harbor, 16 miles, in an hour.
Photo by Tom Janus

Right: A striking note of
bold color is a ferry's
"line," an object often
overlooked by commuters.
Photo by Tom Janus

Opposite page, top: Pier 48, Seattle. In the background is the Smith Tower. At the beginning of the twentieth century it was the tallest building on the West Coast. There is no longer a Victoria car ferry service between Seattle and British Columbia. Photo by Tom Janus

Opposite page, bottom: Feeding the gulls is a common year-round activity; sitting outdoors watching the world go by is seasonal. Photo by Tom Janus

Right: Mosquito Fleet Festival display at Chamber offices in Port Orchard. Photo by Tom Janus

Below: Ferries crossing in the narrow passages between the San Juan Islands. Photo by Tom Janus

Seattle skyline and Colman Dock. Photo by Tom Janus

Chapter 8

A Commuter's Diary

With one eye on a camera viewfinder and the other eye on his watch, photographer Tom Janus has spent the last five years exploring ferryboats on various routes throughout Puget Sound. His purpose was to capture, on film and in the journal that follows, the day-to-day experience of a ferryboat ride. His observations run the gamut from eating cake aboard a catamaran on a politically motivated trial run to a ride with a noisy group of football fans on their way to a Seattle Seahawks game.

In addition to the special events, he has kept a detailed record of the routines and the challenges faced by thousands of Puget Sound residents who make their daily commute to work or school via ferry. Grumblings and complaints are part and parcel of commuting, no matter what the mode of transportation. A 1909 *Charleston Record* newspaper article noted, " The steamer *Kitsap* took the place of the *Kennedy* Wednesday. Some of the trips of the day were badly mixed, and the air is still blue from the gentle cussings of travelers from these parts."

More than 90 years later, today's ferry commuters are little different from their predecessors. The contemporary target for criticism is of course, the Washington State Ferry System—its ships and its crews. Despite the tendency to speak ill, commuters have to admit that ferry travel on Puget Sound is safe, for the most part reliable, and that the hard-working crews are generally friendly, helpful, and compassionate, gaining notoriety only on those few occasions when they fail. Above all, ferry commuting is a rare visual treasure. No bus, automobile, subway, or elevated train can match the experience of watching a 15-pound salmon jump two feet out of the water, or a pod of orcas swimming just off the

ferry's bow. If the sea life is not spectacular enough, there is always the combination of water—beautiful in different ways, depending on the prevailing shade of blue or gray—the evergreen trees blended with the seasonally colored maple and birch, and the mountains. Puget Sound is sandwiched between two magnificent mountain ranges. An eastward commute in the morning can yield spectacular views of the sun rising on Mount Rainier. The evening return westward heads straight towards the Olympic Mountains aglow with the setting sun.

Obviously, ferries have a lot to offer on a variety of levels. They are the state's number one tourist attraction and no visit to Washington is complete without a trip aboard one. The experience is intensified by putting all powers of observation into play and that is what this journal offers. What follows then, are observations, compiled over the course of several years.

12:00 a.m.

Somewhere in the greater Puget Sound area someone must be awake and celebrating. Seattle Mayor Paul Schell has declared that today is "Peter Bevis and the *Kalakala* Day." (7/99)

5:06 a.m. Seattle.

Morning news from T.V. Station Channel 5 indicated that two fast ferries were down with generator problems on the rush hour commute to and from Seattle and Bremerton. Washington State Ferries contacted another company, Clipper Navigation of Seattle, which has been running boats locally and to Canada since 1986. One of their *Victoria Clipper* catamarans came to the rescue. (12/99)

5:15 a.m. Port Orchard.

The weather report on local news stations announced fog all over the Seattle area. Crew on the ferries had to stand on the very front of the car decks and visually look out for things that radar would not pick up—kayakers and rogue logs in the bay. It was announced that ferryboats had not collided in the fog since 1991. (10/99)

5:20 a.m. Vashon.

The loading ramp has a malfunction. Morning news called it a "slow ramp," and passengers were advised of a 20 to 30 minute delay. Vashon Island residents, like those on the San Juan Island routes or Anderson Island, are especially vulnerable when ferries do not run normally. There are no bridges connecting these islands to the mainland. Unless a commuter has access to a private boat, plane, or helicopter when a ferry is down or delayed, there is little choice except waiting. It's a variable one accepts in choosing the relative isolation of island living. Ramp slow; life slow. (12/99)

5:22 a.m. Port Orchard.

The ferries make the morning news on television again. The Feds jump into the ferry funding issue as one local U.S. Congressman, Norm Dicks, a member of the powerful Appropriations Committee, urges the state legislature not to cut funds for the ferry system, which has been threat-

Above: Gulls off the Bremerton dock. Photo by Tom Janus

Opposite Page: The Victoria Clipper is shown here in Victoria's Inner Harbor. Photo by Tom Janus, courtesy, Clipper Narigation

ened with operational shortfalls. Service cuts could jeopardize Bremerton's status as a homeport, create annual difficulties for commuting personnel on the *USS Abraham Lincoln* and generally affect the quality of life in the area. (12/99)

5:30 a.m. Port Orchard.

Last trip for the *Admiral Pete*? A segment on the morning news indicated that this Labor Day weekend would see the last runs for the little ferry that operates during the summer and takes commuters and visitors from West Seattle to downtown Seattle. Along the way are the special sights afforded by the Elliott Bay waterfront.

This probably should not deter Kitsap Harbor Tour's Rick Leenstra Jr., a local businessman. His *Admiral Pete* is one of three boats that provide local tours to the Puget Sound Naval Shipyard and Tillicum Village on Blake Island, and had formerly shuttled commuters and tourists from Bremerton to Poulsbo, a summer destination spot for visitors to the region.

Several local officials and legislators seem to be very much in favor of developing a viable system of water taxis for the region. Rick may be one partner who helps them make it a reality. (9/99)

6:14 a.m. Bremerton.

High winds caused the cancellation of an early morning passenger-only ferry run on the Bremerton–Seattle route. A storm had blown in overnight from the south and carried winds between 40 and 70 knots.

Conversation, as it usually is during trip cancellations, was filled with dismay and travel angst over daily commuter issues. One woman nearby related that she had traveled on the ferries for 20 years, and only once had every boat on all routes been canceled due to weather conditions. Others complained that second-class Bremertonians did not get the service that riders on the Bainbridge route received when trips are cancelled. Someone suggested it might have been better to take the long drive around through Tacoma, but it was un-

known whether the Tacoma Narrows Bridge had been closed due to the winds. So it was best to be patient and wait.

As the winds and rain increased marginally, and the minutes went by more slowly, the ferry *Kitsap* finally appeared and I waited for the burst of applause that was not to come. Finally docked, loaded, and underway, it was now 8:20 a.m. A crew member made a general announcement that there would be a further ten-minute delay as the *Kitsap* detoured around Blake Island in order to avoid the high seas and gusts of 75 knots that been experienced earlier off Alki Point. Amid increasing disgruntlement, the coffee machines were turned off and food service discontinued in anticipation of rocking and rolling seas. People seemed glued at that point to books, newspapers and wrist watches. Cellular phones were out in force as family and employers had to be notified of yet another delay...(3/99)

6:15 a.m. Port Orchard

Light is barely breaking in the east, and there is a stillness between night and morning that is almost reverential. Both the *Retsil* and the *Thurow* are tied up side by side at the ferry landing. There is barely a ripple in the water, and they seem suspended in liquid glass. Both small vessels are now retired from the Horluck Fleet, and there are "for sale" signs posted at the boat yard, as they await their next incarnation.

I liked riding those boats on their 15-minute trip across the inlet to Bremerton and back. I've done it at midnight, the sole passenger, on the almost last trip of the day. I've been one of many on a packed commute at rush hour, when we crammed together, neighborly-like, sardine fashion, 40 or 50 of us. Sometimes there would be bikes on the crowded journey as well, making for more than enough jostling and ill-mannered comments. The best times were the summer rides on balmy mid-afternoons in August, when I sat on the steps and leaned across the metal safety chain that made a barrier in the open door frame. Sitting practically at water level, I'd occasionally catch a small splash or some welcome cooling spray. If I sincerely strained and reached over, I could drag my hand in the water, feeling the breezes and smelling the salty, crisp air.

But those trips are memories now, as our two retirees make way for progress, for bigger, for presumably better. I look over to them, as the sun begins to rise from behind the hills and change the midnight blue sky into hints of daylight, and I think how forlorn they seem to be, and how much I shall miss them. (9/99)

Two of the Horluck ferries at their Port Orchard dock, with the Olympic Mountains in the background. Photo by Tom Janus

Above: Ferry Hyak arriving at Kingston dock. Photo by Tom Janus

Left: A life-ring, a colorful note, on a Washington State ferry. Photo by Tom Janus

Sea lions on buoys are a common sight on the Puget Sound waters during clement months. Photo by Tom Janus

6:40 a.m. Bremerton Ferry Dock.

Hasty and colorful handmade signs covered all the windows at the ferry terminal: "7:15 a.m. Passenger-Only Canceled 3/19." I'd arrived half an hour early, and now there was over an hour to wait for the next boat.

"I heard the engine broke," said someone at my table. Poor old *Skagit*, she's been on this run for almost a month, replacing the local favorite *Tyee*, which has been laid up as well, presumably with a similar broken engine.

Travel concerns would probably keep the WSF phones busy all day, making the commute just that much more haggard. An increase of a hundred plus riders on the next ferry would generate even more body heat in the typically sauna-like passenger cabins of the big boats. I anticipated the marked exodus of passengers fleeing to the outdoor seating areas.

Ironically, we yearn even for the *Skagit*'s rapid return. She's not a comfortable vessel, but at times like this, degrees of inconvenience become relative. While the ferry system prides itself with on-time statistics above 99 percent, that other one percent, when you are in it, seems enormous. There has been a week of incessant wind and rain. Floods and mud slides, increasingly slow and dangerous traffic flow, creek and river overflows cascading into an already supersaturated soil. The annual spring deluge that seems to last 40 days and 40 nights is a way of life in Puget Sound. (3/98)

6:43 a.m. Bremerton.

A writer for a local newspaper cited 27 ferry delays or cancellations on the Bremerton run since the start of the year. Add one to that number for this morning's rush hour. There was no 6:30 ferry—steering problems, presumably—and the next ferry was so crowded that several dozen people missed that one as well.

Local editorialism in the Kitsap papers is calm, but relatively persistent. Both newspaper groups generally support the idea that a bit more competition in the ferryboat arena might be a good thing. There has not been a significantly charged debate on the issue of monopoly or privatization in at least a decade, and I suspect that many of these issues still have sensitive roots in the bitter feelings and political decisions of the late forties and early fifties. (4/97)

6:45 a.m. Bremerton.

This is the first day of the new summer schedule for the Seattle run. There is no *Tyee* in sight, and the *Chinook* is zigzagging in Sinclair Inlet at an unusual hour.

It is clear the *Tyee* will be late. There is no announcement on their service board on the walkway, but the crowd knows. Collective ferryboat wisdom brings grumbled laughter and the rolling of eyes. The *Tyee* has become notorious for its problems, and communication between the ferry system and its riders is often not the model of efficiency.

The line has grown to almost 400 people, and the *Chinook* appears dead in the water off Manette, a half mile away. There is no *Tyee*.

Only the passengers at the very head of the line can see the disruption sign at the point of boarding. If you are not among the first 20 or 30 passengers, you cannot see the posting that it is the *Chinook* that is out of service. You do not see the advisory: EXPECT DELAYS.

The *Tyee*, the boat we love and hate, finally arrives after 7:00 a.m. and departs, loaded, 15 minutes later. Well over 100 riders could not board, but must have been pleased because the *Chinook* appeared to live once more and has resumed service. (7/99)

6:48 a.m. Sinclair Inlet.

It was not bumper-to-bumper, or prow-to-keel, but nonetheless it was a maritime traffic jam in Sinclair Inlet. This long and narrow waterway is a sheltered spot that separates the communities of Port Orchard, Gorst, Manette, and Bremerton. Its gentle waves, even during fierce winter storms, wash around moorings, marinas and warships. These are the waters of the Puget Sound Naval Shipyard.

This is rush hour with a plus, one that we would have for a couple of months.

Recently the aircraft carrier *USS Abraham Lincoln* had come back to the region for an overhaul. The *Clipper* had been leased from Clipper Navigation by the navy to shuttle crew members back and forth between the two bases. The charter would help reduce what a local newspaper suggested could have been a four-hour daily commute for navy personnel. (3/99)

7:00 a.m. Christmas season.

Fog, the kind we call "pea soup" fog, has been covering the Puget Sound area on and off, mostly on, for a week. Weather reporters frequently announced a quarter-mile visibility at the airport. On the ferries, if the fog was at its densest, one couldn't see much beyond the windows. All commuters, land, sea, and air could wisely expect and accept general transit slowness. (12/99)

7:23 a.m. Chez *Chinook* Salon.

The vanity mirror was perched on top of a small bottle

Entering Friday Harbor in the San Juan Islands. Photo by Tom Janus

of water, gourmet Northwest no doubt. To its left, eye-glasses rest on a lipstick smudged tissue, along with a hairbrush, its pink-tipped plastic prongs upright like sea urchin spines. A well-soiled, battery-operated, hand-held hair curler, a lipstick, an eyebrow pencil. War paint had been appropriately applied prior to the application of these most recent tools.

Periodically the mirror had to be adjusted to make visible the increasing mounds of rolled waves of short, sandy blond hair. Pink and well-manicured fingernails matched the hairbrush, now increasingly called into action, a thicket of lost hair added to the brush with each tender stroke.

The ritual precise, practiced, like clockwork, creating a coif in the tall and rounded wave that was stylish in the 1940s, and updated to 1999 with portable cosmetic technology. With more brushing and fine tuning a big hair enhanced fluff of bouffant emerged, round and pouffy and gleaming, its curls now melded into the appropriate helmet of style, with another day's face prepared to meet Seattle under gray clouds and the chilly temperatures of early summer. (6/99)

7:30 a.m. Rich Passage.

Headed into Sinclair Inlet, on the way to Bremerton, was our local favorite carrier, the *USS Carl Vinson*. One of the latest nuclear powered aircraft carriers, it carries so large a crew that it is the size of a small town, and its deck is the length of three football fields end-to-end. There were helicopters overhead, and beside the ship fireboats made a welcoming cascade. The carrier's crew had manned the rails, and many on the *Tyee* made for the nearest windows and the outside compartment to wave and shout

and welcome the big carrier. Several sailors on the *Carl Vinson* returned the salute.

Bremerton is still proud of its century-long naval tradition, and the surrounding country is home for hundreds of navy families. It is always a special event when a ship comes home, and the experience of the passing of boats in home waters, especially when riding the ferries, is a treasured memory for many. (5/99)

7:30 a.m. Bremerton.

The auto holding lanes snaked around the entrance of the shipyard and three blocks up Pacific Avenue. This meant the closest ferry access lanes were filled. I didn't know which ferry was running at this time, and wondered whether the boat would be full by the time I reached the toll booth. Being at the end of the queue brings on a certain amount of commuting anxiety, especially since the wait for the next ferry would be almost an hour and a half.

Our boat however, was the Jumbo Class *M/V Walla Walla*, built along with her sister ship the *M/V Spokane*, in 1973 at the Todd Shipyards in Seattle. For 25 years the jumbos were the largest ferries in the fleet. Today she was quite large enough to accommodate all of us with room to spare.

Larger and full of amenities, the jumbos are a treat for Bremertonians. Aside from greater capacity, the dining area is double the size that locals are used to, with the added perk of having an espresso bar in the Compass Café. But booth seating without tables at the windows does allow for a favorite pastime—using the seats as beds. I counted three dozen sprawled sleepers being rocked by soothing motions, or the steady hum of engines. (11/99)

7:33 a.m. Bremerton.

The Bremerton Sun's bold headline reads "Deep Cuts for Ferries." Last week, Washington voters—57 percent of them—approved Initiative 695, which reduced car license fees for most drivers, and required voter approval on future tax and fee hikes. The initiative passed in almost all of Washington's counties, including Kitsap County, a community significantly affected by transportation issues. What was still left for the future was how the chasm between decreased state revenues and increasing demand for public works would play out.

Opposite page, top:
Carlisle II *regularly crossed Sinclair Inlet from Port Orchard to Bremerton. In 2001 she was assigned to*

other duties in Hilton Smith's fleet, but occasionally fills in on the Inlet. Photo by Tom Janus

Opposite page, bottom:
M.V. Coho *returning from Victoria B.C. to Port Angeles harbor. Olympic Mountains in background. Photo by Tom Janus*

The state ferry system receives most of its operating budget from car license tab taxes. Should the legislature not reapportion its remaining monies, WSF will see a large shortfall. Service cuts have been projected for the entire system. Ferry system Director, Paul Green indicated that all options would be considered so that transportation needs would be met. (11/99)

7:40 a.m. Port Angeles.

A day trip to Victoria, B.C. Another ferryboat ride. We'd decided not to take our car over, so we were able to make reservations and ride the *Victoria Express*, a passenger-only ferry that is part of Jack Harmon's company, Victoria Rapid Transit, Inc.

Above: The California vessel, Intintoli, *docked at the Bremerton Marina. Photo by Tom Janus*

The *Express* runs to Victoria from Port Angeles during the clement weather months, roughly from the end of May through mid-October. During the off season she does charters, special events, and seasonal whale watching. Had we wanted to take a car, we'd need to ride Black Ball Transport, Inc.'s *M.V. Coho*, which accommodates about 100 vehicles and up to 1,000 passengers.

Our smaller ferry, at 105-feet, makes the crossing in an hour, doing 18-20 knots. She is powered by three diesel engines that provide 2,000 HP. The *Coho*, at slightly over 340-feet, with two Cooper-Bessemer diesels, produces 4,000 HP, cruises at about 15 knots, and takes a bit longer to make the trip. We'd leave a few minutes before the *Coho*, spend the day around Victoria's Inner Harbour, see two ferries from Clipper Navigation nearby, and return on the 6:15, in time for a view of the sun going down in the west over the Strait of Juan de Fuca. (8/99)

7:45 a.m. Admiralty Inlet.

A quiet overcast morning on the *Tyee* headed for Seattle. A crew member announced that a fast-ferry, on loan from California, was cruising in the harbor, doing 30 knots on its trials this week in Puget Sound. She's here on a promotional tour, a sister ferry to the type in development for Washington state. These faster passenger-only ferries would carry between 300–400 people on a relatively wake-free commute at 30 knots. This new generation of boats would cut the local one-way commute in half, down to 30 minutes. (2/98)

8:30 a.m. Port Orchard.

The *Mary L* is back in the water at the Port Orchard marine boat shop. She has new paint and a new name. There are two or three guys working on her this morning, sanding down the rough spots and doing odd jobs on her interior. The helm has been ripped apart and rewired,

waiting for finishing touches. The diminutive wheel doesn't appear to be able to turn and steer a boat of this size. More electrical wiring has to be done before the seats can be redone and the galley and the head finished.

Captain Ed Morgan says she'll be certified to carry around 100 passengers, both inside and aft, where a semi-enclosed area is being built for the convenience of bikers, passengers who like the marine air, persons in wheelchairs, and smokers. (8/99)

8:45 a.m. Bremerton.

By 9 a.m., a few locals had begun to queue up under the clock at the ferry terminal. When the M/V *Intintoli* docked a half hour later, the crowd had grown to a hundred. It did not seem a large number for a Saturday morning, but more people were expected for the harbor rides before noon. Bremertonians do not often support special events and the lack of an appreciable turnout might have been expected.

The *Intintoli*, a catamaran on loan from Vallejo, California, sped through Rich Passage on her way to Blake Island at 34 knots. The acceleration was noticeable. I walked around the spacious and uncrowded double decks. Built for 300 passengers, the vessel featured aircraft-like side by side seating, and a range of booths and tables. Designed for a one hour commute in San Francisco Bay, it featured a snack bar. The Bremerton–Seattle version, with a shorter commute, would have no refreshments and would carry 50 more riders. The trip would take half an hour, a marked improvement from current commuting times.

Ferry workers extolled the smooth ride and the reduced wake, even as the boat surged to top operating speed. Less than optimistic guests felt Bremerton would not receive two such boats, and they'd believe it when they saw it. Similarly, a deck hand suggested that homeowners on "the island" would probably complain about the almost non-existent wake and lobby the 35 knot, half-hour journey, back to the stone age. He envisioned these multi-million dollar catamarans caught up in local politics and ultimately reduced to minimal speeds with only negligible reductions in commute time. (2/97)

9:00 a.m.

The *Kalakala*, which had returned to Seattle in early November, and remained moored near the Pike Place Market area of downtown, moved to its new, temporary

Harbor celebration as the Kalakala returned to Seattle on November 6, 1998. Mayor Paul Schell and Peter Bevis accept cheers of the audience. Photo by Tom Janus

Opposite page: At Elliott Bay, crowds await the start of the day's program. Photo by Tom Janus

home at Lake Union. It is still undetermined when restoration will begin and where she will finally reside. (3/98)

9:00 a.m. Bremerton.

This weekend part of the walk-on passenger ferry dock was moved a hundred yards down the boardwalk, a temporary location while construction continued on the site of the new transportation hub. The old dock is slated for removal as design and building continues for the new terminal. During this process, ferry boats were switched to accommodate different loading and unloading needs. (9/99)

10:00 a.m. Bremerton.

A crisp fall morning and the ferry is running late. It is football season and jocks and jockettes of all ages await a replacement boat for the trip to Seattle to watch the Seahawks play Green Bay.

It grew apparent that the boat would be late. Just days earlier, a local ferry had run aground in the fog, and other boats had to be shuffled to maintain schedules. Already it was after departure time, and no boat in sight. But sight did not go far, as pea soup white fog hung dense and deep, insinuating its way into sporting psyches.

Camaraderie boarded with us, late, but still with time to make it to the game. A festive mood filled the ferry, which seemed to be packed way beyond standing room only and the strictures of the Coast Guard's regulations. (9/96)

10:00 a.m. Elliott Bay.

After thirty years of use as a fish cannery and subsequent abandonment, including ten years as a glimmer in Peter Bevis's eye, and several days on the high seas and the Inland Passage, the *Kalakala* was home. Amid a flotilla of small vessels, pleasure boats, water cannons, and kayaks, our *Silver Bird* was towed to dock at the Odyssey Center as the Star Spangled Banner played. Coast Guard boats provided official escort, and when passing ferries detoured and signaled welcome to her, the crowd became one huge wet eye.

Perhaps a thousand people were there for the celebration. Mayor Paul Schell and a half dozen local officials congratulated Peter Bevis as the band played the Black Ball anthem. There was abundant local pride as film crews and reporters staked out vantage points and every corner held an interview in progress.

The *Kalakala* had been stripped down and prepared for her trip from Alaska with a new coat of paint, which appeared to glint when the clouds parted and sun shone through on her hull. Once touted as "First in Style...", she had returned battered, but intact for a welcoming filled with the rosy glow of pride and optimism. (11/98)

10:20 a.m. Port Townsend-Friday Harbor.

We watched for whales out of Port Townsend, and there were none. Or rather, we weren't where they were.

Three pods of orcas stay in the region year-round, not generally venturing into the ocean. They are our resident whales. People in the area, maritime vessels, Coast Guard tour boats and ferries, planes and pleasure craft, look out for them. When spotted, information is relayed to groups in both Washington and British Columbia. Boats can call in and ask for the location of the whales, and when possible, approach them, although they have to be careful not to get too close.

Today the orcas were too far dispersed. One pod was sighted near Neah Bay, another in Haro Straight. The third pod was missing altogether. (6/99)

11:00 a.m. Port Orchard waterfront.

Bob Ulsh is one of the official greeters at the Chamber of Commerce. He is secretary to the local Northwest Mosquito Fleet Society. This is his day. It is the annual Mosquito Fleet Festival, and he is there to answer questions and direct visitors to sites and activities in the area.

At a desk there is his Mosquito Fleet listing. He keeps it filled with relevant information for about 575 of the 1,000 boats that comprised the fleet. Docked outside is the last remaining ferryboat from that era that is still in operation. The *Carlisle II*, built in the San Juans during World War I, works weekends until the end of October, at which point she will retire to the boatyard for restoration. Today she is moored and the pilot house is open to visitors. As a floating museum, her walls are full of framed photos and articles that illuminate the Mosquito Fleet Era. Modern electronics and a contemporary steer-

ing mechanism have replaced the steering wheel I expected to see, but the latter is there in the wooden model of the vessel that Les Johnson has just completed and which is on view at the Chamber office. (9/99)

11:03 a.m.

A month later, and the notices tell us "*Tyee* returns to service." What might have been front page news in happier times, today's announcement has been relegated to page A7 of the second section of *The Sun*, Bremerton's daily newspaper. The *Tyee*, the vessel with whom Bremertonian's have a love/hate relationship, is out of service so frequently on the run that news of her has become banal. (6/99)

12:20 p.m. Sinclair Inlet.

This was the first time I rode the new Horluck boat, the *Mary L.* There are not many passengers at this time of the afternoon. I sat up in the front row and watched Captain Ed fiddle with electronics as Captain Bill watched and tended to his pilot's duties.

The radar box was acting up, although there was no need to use it under today's clear sky. This inlet is considered a protected waterway and small vessels that do not venture out of it are not required by the Coast Guard to carry radar. When the area is covered with fog, it is a blessing. Today was a day for exuberant

salmon. Not far from the dock construction site, what seemed a ten-pound salmon leapt about two feet in the air and landed four or five feet further. These past two weeks, passengers have noticed many jumping fish in the area, and while I've heard the splashes, this is the first time I've seen one. The crew seemed preoccupied with making adjustments to the balky radar device and checking its screen, so there were no salmon announcements. 10/99)

1:00 p.m. Keystone Ferry Dock,

George Terek is suited up and within minutes he'll be in the water off Admiralty Head. A few last questions from well wishers, some moments for the last photos at the shoreline, and then he walks waist deep into Admiralty Inlet. In moments he is 100 feet out, swimming on his back with five and a half miles to go to Port Townsend, just southwest, the other terminus of the ferry run to and from Keystone on Whidbey Island. His support boat, *Island Dream* out of Bothell, WA, carries his wife, daughter and friends. It will keep an appropriate distance alongside him on his swim.

Mr. Terek is a captain for Washington State Ferries, a soft-spoken but intent man. His hope

Above: A tug approaches the Port Townsend waterfront. Photo by Tom Janus

Opposite page: The Tacoma takes on a realistic look at Todd Shipyards. Seattle skyline in background. Photo by Les Morton, courtesy, Todd Pacific Shipyards, Seattle

is to swim all the WSF ferry routes, and this one will get him a swim closer to his goal.

It is Labor Day Weekend, and he has studied the routes and the currents and the tides, anticipating the temperature. Today, Saturday, is overcast with filtered sunlight straining through a broad expanse of flat clouds. The air temperature in the morning was in the fifties, and by noon had warmed up to the mid-sixties. Five or six hours later, when he hopes to reach Port Townsend, it should be ten degrees warmer still, with clear skies and sunshine. George's face, the only part of him that is exposed, is covered with sun block and his nose and lips are white with zinc oxide. On the earlier trip, when he was less prepared, he was seriously sunburned.

I walked with him a hundred yards or so from the head of the campground near the ferry dock, along the rocky beach to a point he found suitable. A writer from the local newspaper also keeps stride, as do a half-dozen people who came out to see him off and impart good wishes. This small band of followers kept a respectful distance as he barreled 15 feel in front of us. There was a short jaunt to the water's edge, a farewell wave;

as we applauded him and his dream, he turned and was in the water. (9/99)

1:00 p.m. Vashon Island.

Vashon and Maury Island sit surrounded by arms of Puget Sound and three counties. A century ago, steamers stopped at more than a dozen points on the Island. Fifty years ago the Vashon community was in the forefront of efforts to change the nature of ferry transportation in the region, the result of which was the state's purchase of the Black Ball fleet.

Today I ride the *Issaquah*, one of four ferries in the *Issaquah 130* series, so called because they carry 130 vehicles rather than the smaller boats of the 100 series. Built in 1979 by Marine Power & Equipment, and rebuilt a decade later, the *Issaquah* is a namesake of a previous ferry which sailed Lake Washington in the early 1900s. (11/99)

2:00 p.m. Everett.

Trips on the *Victoria Clipper III* were part of a special event sponsored by the Kingston Chamber of Commerce, a VIP day as the community's movers and shakers gathered to show support and rally the

region behind efforts to lobby the state Department of Transportation. The goal was to create a bottom-up surge of interest that might cause the state legislature to provide more rapid water transit on new proposed routes.

Chamber members were numerous, and they were joined by reporters and camera crews, business people, interested citizens and commuters, area boosters, and ranking naval officers from Homeport Everett. Miss Kingston and her court offered hospitality to a friendly local congresswoman.

The *Clipper III* had been chartered to provide an example of the beneficial effects of providing similar boats for the region. Seattle's Clipper Navigation operates four high speed passenger-only Clipper catamarans, as well as the *San Juan Explorer* and the larger car ferry, the *Princess Marguerite III*, which once served the Victoria B.C., Seattle, and San Juan Islands routes. *Clipper III*, sleek in blue, white, and red graphics that resemble the Union Jack, is the mid-sized sister of the fleet. At 114 feet, she cruises at 25 knots on local waterways, carrying 231 passengers. (9/98)

2:25 p.m. Entering Bremerton.

I'm standing on the outside deck of the *Sealth* as she prepares to dock. One of the pilings is occupied again this year. It is a sea gull chick, mottled brown and white, just half the size of the attending parent. (6/99)

2:35 p.m. Bremerton.

There was a moment of comic relief—ferry boat humor—as the formerly "fast" new ferry *Chinook* prepared to leave the Bremerton dock for Seattle. One of the crew bellowed from the loading ramp: "Last call for the SLOW ferry to Seattle!"

The past month had seen front page headlines in local newspapers and extensive TV coverage regarding a civil action by a group of waterfront property owners who claimed the *Chinook* was responsible for erosion of their beaches, and who petitioned that the fast-ferry be mandated to reduce its speed in Rich Passage.

The state Supreme Court upheld a lower court ruling mandating the slowdown, with a court date for final resolution to be held in 2000. In the meantime, today was the first day of the slowdown. A one-way commute increased from half an hour to at least 45 minutes. The *Chinook*, which had traveled its run at almost 40 knots, slowed to a more leisurely 12 knots for part of the journey. Its normal speed increased when it was not in the disputed area, Rich Passage.

I had expected pickets and protests and banners when I boarded for the 7 a.m. run, but there were none. The ferry was not quite full the past few days either, and I wondered whether commuters were making alternative travel plans.

Fifteen minutes do not seem like much in the cosmic scheme, but they have been enough to involve courts, counties, chambers, state and federal governments. (8/99)

3:25 p.m. Rich Passage.

Nature abounds in ferry regions. There were pigeons in the passenger compartment again, a not unusual hitchhiking experience. Outside there were salmon escapees.

Coming into Seattle, just beyond Alki Point, there in the distance was a flotilla of small craft. A dozen diminutive vessels, floating gently on peaceful waters, waiting for the fish in a midsummer harvest. Armed with small nets and fishing poles, they waited like a posse to capture rogue, freedom seeking salmon.

Regional news this past week told of ruptured nets in fish holding pens and the loss of 300,000 salmon to the waters and inlets adjoining Bainbridge Island, Bremerton, Port Orchard and other points north, west, south and east. The salmon were being raised off the southern shore of Bainbridge, but a dangerous growth of algae threatened the stock. In the process of towing the fish pens to a safer place, nets ripped in transit. Thus the saga of escaped salmon.

The saga continued in the media with a twist. After a long period of fishing negotiations between the U.S. and Canada, some northerly neighbor fishermen increased the rancor of the debate on overfishing by blockading an Alaska ferryboat for several hours. Diplomatic wires were exchanged, further legal and punitive issues ensued, there was the prescribed 15 minutes of Warholian fame and notoriety. When the ferry and its hostage passengers were finally free to travel, the political and economic realities of salmon continued. (7/99)

3:35 p.m. Bremerton Dock.

Baby chick is two weeks older and now about 2/3 the size of its parents and has outgrown its earlier newborn cuteness. Mottled gray, its head seems too close to the body, the regal neck still unformed. Its caw is incessant as always. The baby bird now actively moved around the nesting area, and I watched as it made two tentative attempts at flying, beating its too small wings. It managed to get airborne for seconds, only a foot or so off solid piling. (8/99)

4:15 p.m. Seattle. President's Day.

The last remnants of an early spring weekend that was ushered in with St. Valentine's Love Day. Clouds broke sporadically into a powder blue sky. Moments of sun shone

off windowpanes sixty stories high in the Columbia Tower.

Ferryboat *Sealth* departed on schedule at 4:15, leaving the Colman Dock for Bremerton. At the end of a three day weekend, the *Sealth* was a true tourist boat. Dozens of hooded, parka-clad visitors stood in the wind of the stern deck. Cameras were in abundance.

In conversation, visitors from Bellingham traded weekend getaway comments with people from Everett. (2/99)

4:17 p.m. Edmonds.

The heat of summer in the northwest begins in the later part of the afternoon, when the sun is at its height and the temperatures reach their daily peak. This may seem strange to visitors and newcomers to the area, folks who are more used to the heat of day occurring closer to noon or early afternoon. It is a matter of geography and latitudes, however. Seattle and the Puget Sound lie across a parallel that place them further north than Minneapolis, Toronto and Montreal.

Riding the ferries at this time, going from east to west, can be a pleasure if you are in line early and can make the connection. It is tourist season, and delays on several routes can reach two to four hours. Though the Super Class of ferries on this run to Kingston can accommodate about 160 vehicles and 2,500 passengers, it is not unusual for many to be left behind, waiting for the next vessel. The system does not have enough boats to accommodate peak summer demands.

On this run, the *M/V Yakima*, one of four vessels in its class, is full. Built in 1967 in San Diego, she and the other Super Class vessels are shorter and lighter in weight than the Jumbos that run between Bainbridge Island and Seattle; they carry more passengers but fewer cars. Both classes are spacious, with two decks for passengers, and lots of outdoor space. Today, under the warm sun and with a cooling breeze, there are many people outside. Seagulls hover, mindful of the desire of passengers to feed them.

These are the better parts of an experience that makes

riding the ferries the major tourist attraction in the Seattle area. Summer over gentle seas. (8/97)

4:30 p.m. Port Orchard.

Grapes, sour. Just days ago, the state of Washington voters pamphlet arrived in our P.O. Box. On the cover was a photo collage, and among the elements was a ferryboat from the Mosquito Fleet. The vessel was *The Virginia V*, steaming in from the right, below a sedate Mt. Rainier and a Boeing aircraft, presumably, among other images.

Today's *Port Orchard Independent* had two paragraphs in its "On the Campaign Trail" column, in which it was noted that the montage's featured boat was NOT the local *Carlisle II*, "the last active vessel from the fleet and well-known to folks here." Locals, of course, would have preferred that "their" boat grace the front cover, rather than the *Virginia V*. (10/99)

4:50 p.m. Bremerton.

I sat on the sun deck of the Horluck Ferry's *Eagle*, and overheard a conversation about the departure of the *USS Abraham Lincoln*. It was an event I'd read about in the papers, but one which I wasn't able to attend.

Earlier this morning, its number "72" was bright in the predawn when I rode across the inlet to catch the 6:30 a.m. ferry to Seattle. The *Abraham Lincoln* had

completed its overhaul at the shipyard and was to leave the area at midday to continue its journey to the homeport of Everett.

Last spring, in March, the navy had leased a catamaran from Clipper Navigation in Seattle to shuttle crew back and forth between the two bases. During the morning rush hour commute, the *Victoria Clipper* became another vessel in what had become a bustling Sinclair Inlet, bursting with boats. In addition to the navy's shuttle, the local waters were filled with other ferries— the big car and passenger boats from the state's system, as well as the passenger-only vessel *Tyee*, and two local ferries from the Horluck Transportation Company which carried shipyard workers and Seattle commuters from the surrounding area to Bremerton. It resembled a two-hour maritime traffic jam, with boats going back and forth between Seattle, Bremerton, Port Orchard and Annapolis.

Now some several hundred riders would be gone until the next ship arrived and the cycle resumed. (9/99)

5:10 p.m. Edmonds to Kingston.

Someone remarked that the latest Jumbo Mark IV ferries were quiet and smooth, almost to the point of being eerie. I sensed this on the *M/V Puyallup*. Whatever the sea currents and winds were doing, I could not feel them. There was motion without movement, it seemed, and any external sounds, waves or the cries of gulls or passing ships, were muffled and screened from the cabins. There was a silence and calm here that is usually found in parts of libraries or places of worship or art museums. On the car deck, with front and rear open to the elements, there was a subtle rocking and the felt force of wind pulled through passageways, still peculiarly quiet. The humming of engines made only scant subliminal impressions. (11/99)

5:48 p.m.

Civility. Horluck Transportation Company style.

Barring storm or calamity, the Horluck boats leave Bremerton for Port Orchard on the quarter hour. Promptly. After all, a marquee says it is a "reliable" ferry. Tonight the captain and crew of the *Carlisle II* waited for late passengers.

My boat, the *Skagit*, just arrived. It was a few minutes behind schedule and her unloading prevented the next arriving ferry from docking on time. since the current temporary dock accommodates one Washington State Ferry at a time. Good neighbor *Carlisle* waited on the other side of the dock those few extra minutes for the *Chinook* to disgorge her riders, and while only a few of them were bound for Port Orchard, they were happy commuters spared having to wait another half hour for the next connection. (11/99)

9:30 PM. Port Orchard.

Since many of our Puget Sound communities are dependent on their ferries, especially where there are no bridges or convenient freeways from one point to another, it is not uncommon for the area's newspapers to cover transportation issues and devote frequent front page space to ferry matters.

Hilton Smith, current owner of Horluck Transportation Company, has been profiled dozens of times in recent years. Referred to as "Ferry Godfather"—in distinction from former state legislator Karen Schmidt, the "Ferry Godmother"—the Horluck side of his enterprises has been taking shots. Today's *Port Orchard Independent* ran, as its headline, "There's trouble aboard the good ship Horluck." The lead-in, "Commuters grumble about service, subsidies," indicates that recent down boats, missed runs and lapses in customer service suggest a certain unreliability, at least according to one quoted commuter. This from a historic little ferry company that prided itself as being "reliable."

Horluck, like many caught in a financial morass because of recent tax-cutting initiatives and the conflicting needs of diverse groups, wonders what to do. Having received "subsidies" to operate their boats on routes where Kitsap Transit, the local bus company, could not provide adequate transportation for its residents, Horluck now finds its revenue source diminished, and its future uncertain.

The issues are complex and frustrating for everyone involved, and there are no immediate solutions.

Whether Horluck remains in the ferry business, or whether it will convert to a cruise and charter operation, is a matter still undetermined. Hilton Smith continued to take meetings daily. Riders around the Sound wonder what the State Legislature and voters will ultimately decide, how their commutes will be impacted, and how much the fares will be. Over a thousand local Horluck commuters take it day by day, waiting for the issue to play out. (1/00)

Above: The newly returned Kalakala was open to the public for two months before she was moved to her Lake Union moorage. Seattle's other icon, the Space Needle, looms in the background. Photo by Tom Janus

Opposite page: The Space Needle and the Smith Tower flank the downtown area of Seattle. Photo by Tom Janus

M/V Snohomish *under-taking maneuvering trials in July 1999. Courtesy, Dakota Creek Industries*

Chapter 9

Ferries and the Future

Ferries of the future and the future of Puget Sound Ferries are two very different topics thoroughly entwined with each other. As the Washington State Ferry System passed the half-century mark, some things had changed drastically, some had stayed the same and the overall future was so murky that many a state legislator, ferry official, island dweller, businessman, and commuter would have loved to possess a crystal ball and a clear vision. One of the things that had not changed was the constant need to maintain infrastructure—boats and terminals, the pressure for more ferries, bigger ferries, or faster ferries on every route, and increasing costs battling against shrinking revenues.

During the controversy over the Issaquah class ferries in the early part of the 1980s, a report on the Washington State Ferry system postulated that many of the system's problems stemmed from an organization which lacked future-oriented focus and therefore found itself overwhelmed by day-to-day activities and constant crises. The failure to anticipate change and the inability to react to change are crippling flaws in any organization. WSF worked diligently to correct problems with the system. More public communication and an emphasis on customer service successfully improved the public's image of ferries and ferry workers, although area press continued to revel in WSF errors, typically giving them front page status.

One of the successes of the Washington State Ferry System in the 1990s was enhanced communications with its customers. Starting with the monthly newsletter, *Inland Crossings*, ferry officials made a concerted effort to acquaint the residents of Puget Sound with their ferries, ferry history, ferry personnel, and ferry news. *Inland Crossings* proved to be a valuable aid in dispensing information to a

society that runs on information. The newsletter was followed by a WSF Internet website which provided schedules and updates to anyone with access to a computer. Subsequently, computer access to WSF evolved to include an e-mail notification system so that commuters could be warned of canceled runs. Global positioning systems (GPS) aboard ferries made it possible for customers to use the Internet to track their ferries en route.

Technology also permeated vessel engine rooms and wheel houses with computerized controls that could perform routine tasks in addition to monitoring the ships' systems. Still, after 50 years of operation, cars are still loaded on boats two at a time Noah's Ark style, and one wonders why more innovations have not appeared. As Washington State Ferries moved toward a more future-oriented focus the system encountered a series of roadblocks. What happened to change the future of ferries is a study of success followed by bitter disappointment and a possible new beginning.

In the early 1990s the future seemed rosy. Plans called for brand new jumbo ferries to ease the load on existing vessels so that the system as a whole could carry more cars and passengers. Weekend travelers to the Olympic Peninsula would no longer be left sitting on the docks waiting for the next boat because the one just pulling

away from the slip was full. On a holiday weekend motorists might face as much as a three boat wait on some ferry routes. Space on the popular San Juan Island ferries was so limited that reservations were required for those seeking passage aboard the vessel.

By June 1995 Seattle's Todd Pacific Shipyards was assembling the units in Washington State Ferries' newest class of vessel, the Jumbo Mark II. Less than four years later the trio of vessels, the *Tacoma*, *Wenatchee*, and *Puyallup*, were sailing the waters of central Puget Sound. At 460-feet, the Jumbo Mark IIs are the longest ferries of their type in North America. They are also the first ferries ever designed in-house by WSF's Vessel Design group. The long planning phase was characterized by the involvement of ferry crews in the initial design ideas. A decision process that relied on inclusion and feedback helped in avoiding the most obvious mistakes of the Issaquah class ferries. Like businesses everywhere, ferries benefited from more enlightened management techniques.

All three ferries were built from the same basic blueprint and employed a new and more efficient unit-by-unit construction process. For each ferry, 116 separate units were pre-built at Todd's Bellingham shipyard and moved to Seattle for assembly on the launchways. The building-block approach creates an entirely different visual pattern for watching a ship come together—different and fascinating. The completed vessels could each carry 2,500 passengers and 218 automobiles.

With a bit of Northwest humor, Todd Shipyard's special supplement to the *Pacific Maritime Magazine*'s October 1997 issue described the new *M/V Tacoma* in great detail, pointing out among other things that the sloping pilot house windows cut down the glare off the water for the 60 days a year when the sun shines in Seattle. Aside from the engine room, bridge, and various other mechanical rooms that ferry travelers never see, the *Tacoma* has crew quarters for up to 26 people although a regular crew would number 15. Unlike the crews of the early steam ferries who were forced to live on the boats, Washington State ferry employees have the option of staying aboard or not. Given work schedules that call for days of long shifts followed by days off, sleeping aboard may be desirable.

Other Jumbo Mark II class amenities not previously seen on Puget Sound ferries, but certainly reflective of modern lifestyles, were the two "baby changing stations" and passenger-cabin table outlets so that travelers with laptops could work while riding the ferry.

For walk-on commuters there was the promise of fast, frequent, and comfortable passenger-only ferries. While island residents like their isolation to varying degrees—some prefer to think of Sound waters as a moat protecting them from the outside world—Bremerton has been somewhat eager to become one of Seattle's "bedroom communities." Local business interests, especially those in real estate, promoted the idea of a fast commuter link to Seattle as a means of attracting new residents to a city

that has been in a tailspin of decline for the past 20 years. South Kitsap boosters, as well, hoped to reap the benefits if new faster ferries resulted in an influx of people fleeing from Seattle's increasingly expensive and urbanized corridor.

When the State of Washington went searching for a design for the passenger-only fast ferries scheduled to be added to the fleet in the late 1990s, there was one major concern—the design had to result in a boat with low-wake action.

The concern over wake-wash has a long history. In 1922, the Puget Sound Navigation Company moved its steamer *Indianapolis* to the Bremerton run in place of the *H. B. Kennedy*. The *Indianapolis*'s blunt bow and deep hull created substantial bow waves when the boat hit maximum speeds. In the narrow waters of Rich Passage at high tides, the bow waves smashed into the shorelines,

M/V Tacoma at Todd Pacific Shipyards, prior to launching. Photo by Les Morton, courtesy, Todd Pacific Shipyards

eroding beaches and damaging bulkheads. Irate water-front residents had raised such a hue and cry, the *Indianapolis* was forced to reduce speeds. The next vocal force heard from were the commuters who resented the effect of the slowdown on ferry schedules. The controversy ended when the *Indianapolis* returned to the wide open waters of the Seattle–Tacoma run and the *H.B. Kennedy*, having been renamed as the *Seattle,* was restored to the route she had traveled since 1909.

In 1935, angry Rich Passage property owners east of Port Orchard on Wautauga Beach filed a lawsuit against Puget Sound Navigation Company. The suit, asking for $26,000 in damages, charged that the ferry *Chippewa* was responsible for heavy swells that damaged beaches, injured clam beds, and destroyed bulkheads. Like the *Indianapolis*, the *Chippewa* had originated as a Great Lakes steamer and the two boats shared the same bow and hull characteristics. The trial ended in a hung jury and the case was dismissed.

In 1991, shortly after the first class of passenger-only vessels, the *Tyee, Kalama,* and *Skagit* were introduced into Puget Sound, there were again complaints from shoreline residents along Rich Passage about the damage caused by ferry waves. Special consultants hired by the ferry system determined that the ferries in question could travel through Rich Passage at a speed of 11-12 knots without damage to the environment. Since boats like the *Tyee* could normally do 21-knots, the study resulted in a significant slow-down—a disappointment to Bremerton commuters who had looked forward to spending less time on the ferries.

The Chinook *under construction in 1997. The underside of a ferry is a view most passengers do not see. Courtesy, Dakota Creek Industries*

The *Tyee* affair—some Bremertonians thought of it as yet another ferry debacle—did serve as a warning to ferry officials that the next generation of passenger-only boats would have to be trouble-free in the area of wake wash. Washington State Ferries' long-range plans called for a fleet of six 350-passenger-only vessels that would serve routes connecting Kingston, Vashon, Southworth, and Bremerton. WSF projected that by the year 2005 the four routes would carry a total of 18,345 people each day. Bremerton alone was anticipated to have 5,140 daily commuters who could reach Seattle in 35 minutes rather than the traditional 50 minutes.

The idea that speed is proportional to wake-wash, particularly in high-speed lightweight vessels, is a misconception. Considerable time and effort were spent in calculating and then testing wake wash action on prospective designs. The 1991 consultant's study had established "no harm" parameters for wake wash in Rich Passage. Using the "no harm" level as a baseline, a sophisticated computer program called Computational Fluid Dynamics was used to match boat design with water characteristics and other factors, such as beach slope, to determine which designs best met the baseline level. Only when they were satisfied that there would be no problem, did state officials select an Anacortes-based company to build one of the ferries with an option to build a second. In partnership with an Australian company, Multi-Hull Designs Ltd., Dakota Creek Industries of Anacortes had come up with a low-wake design based on the Australian model. The international participation is not surprising given that the United States lags far behind other countries in the use of fast ferries.

World-wide, the 1990s saw major developments in the field of fast ferry technology. One of the early designs, a Norwegian concept, made its way to Puget Sound in the design of the *Victoria Clipper* catamarans. The most recent ideas appear in vessels such as BC Ferries *PacifiCat Explorer*, built in Vancouver, British Columbia. That particular ferry is one of the world's largest aluminum-hulled catamarans with space for 250 cars, 1,000 passengers and a speed of 37 knots.

Not that technical and design expertise is lacking in the United States. The problem lies with the caution exercised by the government entities that are the purchasers of fast ferries. Because the price tag is so high, government officials hesitate to try anything that has not already been built, several times over, and successfully operating. The caution with public funds is understandable but it can have the effect of stifling American design innovation unless Americans in the field can sell their ideas to overseas builders. Some pioneering American companies are already working on fast ferries, but there is more room for growth and development in what is destined to be an important process of meeting future transportation needs.

Founded in 1975, Dakota Creek Industries, Inc of Anacortes, Washington is one of the most modern medium-sized shipyards in the United States. Their new construction ranges from high speed aluminum catama-

rans to factory trawlers and ocean-going tugs. The company's work for the Washington State Ferry System produced the catamaran *M/V Chinook*. In her own way, the *Chinook* is just as elegant as the old Mosquito fleet steamers. Although her appearance is more squat, her overall beam of close to 39½ feet is a far cry from the 18 feet that characterized some of the Mosquito vessels, and her $9 million price tag reflects a century of inflation. At the turn of the century, what steamship operators wanted most was speed. The *Chinook* has that—each of her four engines produces 1,800 horsepower for a maximum speed in excess of 40 knots. Her water-jet propulsion system makes the *Chinook* appear to glide through the water with almost no wake.

Probably for the first time since the *H.B. Kennedy* came on the Bremerton run in 1909, Bremerton area commuters were thrilled with a new ferry. Except for the fact that there was no food or beverage service aboard, the *Chinook* was perfect. Diehard coffee addicts could always carry a cup aboard, in their *M/V Tacoma*, *Kalakala*, or even their *Bailey Gatzert* commemorative commuter mugs if they wished. It was only a 35 minute trip and the airline type passenger seats even had drop-down tray tables. Throughout the summer of 1998 commuters reveled in the pleasure of riding on the *Chinook*, whose Indian name was the word for "welcome." For once the "traveling public" had what it wanted.

Washington State Ferry System Director Paul Green welcomed the *Chinook* to the fleet with the comment "Yes, Virginia, Bremerton to Seattle in 35 minutes." There was irony in the words. The *Chinook* had not been in operation long before there were rumblings about unhappy property owners complaining about wake damage. Bremerton commuters greeted the news with grim faces. A group of University of Washington students who traveled daily to Seattle aboard the *Chinook* were overheard, "I can't believe that they're going to make the ferry slow down," groaned one young man.

By March 1999 the rumors had substance. Four Rich Passage property owners filed a lawsuit against the Washington State Ferry System claiming damages and calling for a ferry slowdown. Despite protests from the governments of Bremerton and Kitsap County, the property owners were successful in securing an injunction to force a slowdown until the lawsuit reached court or until an environmental study could be completed. In Kitsap County Superior Court, visiting King County Judge Glenna Hall ordered the *Chinook* to reduce her Rich Passage speed from 34 knots to 12 knots. The 35-minute trip now took 50 minutes.

On land the uproar created waves of its own. The wrath of the traveling public focused squarely on the property owners, who initially remained anonymous for reasons obvious to anyone reading the local papers or attending hearings overflowing with angry *Chinook* riders. Many Bremerton and Port Orchard commuters saw the whole action as another slap in the face to blue-collar workers dealt by wealthy waterfront dwellers. The property owners, bolstered by environmentalists, publicly blasted Washington State Ferries, claiming that the failure to do an environmental review prior to placing the *Chinook* on the run had resulted in damage to sensitive shoreline areas. At its narrowest point where Rich Passage is three-tenths of a mile across, residents claimed that waves from the *Chinook* smashed into bulkheads and washed sand and rock from the beaches.

Local governments appealed to Judge Hall, while commuters considered launching their own class-action lawsuit or asking the governor to call a special session of the state legislature. In rejecting every appeal, Judge Hall also ordered the state to start an environmental review. The Washington State Ferry System appealed to the State

Supreme Court and lost. Included in the appeals were declarations from commuters, some hand-written, testifying to the hardships that the slower ferry service would cause. What on the surface seemed like a commute extended by a mere 20 minutes on each side of the day could in reality mean extra hours of commuting time. Those who had timed their commute to arrive within five or 10 minutes of their work times now had to take earlier boats. Others faced rearranging their schedules to make bus connections, once timed down to the minute. Other commuters who had been drawn to Kitsap County because of the easy commute offered by the *Chinook* faced the prospect of having to sell their houses and move back to King County in order to keep their jobs. For commuters whose lives revolve around transportation issues, the stakes were truly high.

For the first time in years there was talk of bridges. If Bremerton residents were going to lose the comfort of a fast commute, then a bridge to Bainbridge Island would at least let them have easy access to the convenience of that commuter run.

At the end of August 1999, the State Supreme Court upheld Judge Hall's ruling and the *Chinook* slowed to what seemed like a crawl. When the state legislature met for its 2000 session the ferry slowdown should have been a major topic, but the problem of ferry slowdowns was preempted by a bigger problem, one that threatened the very existence of the Washington State Ferries.

The *Chinook being transported to her launch site, February 1998. Courtesy, Dakota Creek Industries*

In the absence of a state income tax, Washington State has a variety of taxes; some are high in comparison to other states. One of the most annoying of these taxes for Washington drivers was the 2.2 percent motor vehicle excise tax. Anyone purchasing a car paid the excise tax plus sales tax at the time of purchase. Depending on the cost of the car, the tax could easily be several hundred dollars. Each year thereafter, the tax was charged when auto license tabs were renewed. Again the amount could be several hundred dollars, although it decreased as the automobile aged.

In the November 1999 state-wide election, Washington taxpayers staged their own tax revolt and passed initiative measure #695. The initiative mandated a flat $30 motor vehicle excise tax (MVET). For the owners of luxury cars and sports utility vehicles, both of which are very popular in the Northwest, I-695 represented a significant savings.

What did all of this have to do with Puget Sound ferries? Approximately 60 percent of the operating costs for the Washington State Ferry System is covered by ferry fares. The rest of the revenue traditionally derived from the MVET, which funded all the ferries capital budget and about 25 percent of the operating costs. Even before the passage of Initiative 695, rising ferry costs were outpacing revenue sources.

In the months after the November election, ferry officials calculated the loss of MVET funds would amount to $52 million in the 1999-2000 budget year. Assuming that they canceled all plans for system expansion and terminal renovation, $30 million in cash reserves could be shifted to cover some of the deficit. In any case, WSF was forced into Draconian cuts. Within weeks, all of the ambitious plans created in the past decade were abandoned. Fifteen years of working towards a fleet of passenger-only fast ferries (POFF) ended when the state announced that it would cancel the four POFFs which were expected to follow the *Chinook* and *Snohomish*. Furthermore, those two ferries, along with their older counterparts, the *Tyee*, *Kalama*, and *Skagit*, were to be pulled from service. Commuters expressed little sadness over the loss of the Calamity and Snaggit as they preferred to call the *Kalama* and *Skagit*; the *Tyee*, built in the early 1980s, had been sidelined with mechanical problems so often that it was possible nobody would even realize it was gone. The *Chinook* and her sister ship, the *Snohomish*, were a different story. The fact that they had been forced to slow down took a second priority position to the idea that they might be gone entirely. The general belief was that once state-operated passenger-only service was dismantled, it would not return.

Further cuts called for pulling boats from the fleet of auto ferries and reducing the number of sailings by eliminating non-peak hour runs late at night. For night-workers dependent on ferries to reach their Seattle jobs the loss of those runs would be devastating. Working people unable to get to their jobs would be in great jeopardy of losing those jobs.

Besides complications in the ferry commute, anticipated cutbacks in public funding for transportation impacted the bus systems as well. Kitsap and King Counties had been moving towards an integrated system of seamless intermodal travel which promised to link ferries and buses into a smooth flow of schedules and fares paid for by smart cards useable in both the bus and ferry venue. Instead, bus service was curtailed on both sides of Puget Sound, and people who relied on public transportation by choice and those who had never had the luxury of owning a car or paying the MVET were the first to feel the impact.

Ferry users organized at the county level into the Ferry Dependent Counties Coalition. With members in Whidbey Island, San Juan, Kitsap, Thurston, Clallam, and Jefferson Counties, they hoped to get the attention of the Olympia Legislature with a "Save our Ferries" Rally in conjunction with a petition drive. Declaring that the ferries were a lifeline, the petition reminded that "ferry riders and supporters depend on ferries every day to access: jobs, goods and services, friends and family, business, schools, tourism and recreation." State legislators were called upon to fund the gap created by I-695, allow for the development of alternatives (including privatization), or create a plan for stable funding of the ferry system. Those attending the rally planned to travel from Bremerton to Olympia by boat, wearing green and white pins and carrying fog horns. One suspects that like the Bremertonians attending the A-Y-P Exposition in 1909, they also had their own chant.

Although state courts eventually declared I-695 unconstitutional, lawmakers acting with the blessing of Washington Governor Gary Locke repealed the motor vehicle excise tax anyway, acknowledging the will of the voters. Ferry service survived intact on a one-time $20 million contribution from the state's general fund and by dipping into the WSF reserves for another $30 million.

The benefit of I-695 may have been that the State of Washington in general and the Washington State Ferry System in particular was forced to reexamine its way of doing things. Clearly the voters' belief that reduced taxes would force the state government to operate more efficiently was in conflict with the government's view that efficiency alone was not the best way to solve problems. Each side had valid points, leaving a special Blue Ribbon Commission on Transportation to arrive at solutions that created greater efficiency and cost less. Ultimately the Commission recommended that ferry users shoulder the cost of ferry operations. The stated measure was for ferry fares to cover 80 percent of the system's cost by the year 2006 and 90 percent by 2012. No one doubted that Washington's ferry riders, long in the habit of enjoying what the industry considers cheap fares, would be bearing more of the actual costs involved in operating the ferryboats that tourists enjoy and commuters sometimes take for granted. Fare increases were an expected, if not popular, solution to part of the ferry-funding crisis.

While commuters would favor more and bigger and faster ferries, those may not be the solution to transportation problems. The answer may lie in diversity—a mixture of large and small ferries running to different communities and operated by private as well as public interests.

In a reversal of nearly 50 years of policy, Washington State Ferries loosened its monopolistic grip on Puget Sound ferry transportation and began to talk about privatization as an option. When what was described as a "deficit-challenged" run through the San Juan Islands from Anacortes to Sydney, British Columbia was about to be abandoned by WSF, public pressure delayed the move and the state adopted a three-year time frame to move the run into private hands. Likewise, in the rest of the Puget Sound area, private operators were now being invited to help out with proposals for supplementing ferry service.

In many ways, the history of Puget Sound ferries may have come full circle and the future may be a return to some of the elements of the past. Private operators, smaller vessels, and service restored to places like Port Orchard, Harper, Everett, Indianola and other communities could all be in the future. The public roads, which made the Mosquito Fleet obsolete, are themselves suffering from crippling gridlock. The answer may be a new Mosquito Fleet, making commuting by boats an attractive alternative to frustration on the freeway.

A crowd begins to assemble in Bremerton for the "Save Our Ferries" rally on February 22, 2001. In the distance is the fast ferry Catalina Jet, which was leased from Seatlle's Argosy Cruises for the event. Over a hundred people would ferry to the state capital at Olympia, and meet with another boatload from Vashon Island. Photo by Tom Janus

Once again the future of Washington ferries is uncertain. Given that Puget Sound is still a watery highway with few bridges, ferries will certainly become a more expensive form of transportation and may have to give way to a demand for some private enterprise to fill the gaps caused by reduced funding.

Puget Sound residents who called on the state to rescue them from what they considered the oppressive monopoly of Alex Peabody's Black Ball Ferries are now demanding to be freed from the iron grip of the Washington State Ferry System, on one hand, and asking for state funding of the system on the other. For its part, the state has discovered that running the nation's largest ferry system is often a thankless task. Washington State ferry riders pay fares that are only a small portion of the operating cost and yet they complain at every fare increase. In the last 50 years ferries have been safe, for the most part functional, and enjoyable to ride. They have been a central feature in Washington State's tourist industry, yet the Washington State Ferry system often seems taken for granted in the good times and subject to harsh criticism in the bad times. Captain Peabody would probably say "I told you so."

There is no doubt that Puget Sound ferries will continue. From canoes to catamarans, the water highway provided by nature is too valuable and too beautiful not to use. The only questions are what kinds of boats and who will operate them? And those questions will undoubtedly be answered in the next decades.

In saying that some things had not changed, another one of those constants was described in an 1889 promotional booklet titled Seattle and published by Charles H. Kittinger. In describing the scenery of Puget Sound the book notes:

"There is no more enjoyable trip than a sail over the placid waters of Puget Sound, on a fine, clear day. Not only is it pleasant, but it is also most interesting to the tourist and sightseer. On one side is the serrated ridge of the Olympic range, on the other the Cascade stretching north and south like two great guardians of the Sound basin, ebbing and flowing betwixt them. At one point can be seen Mount Baker, with its lofty, jagged peaks towering among the clouds; and away beyond Seattle grand old Mount Rainier, rearing its snow-covered head fourteen thousand four hundred and forty-four feet above the sea level....All this can be viewed at a single glance from the deck of the palatial Sound steamers; and the eye is never tired resting here and there on some beautiful point or headland or island which set off the scene. It is, in fact, a charming, ever-changing panorama of beautiful and interesting scenery while sailing on the Sound."

The Athlon was Poulsbo's "other boat" in opposition to the Hyak. Courtesy, Special Collections Division, University of Washington Libraries Neg. 2487

Chapter 10

Patrons of the Ferries

In terms of urban development, the Puget Sound region is relatively young; a century ago it was just emerging from frontier status. Out of the isolation that went along with a location in one of the farthest corners of the United States was born a distinctive Northwest character. Today the industries and people of the area proudly reflect that spirit, a large part of which is commitment to community, environmental stewardship, and the shared goal of preserving a quality of life that can be enjoyed by present and future Puget Sound residents.

The vast forests and deepwater ports that drew the first wave of entrepreneurs from places like East Machias, Maine in the 1850s continue to attract businesses rooted in the maritime trades. The original extractive timber and fishing industries have spawned a host of related activities which serve both local area needs and our Pacific Rim trading partners. And the entrepreneurial tradition remains. Where sailing vessels once hauled timber to San Francisco, today's innovative high-tech companies are spanning the globe in providing internet traffic services.

While the region moves forward conquering new business frontiers, it honors its heritage. Northwest business traditions include longevity of companies, multi-generational ownership, and leadership roles for women.

Heritage is also displayed in the built environment. The spirit that led those early Maine settlers to recreate their New England town on the shores of one of Puget Sound's sheltered bays has remained in the presence of Landmark Historic Districts throughout the region. One such district, Port Townsend, is the only remaining Victorian Seaport on the West Coast. Concern for preserving both the natural environment and the flavor of the area's early settlements is a hallmark of the Northwest.

For those visiting the Northwest for the first time, the most immediate impression—besides the ubiquitous coffee stands which are often the target of humorous comments—is the natural beauty presented by the combination of an astonishing inland sea, ancient green forests, and snow-capped mountains. It is a recreational playground where boating, in everything from kayaks to classic wooden yachts to Washington's own state-operated ferryboat system, is a regional pastime.

Nature has been generous in adding to the richness of the Pacific Northwest, but as in any enterprise, the crucial ingredient is the area's people. In their diversity, friendliness, community involvement, and enterprising attitude, the people of the Puget Sound region personify all the best of past, present, and future traditions.

BOWMAN MANUFACTURING COMPANY

Thomas A. Bowman was born on May 28, 1928 in Berwyn, Illinois. His father was a small town grocer and his mother was a homemaker. In 1940, after the death of his father, Tom and his mother moved to Seattle, Washington where he attended Broadway High School and The Lakeside School. Tom joined Boeing in 1948 where he worked three years in the assembly shops and 12 years as a manufacturing engineer. He left Boeing in 1963 to accept an engineering position at United Control Corporation, later to become Sundstrand Data Control. Tom was elected a senior member of the Society of Manufacturing Engineers in 1969 for his qualifications and knowledge of manufacturing engineering. Tom's experience over the years allowed him to see the demand for a precision sheet metal facility that could respond to local needs. He left Sundstrand in 1971 to form Bowman Manufacturing Company.

Bowman Manufacturing Company initially operated in a 400 square foot shop located at the Bowman home in Lake Forest, north of Seattle. In July 1990 Bowman moved to its current location, Jensen Business Park, a 52,000 square foot facility in Arlington, Washington.

Bowman began operations consisting of mostly hand type work and progressed to computer-controlled techniques. The first machine was a five-ton punch press that was retired in 1985. Beginning in about 1994, Bowman incorporated full electro-mechanical engineering and assembly capabilities which has enabled the company to grow and maintain its competitive edge. In 1997 the company purchased a 2000-watt pulsar laser that enables Bowman to do specialized cutting and has increased the company's ability to proto-type. In response to a rapidly changing global marketplace, Bowman has also

implemented numerous processes, such as ISO-9001.

Tom Bowman started the company as a one-man operation and today Bowman employs nearly 100 people. The payroll has gone from approximately $7000 per year to $52,500 per week and there are about 53 customers serviced by Bowman. Tom retired in 1988 and his daughter Carol and son-in-law Randy Bellon purchased the company. Carol has worked at Bowman since 1984 and controls the accounting portion of the business while her husband, Randy Bellon, is president.

Prior to becoming president of Bowman, Randy worked as a paramedic for King County. As he began to familiarize himself with the sheet metal industry, Randy and his former partner at the paramedic service began to design a device to hold and dispense disposable gloves. After only four months of research and development, Bowman

Bowman Manufacturing Company, Arlington, Washington.

introduced the "Glove Butler" to the medical market in June 1988. The Glove Butler™, a federally registered trade marked product, allows users easy access to disposable gloves. Since the introduction of the Glove Butler™, Bowman has increased the medical product line from one standard type of glove holder to eight styles of medical dispensers. Bowman Medical Products has also expanded the product line to include equipment dispensers for the dental, industrial, food service, high tech, and emergency service markets.

Bowman Manufacturing Company is proud of its community involvement. Bowman has ties with a variety of local high schools offering students part-time work and the ability to gain work experience while learning a trade.

The company also has relationships with two local community colleges that offer courses in math, blueprint, and welding studies tailored especially for the sheet metal fabrication industry. Bowman also participates in the local Stilly Valley Little League providing sponsorship and the use of facilities for league meetings and training. Several Bowman employees have coached little league teams and numerous Bowman "little leaguers" have played on the all-star team.

With no formal training, and only hands-on knowledge and the skill of manufacturing engineering, Thomas Bowman founded and built a prosperous and competitive business. Through hard work and dedication Tom realized the dream of owning and operating his own company—a company that will continue to grow and prosper for years to come.

The original five-ton punch press was the first machine used at Bowman Manufacturing.

Tom Bowman, Carol and Randy Bellon, Bowman Manufacturing Company.

BALLARD SHEET METAL WORKS, INC.

At the turn of the century, Ballard was booming. The area that Captain W.R. Ballard had reluctantly taken in settlement of a debt came to life when it was discovered that it could supply Seattle—burned out in the Great Fire of 1889—with badly needed shingles and lumber. More than 20 sawmills lined the placid shores of Salmon Bay and everyone needed sheet metal work, blowpipe, dust collectors, and roofing metal.

In 1907 two sheet metal workers from Renton, commuting to Ballard each day on the interurban, decided to start their own firm. Oscar Simpson, a 24-year-old Scotch Irishman from Indiana and a friend, Oscar Ranes, formed Ballard Sheet Metal Works.

Oscar's son, Harold Simpson, assumed management of the company during the 1930s.

That same year Oscar Simpson's first son, Harold Simpson, was born.

From their first shop, at 5114 Ballard Avenue, near what is now the Washington Ship Canal, they made their rounds and served the mills. By the mid-teens, the mill work had slowed but the fishing industry was beginning to grow and the firm began building fuel tanks, water tanks, and providing other metalwork for Alaska fishing vessels.

In 1919 Oscar Simpson bought out Oscar Rane and moved the company to a larger facility, in the now historic St. Charles Hotel building, one block south of the company's present location. In the thirties Oscar Simpson died and his son, Harold, assumed management of the firm. By then, the business had changed. The mills had closed, but the fishing industry had continued to grow. Harold Simpson shifted the emphasis of the business to the area's small shipyards, such as the old Sagstad Shipyard, and the canneries of Alaska. This portion of the business has continued to grow through the years. During World War II, Ballard Sheet Metal fabricated and installed ventilation systems and other parts for the U.S. Navy.

In 1957 Donald H. Simpson, grandson of the founder, graduated from the University of Washing-

Oscar Simpson and a partner formed Ballard Sheet Metal Works in 1907.

ton and joined his father in the firm. They worked together until Harold Simpson died in 1971. Donald Simpson assumed control of the company at that time.

Today, the fourth generation of the Simpson family has assumed control of the company. David B. Simpson and Douglas A. Simpson are now operating the business.

Ballard Sheet Metal Works is a complete job shop, but has always specialized in the marine and industrial fields. The company has also become very well known for the fabrication of high quality stainless steel range hoods and counters for residential use.

The company's office is at 4763 Ballard Avenue, still in historic Ballard.

THE CLASSIC YACHT ASSOCIATION

The Classic Yacht Association was founded in 1969 by a group of enthusiasts devoted to vintage wooden power boats. The CYA is dedicated to the preservation, restoration and maintenance of fine, old, power-driven pleasure craft and has become a major influence in the growing awareness and appreciation of the classic yacht. The design and construction of power yachts changed radically in the decades following World War II, leaving the dwindling number of pre-war yachts as the last examples of this era of style and elegance.

The original group of 13 charter members has grown to more than 300 in five fleets. The Southern California, Northern California, Pacific Northwest, Alaska, and USA fleets each organize events within their region. More than 500 classics have been registered, and the Association continues to grow. The CYA's archives preserve significant historical records on fleet vessels and members continue to research the naval architects and boatyards that produced these fine yachts. Members love to talk about history, and many display original photographs and news clippings aboard their vessels.

The Puget Sound region has a rich and illustrious history of shipbuilding and nautical adventure. At one time, there were more than a dozen active boatyards on Lake Union and Lake Washington alone, with names like Blanchard, Schertzer, Grandy, Monk and Shain well known to aficionados of wood on water. Due to its temperate climate, the region has the highest concentration of wooden yachts remaining in the United States. The Pacific Northwest fleet organizes an active agenda of yachting and social activities throughout the year. Fleet activities focus on expanding public awareness through shows, rendezvous and fundraisers. Particular emphasis is placed on the history, craftsmanship

and unique designs of the yachts of the classic era. One of the most popular experiences is the "Bell Street Rendezvous" held each Father's Day weekend on the Seattle waterfront at the Port of Seattle's Bell Street Marina. This event draws 35 to 40 classic yachts from Canadian and Pacific Northwest waters, many of which are open to the public.

The PNW Fleet is active in other areas of maritime history, as well. In 1996, the last steam driven Mosquito Fleet vessel *Virginia V* was named as an honorary member by the Pacific Northwest fleet, and flies the CYA burgee. The association has also raised money to assist in the restoration of this historic vessel, which was

Sueja II at Tacoma Yacht Club, July 4, 1920. Courtesy, Puget Sound Maritime Historical Society.

built on Puget Sound in 1922 and is still powered with an original 1893 triple expansion steam engine. It plied the waters of Puget Sound as a passenger transport from 1922 through 1947 and as a tour boat since the end of World War II.

Qualifications for membership require that a vessel be of good design, construction and maintenance; built prior to December 31, 1942; and show no external alterations that detract from the original intent of the designer. The Classic Yacht Association also accepts affiliate members who may own wooden yachts constructed after 1942 or individuals who are interested in wooden boats. The CYA welcomes membership inquiries and invites other classic yacht enthusiasts to visit its website at http://www. classicyacht.org.

Classic Yacht Association vessels at the Seattle Yacht Club prior to the opening day parade, May 1, 1999.

EAGLE INSURANCE COMPANIES

Few insurance companies in the world specialize in the coverages provided by the Eagle Insurance Companies, headquartered in downtown Seattle, Washington.

Eagle's workers' compensation insurance programs protect companies in high-hazard industries, such as maritime operations. Eagle writes State Workers' Compensation Act, United States Longshore and Harbor Workers Compensation Act (USL&H) and Maritime Employers' Liability insurance along the West and Gulf Coasts, Alaska and Hawaii.

Its roots are deep in traditional blue-collar industries. Eagle customers have been involved in such projects as the Exxon Valdez oil spill cleanup, construction of jumbo car ferries for the Washington State Ferries System, repair of the earthquake-damaged San Francisco Bay Bridge, construction of one of the world's largest fiberglass yachts and wharf construction of the 2020 Pier in Long Beach, California.

Eagle is made up of two carriers—Eagle Pacific Insurance Company and Pacific Eagle Insurance Company. The company first opened its doors in 1972. Its original parent company,

An employee of a local yacht builder insured by Eagle installs interior fixtures.

Eagle provides coverage for Puget Sound's largest shipyards. Here, a shipyard employee prepares to cut through the heavy steel plate of a ships hull.

then the West coast's largest maritime employer, elected to self-insure and self-administer USL&H exposures arising from its stevedoring operations. Through a variety of acquisitions and growth, Eagle quickly became the largest USL&H claims administration firm on the West Coast—and one of the most experienced in dealing with maritime workers' compensation claims.

The Eagle Insurance Companies holding company formed in the late 1980's. Eagle Pacific Insurance Company was purchased in 1982 and later capitalized as a stock insurance company. It issued its first policy, covering its parent company, in January 1985.

Kemper Insurance Companies, a leading U.S. property/casualty insurer, purchased Eagle in 1998. Kemper was formed by James S. Kemper in 1912 to provide workers' compensation insurance for Chicago's lumberyard workers. In 2000 it had revenues of $4.8 billion. It operates countrywide

and in many foreign markets. This acquisition provided increased financial strength and a renewed commitment to the maritime community for Eagle. Capitalizing on its unique expertise, Eagle functions as a separate subsidiary of Kemper.

Today, Eagle Pacific Insurance Company, the primary risk entity, continues to operate as a specialty workers' compensation insurance provider. Pacific Eagle Insurance Company operates as a California domiciled specialty workers' compensation insurer, and Pointsure Insurance Services, a wholly owned managing general underwriter.

Eagle's success is due in large part to its outstanding staff. Many of the company's employees have completed advanced insurance industry coursework leading to prestigious professional designations in underwriting, claims, risk management, accounting, actuarial science and general insurance.

Eagle operates local branch and service offices in California, Washington, Texas, Hawaii and Alaska. These offices offer varying levels of policyholder service including claims, loss control and underwriting. Eagle's branch structure establishes regional strength utilizing individuals with local expertise and brings decision making authority closer to the customer.

Essential to Eagle's success has been its emphasis on developing close working partnerships with clients and their independent insurance agents and brokers. These partnerships yield significant savings in the prevention and management of workers' compensation claims, achieving the lowest possible workers' compensation insurance costs. The process starts with Eagle's underwriters, who work with the insurance buyer

Confined spaces and cramped quarters create unique safety hazards when welding aboard commercial vessels. Eagle assists its clients with specialized training in the selection and use of appropriate safety equipment.

and their broker to develop the right risk transfer mechanism to meet their individual needs. This may be a fixed or guaranteed cost program or a loss sensitive plan where Eagle and the insured share in the financial result or cost of the insurance claims.

Once the account is written, an Eagle loss control professional is assigned and works with the insured's safety representative to analyze its current safety program and identify more effective ways to prevent or mitigate injuries to its employees. Periodic follow-up visits throughout the year offer hands-on assistance in implementing new loss prevention strategies and assuring a strong focus on safety. With Eagle's help, accident prevention becomes the most effective way for any organization to maintain a healthy and productive workforce.

When an employee is injured and a claim reported, Eagle's highly trained, professional claims adjusters take over. Their job is to work with the injured worker and their family to see that all of their needs are met during this difficult time period, and to assure

Marine contractor clients of Eagle often use large cranes to lift structural members into place. Workers stabilize the load using tag lines to assure precise and safe placement of these members.

the worker's speedy recovery and timely return to work. In addition, they have a duty to Eagle and the insured to see that only those costs that are truly the employer's responsibility are paid. These adjusters work closely with Eagle's loss control professionals to understand the details behind the injuries to help ensure that similar injuries can be prevented in the future.

With its rich past and strong financial backing, Eagle Insurance Companies is poised for greatness in the new century. Firmly established as a leading provider of specialty workers' compensation products in the West and Gulf states, Eagle will expand its horizons in the coming years to offer the same exemplary risk management services to new customers in the East and Midwest, setting a new standard against which others will be measured.

F5 NETWORKS, INC.

Imagine this. You're standing in an incredibly long line at the Alaska Airlines ticket counter. The line is in interminable gridlock. Can't we move any faster? Why can't they open other lines and direct us to an available ticket counter?

Now, imagine you're on Alaska Airlines web site to buy that same ticket. And, even though there may be literally thousands more customers making a purchase at exactly the same time, your transaction is completed in mere moments. You have, without knowing it, been seamlessly shuttled through cyber-space by the integration of products and services of an incredibly intuitive helping hand for e-business—a company named F5 Networks, Inc.

While we all expect a certain high level of service from the nearby businesses and services we frequent, no such standard exists for web sites. Yet, in many cases, we achieve quicker, more dependable results when we visit a company's online store. At the heart of this amazing dichotomy are the award-winning products developed and produced by F5, products that act like air traffic controllers, routing client requests through the complexities of a networked environment to dependably produce the desired results. By the intelligent and automated control of time sensitive content and traffic, F5 enables organizations to control, access and utilize the Internet to its fullest advantage, a critical edge in attracting— and keeping—the web-savvy consumer.

As pioneers in this highly specialized field of Internet traffic and content management, F5 is responsible for the creation of integrated products and services for turnkey performance solutions for more than 3000 top corporations with high-traffic Internet sites including , Microsoft, MCI, Motorola, Prudential, Bank of America, USA Today and, yes, Alaska Airlines.

Jeff Hussey, founder and chairman of the board. Courtesy, Lauren McFalls, The Seattle Times.

Their enviable list of industry awards is long and well-deserved, including top accolades from such respected organizations as *Internet-Week, Network Computing* and *Computerworld Magazine.* A live demonstration of their trailblazing content delivery mechanisms captured the "Best in Shownet" award at Interop 2000 in Tokyo.

Steering the success of F5 is a Seattle native whose unwavering vision has long focused on the Internet as the keystone of interactive media. Jeffrey Hussey, F5's chairman of the board, was one of the co-founders of the company in 1996. Born with an insatiable entrepreneurial spirit, Hussey's fascination with technology began early, even as he built a fledgling computer from the same kit as Bill Gates and Paul Allen. He had made the observation that once mass communication moved beyond just one-way broadcast media, like newspapers

and televions into a true interactive environment, an enlightened company's ultimate success would depend on its ability to service customers and respond promptly to their demands— across multiple time zones and even vast geographies. Highly sophisticated products and services would have to be developed to enable these companies to monitor, manage, control and optimize their Internet traffic and content. These products must automatically and intelligently deliver the best possible performance, efficiently handling a user's request through the complex world of geographically dispersed servers. Bolstered by confidence in his theory, a BA in finance from Seattle Pacific University, an MBA from the University of Washington and hands-on experience from his first endeavor as the founder of Pacific Comlink, an inter-

F5 Networks Internet Traffic and Content Management products ensure that mission-critical Internet sites and data centers are available 24 hours a day, seven days a week.

exchange carrier providing Internet access services to the Pacific Rim, Hussey set out to establish F5 as the global leader in its field.

In June 1999, F5 Networks, Inc. made its debut on the Nasdaq as FFIV. Yet, as arduous as the journey to this initial public offering was, Hussey acknowledges the hardest work is still ahead. As he explained to his employees, the company's IPO was anything but the finish line; it was more like an exhilarating leap from the minor leagues to the major leagues. And as gratifying as this move into the public sector appeared to be, Hussey believes an even greater accomplishment was being able to show profitability a full year ahead of Wall Street and shareholder expectations. Indeed, F5 soared from $0 at its inception to a $100 million company in the course of only five years. The challenge now is to add another "0" to the company's market capitalization—a meaningful

Located near Myrtle Edwards Park on Elliott Bay, F5 Networks' offices have a picturesque view of the Puget Sound.

task for the 500 employees of the F5 team.

Hussey's philosophy of total dedication to continually raising the bar for superior performance has proved contagious within his company ranks. And, while he admits that there are many "moments of mirth" within corporate walls, there is also focused diligence, a come-early, stay-late agenda that is commonplace among high technology innovators. Yet F5's management also realizes that each individual programmer, engineer or marketing professional so key to the combined success of the company must be given the unrestricted opportunity for personal as well as professional growth. To that end, corporate attitude leans heavily towards the goal of being incredibly efficient and effective during allotted work hours—the working smarter, not harder mantra that has brought the company to its leading position in the industry today. In addition, company policy strongly encourages each member of its workforce to donate time and talent to one of its many corporate charities, including Habitat for Humanity and the Juvenile Diabetes Foundation.

This respect for each employee's need to grow as a person outside the company as well as a professional within the corporate structure has been rewarded with 110 percent dedication from the entire F5 team. It also plays a major role in the recruitment of new talent, one of the biggest

F5 Networks, cited as one of the fastest growing public companies in Washington by the Puget Sound Business Journal, *maintains a casual corporate culture for its 500 employees.*

challenges facing any high tech development company in this exceedingly competitive market. F5 has created a covetable recruiting environment that entices budding talent to create ever more comprehensive tools to achieve even higher performance within the Internet traffic and content delivery arena.

As a younger man, Jeff Hussey daydreamed that one day he would spend long, languid days sitting alone on a boat making his fortune by quietly trading stocks. Today, instead, he is surrounded by an undulating whirlpool of unimaginable talent, perfecting the proprietary complement of products and services that make waves for the cresting success of many of the world's most progressive companies. All with a steadfast vision and the unbridled energy and intensity of the company namesake—one of nature's most respected powerhouses of velocity and momentum— the F5 tornado.

GRADDON CONSULTING AND RESEARCH

Begun as a land development and brokerage business in 1966 in King County, Washington, Graddon Consulting and Research Company (GCR) has developed its focus upon investigations of the public land records so as to produce evidence that assists in resolving contemporary real estate property issues and controversies in the state of Washington.

Its specialty areas of research and study include historically created rights of way for railroads and public and private road, old legally subdivided lots, previously established vested property rights, and old land use and property laws.

Whether consulting to attorneys or directly to property owners, GCR's examinations of the public land records often span more than 100 years of archives. Equally important, old property and land use laws are also considered.

The Homestead Act of 1862 and the First Transcontinental Railroad Land Grants of 1864 significantly aided the settlement and development of public domain of the western United States. After the establishment of the Territory of Washington in 1853, the General Land Office (GLO) of the Department of the Interior opened a local land office in Olympia in 1854. Duties of that local land office included the management of the earliest public land records including the original government surveys and the documents of the original settlers. Also, it was charged with notification and dissemination of consequential deed information, such as the locations of railroad rights of way.

GCR generally initiates its property research and evidence production assignments with the archived federal and territorial records, documents, maps, and public notices generated both in Washington D. C. and at the Olympia Land Office, Territory of Washington prior to the issuance of the patent. GCR's property research subsequent to the issuance of the patent then covers nearly 100 years of both recorded and non-recorded matters of public record retrieved from many sources, including the many documents stored in GCR's own data bases.

GCR has demonstrated an ability and developed a reputation for its factual historic document production in both subjective investigations and objective and comparative studies. Clients' issues and cases often turn on GCR's ability to discover subjective information and documents that heretofore seem to have been overlooked or were merely absent from the public records. Its objective and comparative studies include those such as the applied uses of historically applied vocabulary and the types of documents and terminology used under certain historic circumstances.

GCR's research and discovery has and continues to greatly benefit its clients by providing them a heightened awareness of their property's history. Evidence production of old documents, records, maps, and laws often serve as evidence to many contemporarily and legally recognized property ownership rights, benefits, and privileges.

The General Land Office was established in the Territory of Washington in 1854.

THE NORTHWEST MARITIME CENTER

Captain George Vancouver, sailing under the British flag, was the first to put the Port Townsend area on the map. He arrived in 1792 and described Port Townsend Bay as "a very safe and capacious harbor." Port Townsend was founded in 1851 and became the state's second city, after Olympia, six months earlier than Seattle. In the 1890s, when Port Townsend was Port of Entry for the entire Pacific Northwest, most ocean traffic was compromised of sailing vessels. The small seafaring town was dominated by warehouses and wharves, saloons and brothels, becoming a thriving international seaport with a reputation as notorious as San Francisco's Barbary Coast.

Horace McCurdy wrote: *"To be in Port Townsend, Washington, at the dawn of the 20th Century was to be born to the sea and to grow up with its stirring sights, its heady smells and its profound mystery soaking into a boy the way the grainy sea salt impregnates a half-tide rock."*

In 1976 the downtown waterfront district was designated a National Landmark Historic District. The city is also recognized as one of only three Victorian Seaports in the nation, and the only one on the west coast. Apace with its evolution into a vacation destination, Port Townsend is establishing international reputation for building fine wooden sailing vessels and state-of-the-art motor yachts. In addition, the Centrum Arts Foundation has established itself as one of the region's major cultural institutions, and attracts audiences from throughout the nation. Annually, over one million visitors come to Port Townsend to experience the artistry, the historic buildings, wooden boats, and to catch a glimpse of the region's maritime past.

The idea of a Maritime Center for Port Townsend was born more than fifteen years ago. In the late 1980s and early 1990s tourism growth in the His-

toric District of Port Townsend, coupled with accelerated demand for condominium and hotel development along the city's working waterfront, displaced many existing water-related uses. In response to the pressures of these market forces, a group of marine trade businesses and non-profit organizations proposed a seaport project at Point Hudson to preserve and enhance the area's identity as a working marina. Due to a lack of funding and governmental support this effort failed, but the idea survived.

During the same timeframe, a key waterfront parcel adjacent to Point Hudson, the Thomas Oil property, faced the prospect of private development which many citizens felt was inappropriate: a 50-unit condominium complex in 1990, and a $20 million luxury hotel in 1993. The public outcry that resulted led to a halt of both proposals and to new zoning and

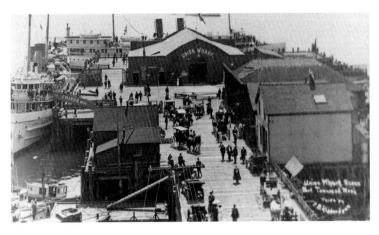

Photo of Union Wharf, from the collection of the Jefferson County Historical Society.

shoreline regulations designed to protect the city's working waterfront.

In the mid 1990s the city and the port of Port Townsend negotiated a purchase agreement for the Thomas Oil property. However, due to a shift in political power, this offer was withdrawn. The Wooden Boat Foundation resurrected the idea for a maritime center in 1997. In 1998, the Wooden Boat Foundation handed off the proposal to the newly formed Northwest Maritime Center, a nonprofit organization, so that the Foundation could continue to focus on providing maritime programs as opposed to buying property and constructing facilities. The Wooden Boat Foundation will be an anchor tenant at the new facility.

The Northwest Maritime Center (NMWC) is a non-profit alliance of community organizations working together to build a multi-purpose, public maritime center featuring education and heritage buildings, on-the-water programs, educational workshops and exhibits, and public access to the shoreline.

McCurdy Boatyard. Courtesy, Jefferson Historical Museum.

POPE RESOURCES

Formation of the Washington State Ferry system was nearly a century away when Port Gamble was established in 1853. Since then, Indian canoes, row boats, sailing ships, steamers, and ferry-boats have shaped the history of that milltown and others once part of Pope & Talbot's family of enterprises.

The tall ship *Julius Pringle* dropped anchor in July 1853, at the head of Gamble Bay, near the mouth of Hood Canal, and not far south of the Straight of Juan de Fuca. The *Pringle*'s captain, William C. Talbot, selected the site for the newly formed Puget Mill Company's first sawmill. It offered protected, deepwater anchorage, and nearby abundant stands of Douglas fir close to the water's edge. Along with experienced millhands, mostly from East Machias, Maine, Talbot and the ship's crew set about constructing buildings, one to shelter a steam-driven sawmill, another to house mill-hands, a cookhouse, and a small shelter for the future mill's manager. First called "Teekalet," a Salish Indian word meaning "brightness of the noonday sun," the site would be renamed Port Gamble in 1868.

Teekalet and the Port Gamble mill, 1863. Courtesy, Port Gamble Historic Museum Archives

In September, only hours after the *Pringle* set sail for San Francisco, Captain Josiah P. Keller and the crew of the *L. P. Foster* anchored at Teekalet. The *Foster*'s cargo included steam engines, boilers, mill machinery, supplies, and merchandise for the store. Captain Keller stayed on as the mill's first manager, and production had begun before the end of the month.

The milltown's population was a scant two dozen men, as well as Captain Keller's wife, son, and daughter. Rowboats and Indian canoes were the most accessible means of travel from place to place for the town's isolated residents. Steamers were of little consequence on the Sound until 1854, when Captain Warren Gove contracted to deliver

mail from Steilacoom to settlements around Puget Sound. One can only imagine how valuable a letter from home might have been for Mrs. Keller, and others at the remote settlement. It took 18 days for a letter from Maine to reach Pope & Talbot's office in San Francisco. Puget Mill Company mail was carried from there by one of the company's ships (a 12- to 30-day trip) or by steamboat to Portland, then to the mouth of the Cowlitz River, by horse to Olympia, and finally upsound by steamer.

Port Townsend was not established until 1854 when the customs house was moved there from Olympia. That year the steamer *Major Tompkins* began regular calls on upsound settlements, including the Puget Mill Company port. But by February of the following year it had sunk at the entrance of

Admiralty Hall from the ferry docks in Port Ludlow, Washington. Courtesy, Port Gamble Historic Museum Archives

Victoria harbor. Other steamers quickly took over the *Tompkin*'s route.

In 1857, not long before a second sawmill was added to the site, Puget Mill Company purchased a half interest in the steam tug *Resolute*. It towed logs purchased from loggers around the sound and assisted sailing ships entering the company's wharf on Gamble Bay. But for millworkers, who sometimes hitched rides, the *Resolute* represented freedom. The company's second tug, the *Cyrus Walker*, was put into service in 1864. It "proved an important link with the outside world for more than one isolated cluster of cabins and cottages," wrote Edwin Coman and Helen Gibbs, in Pope & Talbot's history *Time, Tide and Timber*.

Program celebrating the establishment of the Edmonds-Port Ludlow ferry, May 6, 1925. Courtesy, Port Gamble Historic Museum Archives

Following the end of the Civil War, Puget Mill Company replaced its original sawmill at Port Gamble with a new mill that was able to produce more and higher quality lumber. To supply the company's expanded need for logs, a third tugboat, the *Goliah* was purchased. Although the nation's financial instability suppressed the company's production rate, by 1877 Port Gamble was cutting almost 50 million board feet of lumber annually. The company had markets for more lumber than it was able to produce, so it acquired a bankrupt mill at Utsalady, located on the north end of Camano Island, and equipped it with a new sawmill. (Even with a new mill at Utsalady, the operation lost money, and it was permanently closed in 1890.) A year later, the company purchased the Port Ludlow mill.

By the 1880s, passengers and mail were carried to and from Puget Mill towns by documented steamers as well as a swarm of undocumented vessels that became known as the Mosquito Fleet. One of the best-known steamer fleets was owned by Puget Sound Navigation Company and its steamboats called regularly at Utsalady and Port Ludlow. Puget Sound Navigation's vessels served Port Gamble until 1936, when it sold the route to Olympic Navigation Company of Port Gamble. Olympic Navigation also operated steamers between Port Gamble and Shine on the Olympic Peninsula.

A narrow road connected Port Gamble and Kingston. A landing developed by Pope & Talbot in 1913 linked steamer service from Kingston to Ballard, a fishing port just north of Seattle. The route, along with others that provided freight and passenger service between Seattle, Kingston, and Port Ludlow was owned by the Kingston Transportation Company.

Early automobile ferry service was inventive. In 1921, a lift was used to

Bordner, age class distribution. The photo shows varied growth stages of Douglas Firs from 10 to 60 years old. Courtesy, Tony Johnson, operations forester

load and unload cars from the deck of a scow that was towed between Oak Harbor and Utsalady with a fishing boat. Three years later the ferry company's owners launched the *Acorn*, a motorized ferryboat, and service improved. Berte Olson, the first woman ferryboat operator on the sound, later operated the ferry service across Agate Pass, between the Kitsap Peninsula and Bainbridge Island, where "fast ferry" service to Seattle had been offered by Kitsap County Transportation from Port Blakely since 1923.

In 1925, Puget Mill Company majority owners W. H. Talbot and George A. Pope Sr. sold the lumber empire that their fathers had founded to Chas. R. McCormick Lumber Company for $15 million. But the Great Depression took its toll and in 1938 McCormick defaulted on its note. Following foreclosure, the timberland and mills became the property of the Pope & Talbot Lumber Company, which in 1940 was reorganized and became Pope & Talbot, Inc.

It was not just lumber interests that were reorganized as a result of the Depression. Many ferry services had changed hands, including the once prosperous W. B. Foshay Company. Its assets, including the ownership of Kitsap County Transportation Company and Puget Sound Freight Lines, were assumed by the Seattle First National Bank, then sold to Northland Transportation Company.

After World War II and the rapid population growth around Puget Sound that followed, the ferryboat business became more challenging. Fares raised, but service declined. Fleets aged and operators lost money. In response to growing public pressure in 1951, the State of Washington Department of Highways acquired the Puget Sound ferry fleets and landings. Routes were consoli-

Above: Port Ludlow, 1895. Courtesy, Port Gamble Historic Museum Archives

Below: Captain D.B. Jacson house (1871) at Port Gamble today. Courtesy, Port Gamble Historic Museum Archives

dated, fares fixed, and new, larger, faster ferryboats were ordered.

It's doubtful that the founders of what became known in 1985 as Pope Resources could have predicted the evolution of Port Ludlow or Port Gamble. Port Ludlow's mill had not operated since 1935, but the milltown became a destination resort with an upscale inn, a 27-hole championship golf course, and a 300-slip marina. In 2001, the Port Ludlow resort was sold. The Port Gamble mill was closed in 1995, but the site's New England-style town remains an active community. Its miles of undeveloped waterfront still invite exploration, and the nearby Kingston-Edmonds ferry still afforded the most convenient passage to what was perhaps the most historic of Puget Sound's milltowns.

While some pondered high-speed, passenger-only ferry service between Seattle and Kingston, others took steps to preserve Port Gamble's past. Beginning in the early 1970s, the Port Gamble Museum Committee was formed and, in 1976, in conjunction with the United States bicentennial, the museum opened in the historic heart of the town, below its general store and just above the original millsite. Its founding mission was to conserve and protect Port Gamble's history as it related to the Pacific Northwest and the forest products industry. Its collection includes artifacts from the mill, others contributed by Pope & Talbot's founding families and employees, and the Pope & Talbot corporate archive.

Inside the museum is a full-scale reproduction of Captain Talbot's cabin on the 140-ton brig *Oriental*, the ship that in 1849 carried Talbot to San Francisco from East Machias, Maine. Displays also included replicas of rooms from Port Gamble's famous Puget Hotel, built in 1903, and Admiralty Hall, built in 1887 in Port Ludlow as the home of Cyrus Walker. There are many heirlooms, artifacts, and photographs from the early 1800s.

Pope Resources and its predecessor companies have operated in the Puget Sound area since the company's beginning with the *Pringle*'s landing at Port Gamble. Since then they have logged, milled, and developed such Puget Sound communities as West Seattle, Broadmoor, Washington Park, Sheridan Beach, Sheridan Heights, Cedar Park, Lake Forest Park, Uplake Terrace, Shoreline, Edmonds, Martha Lake, Alderwood Manor, Kingston and others. In fact, they donated the property for the University of Washington Arboretum. One of the company's legendary officers, E. G. Ames, donated what became the official residence of University of Washington's president. The home is still occupied by the University president and it is located in Washington Park, which in 1900 was one of the company's earliest Seattle real estate developments.

Today, Pope Resources is a publicly traded company that trades on the NASDAQ Exchange under the symbol POPEZ. It's principal assets, according to its Chairman and CEO Allen E. Symington, "are both tangible and intangible. Our company owns and operates about 72,000 acres of tree farms in Kitsap, Mason, and Jefferson Counties, and about 2,000 acres designated for residential, commercial or industrial use on the West Side of Puget Sound. It also owns a 44,500-acre tree farm on the western Washington side of the Columbia River. Because of its 150-years of forestry and forest economics experience, and its reputation for habitat and watershed management expertise, the Company manages in excess of 500,000 acres of timberland for other timberland owners."

After Pope Resources was created, its Portland, Oregon-based founding company, Pope & Talbot, Inc., focused its capital and management talents on the lumber and wood fiber businesses. Today Pope & Talbot operates mills manufacturing softwood lumber and wood fiber products in both Canada and the United States, and its shares are traded on the New York Stock Exchange under the symbol POP.

Water transportation has always been an important element in the success of Pope & Talbot, Pope Resources, and subsidiary, Olympic Resource Management. As far into the future as one might view, the Pope companies and Washington State ferries will be an important part of the Pacific Northwest's economy, providing useful products and services to meet the needs of those lucky enough to live and work around Puget Sound.

Pope and Talbot Pioneer *with a log raft, 1951. Courtesy, Port Gamble Historic Museum Archives*

OLES MORRISON RINKER & BAKER LLP

Oles Morrison Rinker & Baker LLP is one of Seattle's oldest law firms, dating from 1893 when the first partners shared an office under the name Condon & Wright. From the days of John Condon (after whom the existing University of Washington Law School is named) and George Wright, the firm has maintained a commitment to high professional standards.

The firm name changed to Wright, Kelleher & Allen in 1916, with the addition of partner Edward Allen. Beginning in the 1920s, Mr. Allen developed a substantial fishing industry practice which ultimately brought him national recognition and a leading role in international fisheries control.

Growth of heavy construction in the 1930s signaled new prosperity for the Pacific Northwest and a new focus for the firm. The firm became Allen, Froude & Hilen. During that time, the firm's practice continued to grow and Gerald DeGarmo joined the firm as a partner. His practice emphasized disputes involving the fishing industry, with clients in Alaska and the Pacific Northwest. As the region became a center for development of hydroelectric power, Gerald DeGarmo rose to national prominence as counsel for the leading contractors on the most ambitious of these projects—Grand Coulee Dam. By the time the dam was built, DeGarmo had established the firm's reputation as the Northwest's preeminent construction industry lawyers. Its prominent clients included Peter Kiewit & Sons, Morrison-Knudsen, Bechtel, and locally owned General Construction.

Meanwhile, downtown Seattle was growing, too. The firm helped incorporate the Nordstrom stores and represented Alaska Airlines in the early years before both had in-house counsel. While Northwest businesses have grown to serve a rapidly expanding regional market, the firm has played

John Condon.

George Wright.

an important role in their commercial transactions.

In 1950, Stuart Oles and Seth Morrison joined the firm. Augmenting the construction practice of Gerald DeGarmo, Stu Oles litigated some of the most prominent cases in the firm's history. As a result, he developed a philosophy about the practice of law that contributed significantly to the firm's success— the function of a lawyer is to help people who have a problem.

In the late 1960s, Bruce Rinker joined the firm. An accomplished litigator of construction disputes, he was the firm's ethics monitor. His care in this regard was born out of his abiding concern for the clients as well as his interesting life experiences, which included being a prisoner of war in 1943-44. Mr. Rinker developed a significant construction law practice in Alaska.

In 1971, fresh out of law school, Sam Baker joined the firm. It was natural that he gravitate towards a construction practice—his father was a well-known contractor. During the 30 years of Mr. Baker's tenure with the firm, its lawyers have held to the highest standards of competence and professionalism as the premier construction law firm in the Pacific Northwest.

The firm has continued to embrace the philosophy of its founders and its

significant members, finding practical approaches to its clients' legal issues. In recent years, the firm has expanded its representation to serve the growing regional, national and international activities of its clients. This practice encompasses all of the western states and occasionally other state courts, all federal courts and state and federal administrative and adjudicatory tribunals of all types. The firm is also involved in international practice extending from the Pacific Rim countries to Europe and the Middle East.

In the 100 plus years since the first partners opened their general practice, the Seattle metropolitan area has increased its population from roughly 80,000 to more than two million. In the 1890s, it was still feasible for a single lawyer to practice in every area of law. Today, the firm offers the combined experience of more than 25 attorneys to deal with the complex laws and regulations of our modern era. The firm has a solid base of litigation attorneys with expertise in construction, supply and service contracts; corporate practice, insurance coverage matters; and commercial law. As in the beginning, however, Oles Morrison Rinker & Baker LLP remains committed to traditional standards of technical excellence and professional service.

PRESERVATIVE PAINT CO.

In Georgetown, a small village adjacent to Seattle, Asphaltum Products Company began selling asphalt and coal tar products in 1908. Six years later, in response to increasing public demand for bright, colorful paints, it rechartered as Preservative Paint Company. But the story of the company's success and growth began the following year and involved some courageous decisions by a talented young woman.

In 1913, 19-year-old Carrie West exaggerated her age to 25 to get a job as the firm's bookkeeper. Eleven years later when Cash Williams, the company's owner, died, the business was near bankruptcy. Carrie West bought the company, went to San Francisco, and made payment arrangements with the firm's creditors to prevent foreclosure. She brought in her brother, Frank, who was then a student at the University of Washington, and the two of them instituted cost and production controls that resulted in turning the business around and keeping it solvent.

The firm had fully recovered by the late twenties and Carrie's other brother, Robert, joined the venture. For the following years, even through the Depression, the company prospered, selling retail products at its factory outlet and wholesale to dealers, shipyards, and local industries. It prided itself then, as it does today, on being a Northwest company catering to the Northwest.

In 1938 Carrie sold her interest in the business to her brother, Frank, so that she could enjoy retirement with her husband. In the 1940s, the company began opening stores in the Puget Sound area to serve customers directly and continued to grow. In the 1950s, it extended its distribution to Alaska.

Frank West passed away in 1969 after nearly 50 years with Preservative Paint. For several years the ownership of the firm was tied up in pro-bate and held in trust. In 1972, eight key employees of the company and Ron West, Frank's nephew and Robert's son, who had started his own business processing waste chemicals, bought the firm. The company expanded the employee-ownership concept in 1975 by extending ownership to eligible employees via an employee stock ownership trust.

In 1994, Preservative Paint Co. was acquired by Kelly-Moore Paint Co. Kelly-Moore Paint Co. was established in 1946. In addition to its success, the company takes great pride in its heritage, in that it still manufactures and sells paint in Georgetown, and in the same building in which it started business 93 years ago.

Above: The original plant, 1908.

Below: Free monorail rides, 1962.

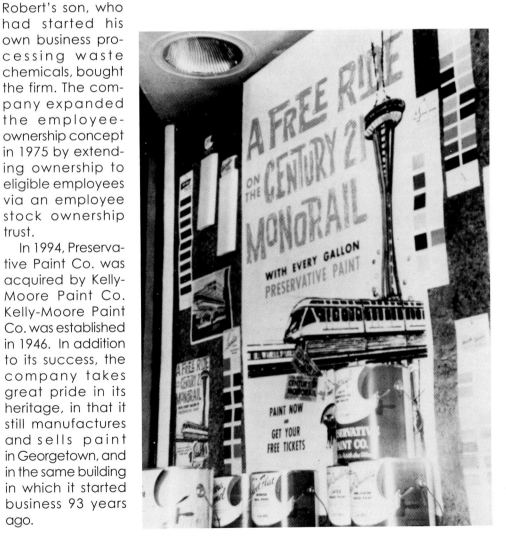

TRENDWEST RESORTS, INC.

In the business world, there are some individuals who influence industries, but few who are able to redefine them. Just as Walt Disney once turned amusement parks into theme parks, Trendwest Resorts—under the leadership of Bill Peare, president and CEO—led the transformation of timeshare into a vacation ownership lifestyle.

Two condos, one hotel room, and an idea. It doesn't sound like much, but from these modest beginnings grew an exceptional network of vacation resorts and experiences. In 1989, Jeld-Wen, Inc., one of America's top 100 privately owned companies, made its entrance into vacation ownership. Jeld-Wen recognized Bill's expertise and recruited him to develop the new timeshare organization. From his many years listening to travelers in the vacation industry, Bill knew firsthand their wants and needs. One feeling they made perfectly clear was the fundamental problem with traditional timeshare—lack of flexibility. Buyers didn't want to be "locked into" a particular vacation destination or

Above: The inviting interior of WorldMark at Depoe Bay.

Below: WorldMark at Rancho Vistoso captures the lure of the desert.

time period. But before Trendwest could complete in the vacation ownership market, it needed a unique business plan. Bill recruited Mike Moyer, Jeff Sites, as well as several other industry experts. Together they conceived a distinctly different product from existing point-based systems. During the sales presentations, potential owners were polled about how they like to vacation. Bill and his team discovered that people generally preferred shorter, more frequent vacations to varied destinations within driving distance of their homes. And on that idea, Trendwest was born.

Trendwest developed WorldMark, The Club, a California nonprofit mutual benefit corporation, to own and operate the resorts within this innovative vacation system. All of the resort properties would be deeded to the owners—debt free. The Trendwest concept combined the flexibility of "vacation credits" with ownership in a network of drive-to resorts, and choices from a variety of worldwide destinations. Suddenly timeshare owners could customize their vacations—choose their resort, stay in any size unit, and stay for as long as they liked—in resorts that were as close as a two-hour drive away or as far away as Fiji. It was vacationing just the way people wanted.

Trendwest Resorts is one of the most successful companies in the vacation ownership industry. The company has experienced phenomenal success since it was established in 1989. Its network of vacation resorts is located in the Continental United States, Hawaii, Canada, Mexico and the South Pacific. The company listens to its owners, and continually evolves to anticipate and accommodate their vacation needs. The consumer-driven product, combined with employees dedicated to delivering the highest levels of customer service, has contributed to the success of the resort system.

As the company has grown, the majority of positions have been filled by employees promoted from within. Trendwest is proudly committed to employee education and spends a large amount of money each year on training and leadership programs. Most importantly, every employee is in sales and service and is responsible and accountable for owner satisfaction.

Trendwest is also committed to its local resort, sales office and corporate communities. Resort managers join local chamber of commerce organizations and become closely involved in community affairs. The company also has an established policy of hiring locally.

Today, Trendwest, a NASDAQ Financial-100 company, is one of the most successful businesses in the va-cation ownership industry, with resorts in the continental United States, Hawaii, Canada, Mexico, Australia and Fiji. The company's

ambition will always remain to be the best—in product, service and financial performance. For Trendwest Resorts, success is measured by the ability to provide their owners with vacation perfection—time after time.

Above: WorldMark at Denarau Island, Fiji, embraces the local style.

Below: WorldMark at Coral Baja in San Jose del Cabo, Mexico.

Capt. Bill Nearhoff and deckhand Michelle Rickmann on the Carlisle II at the holiday season. The vessel is usually decked out with lights around her railings and holiday wreaths in the windows. Carlisle II regularly participates in the Christmas boat festival. Photo by Tom Janus

ACKNOWLEDGMENTS

The authors would like to give special thanks to the staff and volunteers at the various local historical societies, associations and museums, especially Carolyn Marr at MOHAI, for her professionalism and grace under fire and Pamela Kruse-Buckingham at the Kitsap County Historical Museum; George Bigley of Deltoid Images, for his assistance and encouragement on board the *Kalakala*; Robert Ulsh, steamboat historian and artist/conservator, so generous with his time and expertise; Ed Morgan, manager at Horluck Ferries; Les Morton, from the photo-lab at Todd Pacific Shipyards in Seattle; George Terek, ferryboat captain; and all of the ferryboat community, employees, friends and passengers, for their spirit, enthusiasm, and patience in a glorious and often trying transportation environment.

BIBLIOGRAPHY

Books:

Barkan, Frances B., ed. *The Wilkes Expedition: Puget Sound and the Oregon Country*. Olympia, WA: Washington State Capital Museum, 1987.

Bennett, Robert A., comp. *A Small World of Our Own: Authaentic Pioneer Stories of the Pacific Northwest From the Old Settlers Contest of 1892*. Walla Walla, WA: Pioneer Press Books, 1985.

Binns, Archie. *Sea in the Forest*. New York: Doubleday, 1953.

Blaine, David. *Memoirs of Puget Sound: Early Seattle, 1853-1856: The Letters of David & Catherine Blaine*. Edited by Richard A. Seiber. Fairfield, WA: Ye Galleon Press, 1978.

Blankenship, George E. *Lights and Shades of Pioneer Life on Puget Sound*. Seattle: Shorey Book Store Reprint, 1972.

Burns, Robert. *The Shape & Form of Puget Sound*. Seattle: Washington Sea Grant: Distributed by University of Washington Press, 1985.

Carey, Roland. *The Sound of Steamers*. Seattle: Alderbrook Publishing Company, 1965.

DeMoro, Harre. *The Evergreen Fleet; A Pictorial History of Washington State Ferries*. San Marino, CA: Golden West Books, 1971.

Denny, Arthur Armstrong. *Pioneer Days on Puget Sound*. Fairfield, WA: Ye Galleon Press, 1979.

Doig, Ivan. *Winter Brothers: A Season at the Edge of America*. New York: Harcourt Brace Jovanovich, 1980.

Droz, Dwight. *One for the Weather, One for the Crow*. Poulsbo, WA: Scandia Patch Press, 1996.

Evans, Jack R. *Little History of Gig Harbor, Washington*. Seattle: SCW Publications, 1988.

Faber, Jim, with a foreward (sic) by Murray Morgan. *Steamer's Wake*. Seattle: Enetai Press, 1985.

Gorst, Wilbur H. *Vern C. Gorst, Pioneer and Grandad of United Airlines*. Coos Bay, OR: Gorst Publications, 1979.

Haeberlin, Herman Karl, and Erna Gunther. *The Indians of Puget Sound*. Seattle: University of Washington Press, 1930.

Harlan, George H. *San Francisco Bay Ferryboats*. Berkeley: Howell-North Books, 1967.

Harmon, Alexandra. *Indians in the Making: Ethnic Relations and Indian Identities Around Puget Sound*. Berkeley: University of California Press, 1998.

Hershman, Marc, Susan Heikkala, and Caroline Tobin. *Seattle's Waterfront: The Walker's Guide to the History of Elliott Bay*. Seattle: Superior Publishing Co. 1966.

Judson, Phoebe Goodell. John M. McClelland Jr., ed. *A Pioneer's Search for an Ideal Home*. Tacoma: Washington State Historical Society, 1966.

Kitsap County Historical Society Book Committee, Evelyn Bowen, comp. *Kitsap County History: A Story of Kitsap County and Its Pioneers*. Silverdale, WA: The Society, 1977.

Kline, M.S. (Mary Stiles), and G.A. Bayless. *Ferryboats: A Legend on Puget Sound*. Seattle: Bayless Books, 1983.

Kolb, James A. *Puget Soundbook*. Poulsbo, WA: Marine Science Center, 1991.

Kruckeberg, Arthur R. *The Natural History of Puget Sound Country*. Seattle: University of Washington Press, 1991.

Kvelstad, Rangvald, ed. and comp. *Poulsbo, Its First Hundred Years*. Poulsbo, WA: Poulsbo Centennial Book Committee, 1986.

Leighton, Caroline C. Introduction and notes by David M. Buerge. *West Coast Journeys 1865-1879: The Travelogue of a Remarkable Woman*. Seattle: Sasquatch, 1995.

Lincoln, Leslie. *Coast Salish Canoes*. Seattle: Leslie Lincoln, 1991.

Marshall, James Stirrat, and Carrie Marshall. *Adventure in Two Hemispheres including Captain Vancouver's Voyage*. Vancouver, Canada: Talex Printing Services, 1955.

McDonald, Lucile. *Early Gig Harbor Steamboats*. Gig Harbor, WA: Mostly Books, 1984.

_____. *Swan Among the Indians: Life of James G. Swan, 1818-1900; Based Upon Swan's Hitherto Unpublished Diaries and Journals*. Portland, OR: Binfords & Mort, 1972.

Meany, Edmond, S. *Vancouver's Discovery of Puget Sound; Portraits and Biographies of the Men Honored in the Naming of Geographic Features of the Northwestern America*. Portland, OR: Binfords & Mort, 1957.

Morgan, Murray. *South on the Sound: An Illustrated History of Tacoma and Pierce County*.

Woodland Hills, CA: Windsor Publication, 1984.

Neel, David. *The Great Canoes: Reviving a Northwest Coast Tradition*. Seattle: University of Washington Press, 1995.

Neil, Dorothy, and Lee Brainard. *By Canoe and Sailing Ship They Came: A History of Whidbey's Island*. Oak Harbor, WA: Spindrift Publishing Company, 1989.

Newell, Gordon, ed. *The H.W.McCurdy Marine History of the Pacific Northwest*. Seattle: Superior Publishing Co., 1966.

Newell, Gordon R. *Pacific Steamboats*. Seattle: Superior Publishing Co., 1958.

_____. *Ships of the Inland Sea: The Story of the Puget Sound Steamboats*. Portland, OR: Binfords & Mort, 1960.

Orr, Elizabeth L. and William N. Orr. *Geology of the Pacific Northwest*. New York: McGraw-Hill, 1996.

Price, Andrew. *Port Blakely: The Community Captain Renton Built*. Seattle: Port Blakely Books, 1990.

Ruby, Robert H. *Myron Eells and the Puget Sound Indians*. Seattle: Superior Publishing Co., 1976.

Seattle. Seattle: Chas. H. Kittinger, Publisher, c. 1889.

Shrader, Grahame F. *The Black Ball Line, 1929-1951*. Seattle: Shorey Book Store, 1980.

Skalley, Michael. *Ferry Story: The Evergreen Fleet in Profile*. Seattle: Superior Publishing, 1983.

Steber, Rick. *The Pacific Coast*. Oregon Country Series, vol. 2. Prineville, OR: Bonanza Publications, Ltd., 1987.

Stewart, Hilary. *Cedar: Tree of Life to the Northwest Coast Indians*. Seattle: University of Washington Press, 1984.

Swan, James G. *The Northwest Coast, or, Three Years' Residence in Washington Territory*. New York: J.& J. Harper Editions, Harper & Row, 1969.

Thompson, Wilbur. *Steamer to Tacoma*. Bainbridge Island, WA: Driftwood Press, 1993.

Thorniley, William O. *Famous Pioneer Steamboats of Puget Sound; Marine Digest, April 8, 1944-November 11, 1944*. Seattle: Marine Digest, 1944.

Williamson, Joe, and Jim Gibbs. *Maritime Memories of Puget Sound in Photographs and Text*. Seattle: Superior Publishing Co., 1976.

Wing, Robert C. *Peter Puget: Lieutenant on the Vancouver Expedition, Fighting British Naval Officer, the Man for Whom Puget Sound was Named*. Seattle: Gray Beard Pub., 1979.

Winthrop, Theodore. *Canoe and Saddle*. Nisqually ed. Portland, OR: Binfords & Mort, 195-?

Wright, E.W., ed. *Lewis & Dryden's Marine History of the Pacific Northwest*. Seattle: Superior Publishing Co., 1967.

Articles:

Alcorn, Rowena, and Gordon D. Alcorn. "Puget Sound's Great Sternwheeler Days." *Sea Chest* 15, no. 3 (March 1982): 86-90.

Bate, Alison. "The *Kalakala* Returns Home." *Marine Digest and Transportation News* 77, no. 4 (December 1998): 5-6.

Callaghan, Carolyn W. "Puget Sound's Mosquito Fleet: Maritime Memories of Early Steam-Driven Saltwater Transit." *Columbia* 13, no. 2 (Summer 1999): 40-43.

Carey, Roland. "Virginia's First Twenty Years." *Sea Chest* 5, no. 4 (June 1972): 130-139.

Chasan, Daniel Jack. "In the Wake of the *Issaquah*." *Pacific Northwest* (May 1981):13-16.

"Curvy Ferry *Kalakala* is For Sale Again. *Marine Digest* (March 16, 1985): 4.

Hatch, John. "*Kalakala* Spawns New Life Form!" *Streamline News* 1, no. 2 (March/April 1999).

Heath, Mary. "The Wide-Angle Lens of Joe Williamson." *Enetai* (May 12-26, 1980): 15.

Johnson, Ralph. "The Indomitable Mosquito." *Sea Chest* 12, no. 2 (December 1978): 79.

Langlie, Arthur S. "A Short History of Indianola's Long Dock." *Sea Chest* 23, no. 1 (September 1989): 34-41.

Leithead, Robert C. "The Navy Yard Route." Part one. *Sea Chest* 2, no. 3 (March 1969):98-117.

_____. "The Navy Yard Route." Part two. *Sea Chest* 2, no. 4 (June 1969): 153-166.

_____. "The Navy Yard Route." Part three. *Sea Chest* 3, no. 1 (September 1969): 21-40.

_____. "The White Collar Line." *Sea Chest* 5, no. 1 (September 1971): 4-13.

"Maritime Happenings." *Sea Chest* 1, no. 3 (March 1968): 13.

Mason, Theodore C. "The 'Flying Bird' of Puget Sound." *Proceedings* (January 1984): 62-68.

McDonald, Lucile. "The Famous Williamson Photo Collection." *Sea Chest* 13, no. 2 (December 1979): 53-60.

Mortenson, Lynn Ove. "Steamship Summers." *Peninsula Magazine* (Fall 1990): 54-56.

Newnham, Blaine. "Back to the Future." *Seattle Times/Seattle Post-Intelligencer Pacific Magazine* (August 9, 1992):10-17.

Scott, George W. "The Politics of Transportation." *Columbia* 9, no. 1 (Spring 1995): 13-19.

"Seattle is Home of World's First Streamlined Vessel." *Port of Seattle Bulletin* (July-August 1935).

Spitzer, Paul. "Harsh Ways." *Pacific Northwest Quarterly* 90, no. 1 (Winter 1998/99): 3-16.

"Storm Warnings: A P-I Special Report on Washington State Ferries." *Seattle Post-Intelligencer* (January 8, 1986): C1-C16.

Thompson, Wilbur B. "M V *Suquamish*." *Sea Chest* 1, no. 2 (December 1967): 25-27.

Todd Pacific Shipyards. "Jumbo Mark II Class *M/V Tacoma*." Special supplement to the *Pacific Maritime Magazine* (October 1997).

Warner, Katy. "Marine Disasters *Tolo, Dix*." *Sea Chest* 1, no. 2 (December 1967): 3-5.

Warner, Katy. "Steamer *Dix* Tragedy of 1906 Recalled." *Marine Digest*, 42, no. 22 (July 6, 1968): 12-13.

Yohe, Ward J. "*Kalakala*: Workhorse of Puget Sound." *Undersea Quarterly* (Spring 1999): 4-6.

Brochure:

"*Historic Old Colman Dock Exhibit*." Brochure. Seattle: Waterfront Awareness, 1982.

Published Reports:

Andrews, Charles E. *Second Preliminary Report on the Engineering and Economic Phases of Bridging Puget Sound in the Vicinity of Seattle, Washington*. Submitted to the State of Washington Toll Bridge Authority, February 7, 1951.

Gilman, W.C. *Washington State Ferries Report on Traffic and Earnings*. New York: W.C. Gilman & Company, April 20, 1951.

Gore, William J., and Evelyn Shipman. *Commuters vs. the Black Ball Line: Washington Purchases the Puget Sound Ferries*. Inter-University Case Program #42: University of Alabama, 1959.

Unpublished Sources:

Holbrook, F.W.D. *Scrapbooks 1901-1915*. Photocopy. Puget Sound Naval History Collection, Kitsap Regional Library, Bremerton, WA.

Lasker, Bruno, comp. "Poulsbo, Kitsap County, Washington Information on the Social and Economic History of the Community and Its Vicinity." 1957. Photocopy. Kitsap Regional Library, Bremerton, WA.

Nickum, George C. "Puget Sound Automobile Ferries, Their Evolution and Design." Paper presented to the Society of Naval Architects and Marine Engineers Pacific Northwest Section, Harrison Hot Springs, British Columbia, Canada, Sept. 25, 1965.

Simonton, Catherine. "A Study of Reaction to Change; The Washington State Ferry System.: Seattle University, June 1983. Photocopy. Ralph White Collection, Kitsap Regional Library, Bremerton, WA.

Waring, Josephine. "Early Pioneering at Keyport, Washington." circa 1956. Photocopy. Kitsap Regional Library, Bremerton, WA.

Newspapers:

Bainbridge Review
Bremerton Searchlight
Bremerton Sun
Central Kitsap Reporter (Silverdale, WA)
Columbian (Vancouver, WA)
Kitsap County Herald (Poulsbo, WA)
Port Orchard Independent
San Francisco Examiner
Seattle Post-Intelligencer
Seattle Star
Seattle Times
Sun (Bremerton, WA)
Tacoma News Tribune
Vashon Island News-Record

Newsletters and Trade News:

Inland Crossings : A Monthly Newsletter for Riders and Staff of Washington State Ferries (Seattle), 1997-2000
Marine Digest (Seattle), 1942-1948

Websites:

Kalakala Foundation, www.kalakala.org
Steamer *Virginia V* Foundation, www.virginiav.org

BIBLIOGRAPHIC ESSAYS

Chapter 1
From Canoe to Steamboat

Like Puget Sound itself, the study of the region's geology is an ongoing process. For an overview of the region see *Geology of the Pacific Northwest* by Elizabeth L. Orr and William N. Orr (New York: McGraw-Hill Companies, Inc., 1966). For sources focused more directly on Puget Sound, two of the standards are Robert Burns's *The Shape and Form of Puget Sound* (Seattle: University of Washington Press, 1985) and Arthur Kruckeberg's *The Natural History of Puget Sound Country* (Seattle: University of Washington Press, 1991). A brief but entertaining look at Puget Sound can be found in *The Puget Soundbook*, written by James A. Kolb and published in 1991 by the Marine Science Society of the Pacific Northwest.

The renaissance of the canoe culture on Puget Sound was the impetus for *The Great Canoes: Reviving a Northwest Coast Tradition* by David Neel (Seattle: University of Washington Press, 1995). The book is not only a visual feast, but also a reminder of the emotional links forged by heritage and tradition. For a literary and artistic celebration of cedar see the classic *Cedar* by Hilary Stewart (Seattle: University of Washington Press, 1984). *Coast Salish Canoes* by Leslie Lincoln (Seattle: Lesley Lincoln, 1991) examines the types, construction, and uses of the various Northwest Indian canoes.

The entire story of the British expedition under George Vancouver and the later American Exploring Expedition under Charles Wilkes are published primary sources. Vancouver's *A Voyage of Discovery to the North Pacific Ocean and Round the World, 1791-1795* and Wilkes's *Narrative of the United States Exploring Expedition. During the Year 1838, 1839, 1840, 1841, 1842,* are available in several editions. Later publications which quote liberally from the journals with the added benefit of commentary and analysis are: Edmund S. Meany, *Vancouver's Discovery of Puget Sound* (Portland, OR: Binfords & Mort, 1957); Frances B. Barkan, editor, *The Wilkes Expedition: Puget Sound and the Oregon Country* (Olympia: Washington Capital Museum, 1987); and Robert Wing, *Peter Puget: Lieutenant on the Vancouver Expedition, Fighting British Naval Officer, the Man for Whom Puget Sound was Named* (Seattle: Gray Beard Pub, 1979).

In reference to the term passed midshipman, the word passed referred to an old navy title meaning a midshipman who had passed his exam and was awaiting a promotion to lieutenant.

For those who have not read pioneer reminiscences or letters—they are a delightful class of literature. *A Pioneer's Search for an Ideal Home: A Book of Personal Memoirs* by Phoebe Goodell Judson, edited by John M. McClelland, Jr. (Tacoma: Washington State Historical Society, 1966) is a warm and cheerful account of life in Washington Territory. Less cheerful, but possibly more honest since the letters were not written with the intent of publishing them, is *Memoirs of Puget Sound: Early Seattle, 1853-1856: The Letters of David & Catherine Blaine*, edited by Richard A. Seiber (Fairfield, WA: Ye Galleon Press, 1978). Another Seattle pioneer who realized how useful his recollections might be to future generations was Arthur Armstrong Denny who wrote *Pioneer Days on Puget Sound* (Fairfield, WA: Ye Galleon Press, 1979). Two accounts written by professional writers and originally published in the nineteenth century are Theodore Winthrop's classic *Canoe and Saddle* (Nisqually ed., Portland, OR: Binfords and Mort, 195-?) and Caroline Leighton's *Life on Puget Sound*, republished as *West Coast Journeys 1865-1879: The Travelogue of a Remarkable Woman* with introduction and notes by David M. Buerge (Seattle: Sasquatch, 1995).

James Swan enjoys the status of not only having written his own voluminous accounts of life in Washington Territory, but also having been the subject of books written by other authors. Together they present an intriguing picture of a fascinating man. Lucile McDonald's *Swan Among the Indians* (Portland, OR: Binfords & Mort, 1972) and Ivan Doig's *Winter Brothers: A Season at the Edge of America* (New York: Harcourt Brace Jovanovich, 1980), use Swan's own diaries to probe his life. *The Northwest Coast ,or, Three Years' Residence in Washington Territory* by James G. Swan (New York: J. & J. Harper Editions, Harper & Row, 1969) gives us the words of Swan himself as well as his drawings.

Washington's foremost territorial newspaper, published in Olympia, started in 1853 as *The Columbian*. By 1854 the paper had adopted the name *Pioneer and Democrat*. The notation of minute travel details and the perennial boosterism make the paper a valuable source for "getting the feel" of the 1850s.

Steamboats hold a continual fascination for many Puget Sound residents. The most passionate aficionados can easily recite the history, dimensions, mechanical details, routes, and whistle sounds of many of the little steamers. Thanks to the devotion of the maritime enthusiasts, there is a wealth of "steamer" literature. Among the favorites are *Maritime Memories of Puget Sound* by Joe Williamson and Jim Gibbs (Seattle: Superior, 1976); *The Sound of Steamers* by Roland Carey (Seattle: Roland N. Carey, 1965); and *Steamer's Wake* by Jim Faber with a foreward by Murray Morgan (Seattle: Enetai Press, 1985).

Chapter 2
The Mosquito Fleet

The Northwest is blessed with a number of steamboat enthusiasts—some work in local museums and historical societies, some are artists, and some are just plain fans with a thirst for knowledge. The Port Orchard-based Mosquito Fleet Association, the *Virginia V* Foundation, and Bill Somers's Museum of Puget Sound are all devoted to keeping memories of the Mosquito Fleet era alive. One local society, the Bainbridge Island Historical Society, even has a tape of various historic steamboat whistles and a catchy song about the *Virginia V* that, once heard, cannot be forgotten. Incidentally, *Virginia V* website, can be found at www.virginiav.org and offers updates on the progress of the vessel's restoration.

The general reference sources for maritime history on Puget Sound are the *H.W. McCurdy Marine History of the Pacific Northwest*, edited by Gordon R. Newell, and its companion volume *Lewis & Dryden's Marine History of the Pacific Northwest*, edited by E.W. Wright. Tracing marine events year-by-year, these books are the starting point for any researcher.

Two major periodicals covering Puget Sound maritime subjects are the monthly *Marine Digest and Transportation News* published since 1922 and *The Sea Chest*, the quarterly journal of the Puget Sound Maritime Historical Society. The Maritime Historical Society, incidentally, was founded in 1948 by a group of five men who were appalled to find no local organization devoted to preserving Puget Sound's rich maritime heritage. Their efforts have produced not only *The Sea Chest*, but a treasure trove of maritime materials and photos, including a large and impressive collection of Mosquito Fleet photographs by marine photographer Joe Williamson. The materials are available for public viewing at Seattle's Museum of History and Industry located in McCurdy Park, appropriate since it honors H.W. McCurdy.

One source not heavily used by researchers is a set of scrapbooks compiled by Puget Sound Navy Yard civil engineer F.W.D. Holbrook and available for viewing at the Kitsap County Historical Museum and at Kitsap Regional Library. The volumes cover the time period 1901-1915 and consist mainly of news clippings and ephemera relating to the shipyard, local transportation, and Bremerton history.

One of the ferry system's own, William Thorniley, publicist for Puget Sound Navigation Company, wrote a series of articles for *The Marine Digest* in the 1920s. His detailed profiles of "Famous Pioneer Steamboats of Puget Sound" were reprinted in 1944. If ships could have biographies, this series would be it for vessels such as the *State of Washington*, *City of Seattle*, *Bailey Gatzert*, and others.

For more on the career of shipbuilder Edward W. Heath see Paul Spitzer's excellent article "Harsh Ways: Edward W. Heath and the Shipbuilding Trade", in *Pacific Northwest Quarterly*, Winter 1998/99, pp. 3-16.

Evidence that the Mosquito Fleet truly is a part of Puget Sound lore can be found in the number of magazine articles and newspaper features dedicated to recalling the era. Every decade sees additions to the growing body of literature. It is also a popular topic for school reports. More than one librarian will scramble to find information for an entire class of ninth-graders who want to know "what exactly was the Mosquito Fleet?".

Chapter 3
The Black Ball Line

The development of automobile ferries and the emergence of the Black Ball Line as a near monopoly in Puget Sound transportation represent a crucial turning point in the history of ferryboats in the region. The actual transformation of the vessels is described in detail by Robert Leithead in part two of the three-part series "The Navy Yard Route" written with the collaboration of Captain Louis Van Bogaert, and published in the Maritime Historical Society's *Sea Chest* (March–September 1969). The series traces Puget Sound ferry service from 1885 to 1969.

In a similar vein, George Nickum's "Puget Sound Automobile Ferries: Their Evolution and Design" paper presented to the Society of Naval Architects and Marine Engineers Pacific Northwest Section, Harrison Hot Springs, British Columbia, Canada in 1965 explains the Whatcom's conversion and then follows the building of the first ferries actually designed to carry automobiles

As it is with everything maritime, *H.W. McCurdy's Marine History of the Pacific Northwest* is a valuable source for following not only individual vessels but the travails of the men (and occasional woman) who owned and operated them. The Hunt brothers, Skansie brothers, and Harry Crosby's enterprises are chronicled there. So is the maritime career of Joshua Green, although his later fame as preeminent banker, community leader, and centenarian also garnered much press coverage.

Kitsap County newspapers' periodic feature articles on the Horluck Transportation Company, Mary Lieseke, and current owner Hilton Smith offer enough background to piece together a tribute to the veritable ferry company which has linked Bremerton and Port Orchard for most of the twentieth century and continues into the twenty-first.

Another Kitsap ferry operator, Berte Olson, a shrewd businesswoman in an overwhelmingly male occupation, is a subject for further exploration. Kline & Bayless's masterful comprehensive history, *Ferryboats: A Legend on Puget Sound* (Seattle: Bayless Books, 1983) gives a brief account of her career, but a fuller treatment is needed.

Changes in the vessels led to dramatic realignments in the various ferry companies based in Puget Sound. Grahame Shrader's concise but valuable history, *The Black Ball Line, 1929-1951* (Seattle: Shorey Book Store, 1980) highlights Alexander Peabody and the growth and development of Black Ball Line. Additionally, another article by Leithead, "The White Collar Line," *Sea Chest* (September 1971), provides some of the background on the Kitsap County Transportation Company and its competition with Black Ball.

Finally, various activities of Puget Sound Navigation, i.e. schedules, fares, and vessel acquisitions including the building of the luxurious *Chinook* were commonly reported in area newspapers and in the trade periodical *Marine Digest*.

Chapter 4
Kalakala: A Class of Her Own

Because she has always been a "celebrity," much of the *Kalakala*'s story can be found in newspaper coverage. Beginning in San Francisco with the tragedies that befell the *Peralta*, followed by Seattle and world press

coverage of the dramatic introduction of the streamlined *Kalakala* in 1935, and continuing throughout her career until her resurrection in 1998, the *Kalakala* has left a wake of press clippings. Each step taken toward the vessel's restoration is noted in the media and even the bacteria in the ferry's bilge water has made news.

The former ferry's status as a tourist favorite is evidenced by the *Kalakala* memorabilia available on Internet auction sites. Not only is it plentiful, it can be found throughout the United States. Today the *Kalakala* postcard mailed home by a vacationer in the 1930s is not only a source of information but a collectible worth a hundred times more than its original purchase price.

Her contemporary story is best related by those in whose care she currently resides. The Kalakala Foundation is in the process of gathering photos, written recollections, and artifacts relating to the vessel. Their website at   updates the *Kalakala*'s present status and explains her history to the uninitiated. The site also includes an online version of the Foundation's newsletter, *Streamline News*.

Nearly every published work on Puget Sound ferries includes material on the *Kalakala*. Harre DeMoro's *Evergreen Fleet* (San Marino, CA: Golden West Books, 1971), Kline & Bayless's, *Ferryboats: A Legend on Puget Sound* (Seattle: Bayless, Books, 1983), and Jim Faber's *Steamer's Wake* (Seattle: Enetai Press, 1985) all have sections devoted to the vessel. Add to those, George Harlan's *San Francisco Ferryboats* (Berkeley: Howell-North Books, 1967), which describes the dramatic history of the ferry in her first incarnation as the *Peralta*.

Of the numerous articles, Theodore C. Mason's "The 'Flying Bird' of Puget Sound" (*Proceedings*, January 1984), Robert Leithead's "Navy Yard Route" (Sea Chest, June 1969 and September 1969), Alison Bate's "The *Kalakala* Returns Home" (*Marine Digest and Transportation News*, December 1998), and Ward J. Yohe's "*Kalakala*: Workhorse of Puget Sound" (*Undersea Quarterly*, Spring 1999) are worthy of note. One of the earliest articles, "Seattle is Home of World's First Streamlined Vessel" (*Port of Seattle Bulletin*, July-August 1935) portends the ferry's fame.

Chapter 5
Washington State Takes Over

Much of the impetus for the state takeover of the ferry system came from the ferry-riding public who believed that replacing the Black Ball line with a state-run system would result in lower fares and more modern vessels. Their viewpoint is aptly represented in a myriad of newspaper accounts covering the years 1947-1951.

On a more official level, one of the determining factors in whether or not a state operation of the Black Ball ferry system was feasible was the state-commissioned independent study done by the New York consulting firm of W.D. Gilman and Company in 1951. Their report, *Washington State Report on Traffic and Earnings*, provided the numerical data which influenced the state in making its decision to purchase the ferry system.

An excellent and detailed analysis of the steps leading to the sale of Black Ball to Washington State can be found in a public policy case study done by William J. Gore and Evelyn Shipman. Their work, *Commuters vs. the Black Ball Line: Washington Purchases the Puget Sound Ferries* (University of Alabama, 1959), has been quoted throughout the chapter. Another brief account sympathetic to the Peabody position is Grahame Shrader's, *The Black Ball Line 1929-1951* (Seattle: Shorey Book Store, 1980).

Chapter 6
The Evergreen Fleet

For more information on one of the earliest concepts for cross-Sound bridging, see Charles E. Andrews' February 7, 1951, report to the Washington State Toll Bridge Authority entitled "Second Preliminary Report on the Engineering and Economic Phases of Bridging Puget Sound in the Vicinity of Seattle, Washington." The plan, one of many over the years, included four possible routes and a combination of suspension bridges, floating bridges, and underwater tubes that would allow for the unobstructed flow of surface shipping.

Ferries are one topic never ignored by the Puget Sound area press. That fact alone is testimony to the importance of the ferry system. Ferries have always been the lifeline that connects the broken geography of Puget Sound; modern highways and bridges have not totally eliminated that role. To the frequent reader it appears that local press revel more in the bad news connected to the operation of Puget Sound ferries, although the introduction of new vessels certainly receives equal attention.

The Issaquah class ferries represent an anomaly in the

sense that they were eagerly anticipated new boats which spawned an abundance of bad press, legislative investigations, and lawsuits. Daniel Jack Chasan's investigative report, "In the Wake of the Issaquah", (*Pacific Northwest Magazine*, May 1981) is an excellent start at explaining the debacle resulting from Washington State's vessel expansion program of the early 1980s.

Another report which explored the problems plaguing Washington State Ferries in the 1980s was the *Seattle Post-Intelligencer's* special report "Storm Warnings" published on January 8, 1986. In recapping thirty-five years of state ownership, the newspaper's staff examined safety, finances, salaries, customer satisfaction, fares, and the future of ferries.

Chapter 9
Ferries of the Future

The future of Puget Sound ferries is currently being written in the courts, in advisory groups and citizen committees, in the media, and in the opinions of experts and those who depend upon ferries for commuting or for attracting tourist dollars.

Promotional materials generously provided by Todd Pacific Shipyards serve as a major source for information about the Jumbo Mark II Class ferries—the largest in the ferry system. Likewise, Dakota Creek Industries of Anacortes, Washington, graciously supplied materials relating to their vessels—the passenger-only fast ferries. Other documents relating to the construction and projected use of these new ferries are published under the auspices of the Washington State Ferries and Washington State Department of Transportation.

Much of the material in this chapter is courtesy of the insight of Eric Anderson, President of Art Anderson Associates a marine and facilities architecture and engineering firm and a mainstay in the Puget Sound business community for more than forty years. His clear vision and gift for explaining something as scientific as wake wash and no harm zones to a layperson has been tremendously helpful. Furthermore, Anderson's concept of intermodal travel and the potential benefits of public-private cooperation in providing transportation on Puget Sound's waters are undoubtedly a good representation of the future of ferry service.

INDEX